A

ROSE

BLOOMS

in

TEXAS

*Coming of Age in the
Civil War Era*

bright sky press
HOUSTON, TEXAS

2365 Rice Blvd., Suite 202
Houston, Texas 77005

ISBN: 978-1-931721-04-2

10   9   8   7   6   5   4   3   2   1

Library of Congress Cataloging-in-Publication Data on file with publisher.

Editorial Direction, Lucy Herring Chambers
Editor, Cristina Adams
Design, Marla Y. Garcia

Printed in Canada through Friesens

A ROSE
BLOOMS
in
TEXAS

Coming of Age in the
Civil War Era

CARLOS R. HAMILTON JR.

bright sky press
HOUSTON, TEXAS

TABLE & CONTENTS

PREFACE

In 1974, after the completion of my military service, our family returned home to Houston to establish our young children in a new school and to begin my medical practice. The following year my grandmother, Frances Wootters Denman, reached the end of her long life at the age of ninety-four years. Shortly thereafter, I discovered that she had left me a piano in her will, and arranged to have it moved to our new home. It was with surprise that I recognized the instrument from my childhood, an upright piano that had resided in a parlor in her home.

During World War II, when my father was serving as the medical officer for an artillery battalion in Europe, my mother and I moved to an apartment behind my grandparents' home in Houston. Although I was very young at the time, my memories of those years are distinct; I clearly recall the piano, a towering, antique giant of nine and a half feet that, due to its age, could not be appropriately tuned. I must have commented to my grandmother that I was fond of the piano, even though it had no apparent use, and she must have remembered my comment well enough to count on me to provide a home for the instrument, at least for another generation.

The difficulty in moving and accommodating the over-sized instrument, even in the twentieth century, was evident.

It also made me wonder how—and why—a family would move it from North Carolina to a rural east Texas plantation in 1857 so that a ten-year-old child could continue her musical studies. That child, my great-grandmother as it turned out, eventually became the mother of seven children, including my grandmother. And although Berta Smith Wootters had died many decades before I was born, her children continued to express great affection and admiration for her. My great-grandmother became a single parent when her husband, John Wootters, died at the age of fifty-two, likely from complications of a wound received during the Civil War. Even so, Berta Smith Wootters persevered, managing her affairs, nurturing her children, and guiding all of them to university educations and productive lives as adults.

Some years after the silent musical instrument had been situated in our home, it occurred to me that I had little information about the original owners and the circumstances of their lives. When I expressed an interest in learning about them to a cousin, Dr. John H. Wootters, a grandson of Berta Smith Wootters, I was invited to visit him in Crockett to learn what I could about that family. Dr. Wootters and his wife had moved to Crockett, Texas after his retirement from a distinguished practice of general surgery in Houston. He informed us that, although he wasn't certain of the plantation's exact location on the Trinity River, he knew someone who could help. As luck would have it, a man named Mr. Edgar Pouncey knew the way to the property and the site of the graves of Major John Smith and Anna Jane Smith.

Mr. Pouncey not only directed us to the plantation site and the graves, but he shared new information about the Smiths that their descendants didn't know. Edgar Pouncey was a descendant of a family of slaves who had come to Texas with the Smith family and whose own ancestors had served earlier generations of Smiths. As he related stories of the Smith family, he spoke with great respect and warmth.

All of us recognized the institution of slavery as a tragic mark on American history, a blight with no redeeming qualities whose effects will take generations to heal. Even so, according to Mr. Pouncey, the Smiths had assured at least some of their slave families that they and a child that was apparently mentally impaired would always have a secure home with their family. A site for a church had been dedicated for the use of the slaves and, at the time of emancipation, ownership of homesites was transferred to the freedmen. Educational opportunities had been encouraged and a Cedar Branch School was eventually created near the church. Edgar Pouncey had served as a Trustee of the Grapeland Independent School District with which the school was affiliated. He was rightly proud of the opportunities that had been offered to many children through the school.

This information, unexpected and thought-provoking as it was, motivated me to learn what I could about the Smith family as well as the turbulent and tragic times in which they lived. One can often understand more about a person's character and personality by reading what they have written or said and two items in Appendix I may illuminate these aspects of John Wootters and Berta Smith. These are the comments of John on receiving the company flag for the Crockett Southrons and the essay of Berta at the graduation ceremony of Fairfield Women's College.

Special appreciation must be given to my assistant, Jasmin Dimayuga, for her help in the preparation of the manuscript; to my reviewer, Eileen Flynn DeLaO for her patient and thoughtful suggestions; to Dr. John Boles, professor of history at Rice

University and the Susanne M. Glasscock School of Continuing Studies; and to the Texas State Historical Association and other sources of information mentioned in the bibliography. A special thanks to Cristina Adams, my very helpful editor and to Lucy Herring Chambers, Publisher, Bright Sky Press. This work could have never been completed without the support of my wife, Carolyn Burton Hamilton, who recognized that the story of these families, borne out during the most difficult era in American history, needed to be told and encouraged me to try to tell it in the best way I could.

DEDICATION

*This work is dedicated to the present generation of
ladies in my family who carry on the spirit, values and
devotion reflected by the subjects of the story:*

*My wife, Carolyn Burton Hamilton; our daughters
Patricia Hamilton Dewhurst and Marci Curry Hamilton;
and our granddaughters Madeleine Janes Hamilton,
Grace Elizabeth Hamilton, Frances Carolyn Hamilton
and Carolyn Hamilton Bivins.*

MAY 1863
FAIRFIELD, TEXAS

BERTA WAS STARTLED AWAKE with an intense sensation that she could hardly describe. It wasn't a feeling of fear or dread, but one of acute expectation. Sleep came easily for the fifteen-year-old, so she wondered what could have roused her on this night. Did she have a nightmare? Maybe, but she could not remember. Brushing a few wayward strands of hair from her eyes, she sat upright on her bed, concentrating, the fading light of a gibbous moon in the western sky illuminating the room and her pale face. No dream came to mind, but as she gradually awoke, she sensed that this day would be unlike any she had ever experienced. This was the day she would return home to the Smith Landing Plantation. Her first session at the Fairfield Female College was ending, and the seniors would have their farewell ceremony that afternoon.

Berta could hear birds singing in the oak tree outside her bedroom window. She quickly put on her robe and slippers, and stepped through the French doors that opened onto the veranda, which extended around the entire second story of the college. It was the largest building she could remember, although the Tremont Hotel in Galveston, where she and her family had stayed on their arrival from North Carolina six years earlier, may have been of similar size. The Fairfield College[1] building and its views of the surrounding fields and forest had been her home since January. Berta walked around the veranda and saw the morning mist rising from the pasture, the small creek that ran across the back of the property, where a small group of deer were quietly browsing near the water.

As she reached the south side of the building, she noticed three raccoons heading away from the building, likely lumbering back to their dens after feasting on scraps left for them by the kitchen workers. Stone pillars formed the foundation of the building, and the first floor was above the ground such that small creatures could easily hide underneath. Towards the rear of the building, the cave-like cellar connected to the pantry on the first floor, providing a cool storage room for preserved foods. Given the early morning hour, Berta knew she would soon hear the first bell ringing to awaken the students and signal the beginning of the day's activities.

As her stroll carried her to the east side of the building, she marveled at the beauty of the impending sunrise, at the

[1] *Appendix II, Item 1. Fairfield Female College.*

rose-colored reflections from strands of clouds considered by the ancients as the fingers of Eos, goddess of the dawn. On this morning, she and her classmates would be meeting with their instructors for a final review of their efforts during the session. Berta continued to feel an unexpected sense of excitement and anxiety about the day. Perhaps it was the idea that school was ending and she would soon return to her beloved family, or perhaps it was the anticipation of meeting one last time with her music instructor, who would be leaving Fairfield College at the end of this session.

The helpers at the college had cleaned and pressed her clothes for this special day, and Berta took greater care than usual to arrange her lustrous red hair atop her head in a neat bun. She had a vague sense of guilt about the pride she took in her hair, as its unique hues were a trait she shared with her mother. She had also inherited her mother's pale skin, which would only glow pink when she became overheated. Berta's complexion made it impossible for her to hide her emotions, as she would blush at the slightest provocation. Her father often teased her about this. Guile, he said, was not a trait that she should cultivate because her face would always reveal her true feelings.

The final detail of her preparation was to see that her hands and nails were presentable, as every pianist should. Although she didn't expect to perform on this occasion, she refused to neglect this detail of her routine. Her hands were smaller than she would have liked, which limited her ability to play some of the more intricate chords in her pieces, and her pinky finger extended outward noticeably. As she studied her hands, she thought, with a brief twinge of sadness, of her dear departed brother Lucius, who, because of the shape of her hands, had often teased her about having four thumbs.

Shaking off the sad thought of her absent brother, Berta turned to anticipating the final meetings with her instructors. The senior girls had already finished their meetings; the only activities left were to prepare for the trip home and the closing ceremonies that afternoon.

Not all the girls were enthusiastic about the immediate future. Berta's friend, Molly Rather, whose family had sent her to Texas to avoid the anticipated warfare in their home state of Mississippi, was one of those girls. She was graduating now, but the future was looking uncertain, as the Rathers had fled their home following the Union army's push into Mississippi after the Battle of Shiloh in Tennessee the previous year. Molly's family had relocated to an area on the Brazos River in Texas, where her mother's relatives had settled some years earlier when the state was still part of Mexico.

Berta's first meeting of the morning was with her piano instructor, Count Rudolph von Godski. The Polish aristocrat sported a slight limp from the battle at Shiloh and an exuberant mustache, held in place with beeswax, which threatened to catch fire every time he leaned over the candelabra on the forte-piano. The Count eased her anxiety that morning by pronouncing her talent exceptional and her performance technique excellent. But he then went on to suggest she would need to work harder to reach her full potential; she was very good, he noted, but she could be even better.

After thanking him for his encouragement and instruction, Berta thought about what activities she could give up to follow his advice. She already spent several hours every day practicing different pieces, such as etudes, mazurkas, waltzes and barcarolles. Her other pursuits, which included reading for pleasure and visiting with friends, played an important role in her life, and she wouldn't want to give them up. Music was wonderful, even necessary, Berta decided, and she would continue to develop her musical skills. But her playing would be for pleasure, not as a full time effort.

Between meetings with faculty members that morning, she encountered Betty Graves, the older daughter of the college president, Dr. Henry L. Graves. Betty taught younger students at the academy and had become her friend. Dr. Graves and his family which included his wife Rebecca and their children lived in the college building. Betty was the oldest and Ophelia—who preferred to be called Mollie—was in her class. A younger son, Henry, attended the academy. In addition to teaching the younger students, Betty had assumed the responsibility of protecting and cultivating a rose garden that seemed to flourish in the Freestone County environment. She would permit older students to walk among the bushes and occasionally pick a bloom. When Betty had learned that Berta had lost her brother, Lucius, in the war, she went out of her way to show her kindness and compassion, even teaching her some of the gardening techniques she used.

That day, Betty was beautifully groomed, as usual, with her abundant dark hair neatly arranged atop her head and her long dress adorned with a colorful ribbon that matched the one in her hair. Berta was surprised when her friend offered up a rose plant to take as a reminder of her happy years at Fairfield Female College and a token of Betty's affection and respect.

"I know you have experienced a great loss with the death of your brother," Betty said. "I have marveled at the resilience of your spirit and your thoughtfulness toward others. Give this small plant similar attention, and it may grow and bloom as I know you will."

Touched by her friend's words, Berta promised to nurture and treasure the plant, even as she wondered aloud why her friend seemed a little unsettled. As Betty looked around to see if anyone was within earshot, it was clear that she wanted to talk to her about something other than the weather and the garden.

"I do have something I want to discuss with you, and I must ask you not to reveal to anyone what I'm about to tell you," Betty said.

Berta flushed, slightly indignant at the notion that she couldn't keep a secret, but Betty shook her head and continued.

"Do you recall the flag ceremony earlier this spring? And if so, do you recall the man at the end of the procession who was somewhat taller than the others?"

Berta nodded, not certain that she remembered all the details and every soldier, but eager to hear the rest of the story. Betty obliged by telling her that the tall soldier, William, who had been away for training since the flag ceremony, was returning to Fairfield that evening. He would remain there for two days with his company before heading east to fight in the war. While this was somewhat interesting to Berta, she couldn't understand what about this solider and his company was making her friend anxious. And then Betty revealed her splendid secret.

"This evening, after the graduation ceremony, William and I will be married," she said. "Except for the two of us and the minister at the church in town, you are the only person who knows of it."

Berta's surprise left her breathless. "Oh! I cannot get my breath from such a shock," she gasped. "I don't know what to say!"

"Dear Berta, you don't need to say anything," Betty replied. "It would perhaps be best if you didn't respond immediately to what you have been told. My purpose in telling you this is that I trust you to keep the secret and to comply with my next request."

Betty then gave Berta a sealed letter to deliver to her parents the following morning, when they were likely to be alone. If pressed to answer questions, Berta was to say that their daughter and her fiancé were very much in love and that, given the war and the resulting uncertainties that accompanied daily life, they didn't want to be apart for even one more day. With William going away to war, there was simply no time for the formalities of a traditional wedding. Happily, the minister at her family's church had agreed to marry them, despite the possibility of upsetting her parents.

"Whatever the future may hold, we will always know that our love has been declared and blessed and that no human act can ever disrupt that bond," Betty said.

The two young women walked over to a garden bench and sat down together. The morning sun brushed the treetops of the surrounding forest, chasing away any lingering clouds. Berta gently grasped her friend's arm.

"With William going away to war, where will you live?"

"William has property of his own with a house that will be adequate for my immediate needs if my family does not want me to stay," Betty smiled. "I am confident that I can support myself in some fashion by teaching young children somewhere. With that and my faith, I do not fear the future."

Berta, however, had enough fear for both of them. She would not hear of her friend living alone and insisted that Betty return with her to Houston County, as her own family had rooms available and was always welcoming to both visitors and family. Smith Landing Plantation wasn't too far from Fairfield, and if Betty wanted to open a school, there were plenty of children who could benefit from experienced instruction. It was a heartfelt offer, one that Betty graciously refused.

"You are as thoughtful as you are gentle, however, having faith means that I look forward even though I have no idea what the future holds," Betty said, standing up.

She pressed the letter into Berta's hands, asking her again to keep it safe until the following morning, and promised to return in two days. The young women then bade each other a tearful goodbye as they walked toward the college building.

Until she could calm her racing heart and flushed face, Berta knew she was in no condition to have a review session with Dr. Graves. As she waited in the foyer, she distracted herself by recalling his lectures on the botanical sciences and the beauties of natural philosophy as portrayed by the Swedish scientist Carl Linnaeus. As she held the rose Betty had given her, she tried to remember how it would be classified but gave up after several minutes, concluding that its greatest significance was as a token of affection from a dear friend.

When she was called into Dr. Graves' office, Berta did not know what to expect from the meeting but the conversation that ensued caused her to blush with surprise. He congratulated her on being admitted as a member of the local Baptist church one month earlier in April.[2] As happened with all those seeking new membership in the faith, she was required to meet with the minister and at least two of the deacons of the church who would question her about her faith, her understanding of the Scriptures and the significance

[2]   *Berta Smith was baptized into church membership April 26, 1863.*

of membership. She remembered the evening very well, as they had asked her some difficult questions, and she had replied with answers that were, on occasion, somewhat unexpected. Dr. Graves, who had recommended her to the church for membership, already knew about her responses and was curious to hear Berta's side of the story.

It was a tale of faith and will, of a congregation that thought a fifteen-year-old too young to understand the importance of spirituality, and of a young woman whose unshakeable faith and cast-iron will proved them wrong. The questions were, in Berta's mind, at times pointless and puzzling. Did she think it was God's will that she publicly declare her faith? She did. Did she think it was God's will that she attend the College? She did. Was it also God's will that the Confederacy and the Union go to war? Her answer—that God would want people to treat each other with love and respect, and would never want the world to be at war—no doubt perplexed the interrogators.

"Tell me," Dr. Graves said. "How do you think we should react when bad things happen to us or our loved ones?"

Berta chewed her lower lip slowly as she composed a response.

"I don't think God wants bad things to happen to us," she shook her head. "But they will anyway, so His presence and comfort are available to help us deal with what does happen. Sometimes God can use those things to achieve good results, although we may not understand or believe it at the time." Using her own family as an example, Berta pointed out that her mother, despite ongoing illness and a lack of strength, refused to let the situation overcome her. The illness might weaken her body, but not her spirit.

"They even wanted to know if I thought slavery in the Southland was also God's will," Berta said. "And I am sure that my answer was not what they expected from a girl like me."

"It is an unusual question for such a situation," said Dr. Graves. "What did you tell them?"

"I told them about Hannah, a slave who especially helps mother and who has more faith in God than anyone I've ever known," she said. "I told them that when we march through the gates of Heaven someday, Hannah will be near the front of the procession."

Berta's opinion of slavery was unusual, if not downright unconventional. She suspected that slavery had begun long ago as a result of sin, between two groups of people, and that subsequent generations had been unwilling to remedy the situation. God may not have placed Hannah in a perfect world, but she was certainly a blessing to those who lived in this one. And while the deacons might not have approved of her opinions, they had accepted her into the congregation, and for that she was grateful.

"I presume that church deacons don't think women reflect on faith and public matters very often," Berta frowned. "So I believe that most any answer they agreed with would have been adequate."

"You have considerably greater insights than most people your age," Dr. Graves smiled, clearly showing his approval. "Now on to lighter matters, such as that lovely rose bush you came in with. I recall that Betty mentioned your interest in gardening."

"Yes, by happy coincidence, Betty gave me this plant just now," she said. "I'll plant it at our home in Houston County and call it the 'rose of love.' As Betty has taught me how to provide for the plant, she has also taught me about love, and

I will do my best to keep these lessons in my mind and heart."

The implications of what she had said didn't hit Berta until it was too late. The words were out, and she couldn't take them back. Fortunately, Dr. Graves just seemed bemused by her thoughts on love.

Realizing that the conversation had gone on too long, Berta excused herself, noting that she needed to place the rose bush in water until, once back home, she could properly plant it. Dr. Graves excused her, cautioning that he expected a report on the health of the plant, her mother and Hannah when she returned to school in the autumn. With the good-byes finished, Berta slipped out the door before she could say anything else.

A large gathering of family and friends, faculty and staff of the college, and town residents attended the Fairfield Female Coliege graduation ceremony that afternoon. The building's front veranda served as a stage for the proceedings as well as the seating area for Dr. Graves, his wife, several members of the school committee and the minister of the Baptist church. Girls from the other classes sat in the audience, in neat rows just behind the new graduates, perhaps so that they would be impressed by the gravity of the moment and therefore eager to continue their own studies. Behind the rows of students were the families, friends and supporters who had come to enjoy the celebration. Several visitors in the audience were young men wearing their Confederate Army uniforms; Berta could not help but wonder which one might be Betty's co-conspirator in the secret wedding plan. Even though she realized that her ruminations on the rose plant must have seemed odd to Dr. Graves, she was grateful not to have inadvertently revealed anything. As she watched the different people on the stage, she understood for the first time how many would be affected by that evening's events, and could only admire the minister for being so sympathetic to the young couple.

It was anticipation and daydreams of young love that kept Berta's mind from becoming too restless during the lengthy ceremony. But not everyone had something else to think about. In a sign that the introductions, prayers and admonitions had gone on too long, some of the younger children and students were beginning to fidget. Just as she wondered whether the fidgeting would become a disruption, a final amen was spoken and the tearful graduates joined their families for a reception in the grand hall and chapel of the college.

Following the reception and a light supper, Berta went back to her room to arrange her belongings in preparation for the arrival of Hannah and her son, Edgar, the next morning. They would pack her things, load the carriage and then, together, they would all make their way home. At first, sleep was impossible, so she turned to writing. In the flickering candlelight, she composed a letter to Betty, who by this time was a married woman:

My dear Betty: It is late in the evening, and I know that you and William are now man and wife. I want to wish you the greatest happiness and joy on this day, which will be forever in my mind. You will both be in my prayers daily. Please tell William that his safe return to you from the war will be my greatest wish. Remember that you are always welcome at the Smith Plantation and in Houston County for a visit of any duration. Thank you for the rose bush. I will cherish and nurture it as a symbol of the love that you have shown me and will share with your beloved

William. I will ask your parents to give this letter to you on your return, and I expect that they will feel the same happiness about you and William that I do. Love from your friend and admirer, Berta.

She sealed the letter with drops of wax from the melting candle, and was soon overtaken by sleep.

A familiar voice awoke her the next morning; Hannah and Edgar had arrived, and it was time to go home. In an instant, Berta remembered her obligation, and the promise she'd made to Betty. She dressed quickly and, with Hannah's help, finished packing all of her belongings. Even as Hannah assured her that Edgar would carefully move her trunks to the waiting carriage, Berta fairly ran down the broad stairway to Dr. and Mrs. Graves' rooms. There was no time or inclination for breakfast; the tension and excitement she felt about delivering her news had banished her appetite. She found the couple on the veranda and noted, with some relief, that they were enjoying a quiet breakfast alone. That would make her job easier. With a combination of uncertainty and nerves, she approached their table to deliver the letter that Betty had given her.

"Won't you join us for breakfast?" Dr. Graves said, motioning to an empty chair at the table.

"Yes, please join us," Mrs. Graves said. "We haven't seen Betty this morning, have you?"

"Thank you so much for the invitation, but I really can't linger," Berta said. "I have a note to give you, but I don't want to delay our leaving for home as Hannah and her son are already loading the carriage."

Dr. Graves opened and read the letter before Berta could gracefully exit the scene. His usually stoic expression quickly changed, as his eyes filled with tears and a genuine smile crossed his face. Mrs. Graves took the letter from him and read. Her reaction was equally emotional, confirming that Betty and her new husband would find only love and acceptance in her family.

Dr. and Mrs. Graves were understandably full of questions. Did Betty share their plans? Did Berta know when they were returning? Berta answered simply what Betty had told her, that their daughter's love for William and the uncertain future had spurred them to the altar without delay. The bride's parents smiled; the marriage had their blessing. They understood the decision and approved, but they would have enjoyed taking part in the celebration.

Betty, they said, was twenty-three years old and capable of making her own choices, and William's family was highly respected in Freestone County. All in all, it was a wonderful step in their daughter's life, and they looked forward to seeing her soon. In two days, Berta told them, convinced now that Betty and William would receive an enthusiastic welcome. It had been a day of revelations, but none more puzzling than the discovery that love was a matter of both one's mind and one's heart. As she left, Dr. Graves called out to her, "Berta, be sure to tend to your rose of love and we will all look forward to your return in September."

The carriage ride to Houston County passed in the blink of an eye, and Berta soon spied her parents standing on the embankment as the ferry approached Smith Landing Plantation. The journey had given her an opportunity to think about the past few days and to wonder whether she would ever feel about someone the way Betty felt about William. Perhaps it would happen sooner than expected. The only person out-side her family that she had ever had any such interactions with was her friend John Wootters, and her feelings about him had grown in the nearly two years since he had left to fight with the Crockett Southrons.

The last time she'd visited with him was at a church ser-vice in Crockett. He had exuded a strength and confidence she couldn't easily forget. The words he had spoken the next day at the flag ceremony remained prominent in her mem-ory and reinforced her daily prayers for his safe return. He even wrote to her with stories about life in the army camps and on the battlefield. Those rare letters had an effect that she knew would take time to resolve.

JULY 1861
CROCKETT, TEXAS

TUESDAY MORNING DAWNED warm and humid as the Smith household rose early to prepare for a trip to Crockett that afternoon. The family anticipated the next day's celebration with a mix of pride, hopefulness and concern. The occasion, deemed patriotic by politicians and local citizens alike, featured the presentation of a special flag to the first unit of volunteers to leave Houston County for the war in Virginia. Sewn by a group of ladies from the Baptist, Methodist and Presbyterian churches, this flag would be carried by the company and serve as a rallying point for the troops.

John Smith had seen the banner and had told his family that it was a replica of the Texas flag with the name Crockett Southrons embroidered in an arc across the top. It was to be presented by Miss Sarah Jane Monroe, an articulate young lady and a contemporary of many of the departing troops. Her family boasted a storied patriotic heritage: her father, A.T. Monroe, who had relocated to Houston County from Virginia in 1854, was the grand-nephew of former U.S. President James Monroe. It seemed ironic to John Smith that a descendant of one of the country's founding fathers would advocate so fervently for the dissolution of that country.

John Wootters, who had been elected by the troops as their First Sergeant, would accept the flag on behalf of the company. Well known to the Smith family, John was the nephew of Lodwick Downes, an owner of the Long and Downes mercantile business in Crockett. Downes was a friend of John Smith's and a fellow Mason. Wootters, who attended services at the same Baptist church frequented by Berta and her family, also worked at the mercantile store as a clerk. He graciously tended to the needs of Berta and her mother whenever they stopped by the store.

The nearly fourteen-year-old Berta had been surprised by both the courtesy and congeniality of this young man, seven years her senior, who had expressed interest in her musical talents. She had been both flattered and flustered by his attention and approval. She also noted and appreciated the courtesy he had shown to the slaves, Hannah and Oscar, who were so important to her family's household.

The Houston County company of soldiers to be honored had been organized by Dr. Edward Currie, who was also their captain. On Wednesday, the company would leave for New Orleans, where they would officially become part of the Army of the Confederate States of America. While their exact assignment and command wasn't yet clear, similar groups from other Texas counties had become part of the First Texas Voluntary Infantry Battalion. As Captain Currie believed they would become Company I of that group, they had selected the name Crockett Southrons to identify their unit. Once officially mustered into service in New Orleans, they would travel by railroad to Virginia to join the battalion being organized by Col. Louis T. Wigfall.

This last bit of news worried Berta's father somewhat since Wigfall, a South Carolina native, was widely known as a fire-breathing secessionist whose enthusiasm for war with the Northern states predated the hostilities at Fort Sumter. His career as a lawyer and politician had been marred by a propensity for dueling, and his military experience was limited to brief participation in the Seminole Wars. That did not dampen his enthusiasm for combat. Indeed, perhaps no one welcomed the events the past six months more than Col. Wigfall. He had been present in Charleston during the bombardment of Fort Sumter and had personally received the truce and surrender of the fort from U.S. Army Major Robert Anderson. As a member of the Texas Legislature, Wigfall had been a staunch opponent of Governor Sam Houston.

On the other hand, Smith believed that quick and decisive victories by the Confederate army would encourage the Federal leadership in Washington, D.C. to be more accepting of an independent Southern nation. To that end, Wigfall's intensity and zeal for action could help the Confederacy succeed. However, Smith also knew that military victories were achieved, not by colonels, but by committed, well-trained army officers and troops. He could only hope that Wigfall would provide that type of leadership. Thanks to the military background of the Confederacy's provisional president, Jefferson Davis, Berta's father was confident in the fledgling nation's prospects.[3] He felt certain that Davis would appoint experienced senior military leaders capable of channeling secessionist enthusiasm in a more productive direction.

So it was with a sense of hope that the Smith family arrived in Crockett for a prayer meeting at the Baptist Church the evening before the big event on Wednesday. John, Anna, Jane and Berta had been warmly received by the church's membership after their move from North Carolina. And although the distance from their plantation home to town precluded their regular attendance, they were held in high regard by the congregation. Some members of the church were aware of Hannah and Oscar's deep faith and spirituality, as the slave couple usually accompanied the Smiths to town and often attended church services with them. Like all slaves in attendance, they were expected to sit in a designated balcony area; some meetings, they would have their own church services either outdoors or in a nearby building. When not in Crockett with the Smith family, they would be leading services for slaves at the church building on the Smith Landing Plantation.

Hannah and Oscar had encountered Mr. Wootters at the mercantile store and been surprised by the courtesy he showed to them. Slaves, who were expected to act deferentially toward all white people, were accustomed to a level of indifference or rudeness from that segment of the population. What they weren't accustomed to was being treated with respect; Wootters' attitude was a surprise, albeit a pleasant one. It meant that Hannah and Oscar were looking

[3] *Appendix II, Item 2*

forward to attending the church service and celebration, and recognizing his leadership.

The prospect of war left many slaves feeling uncertain and anxious. Even after two centuries and many generations of slavery, the hope for freedom burned brightly. While some of the Smith Plantation slaves understood their good fortune in having generous and temperate owners, kindness was no substitute for the freedom to determine one's own future.

The impending war could actually harm their interests. Even if they did shake off the shackles of slavery, it would mean entering a world of hostility and danger, especially for the very young and the very old. Either way, one thing was certain: opposing their owners' immediate interests could only lead to trouble. The possibility of obtaining their freedom by peaceful means had vanished with the onset of the war; now, they could only depend on their faith in God to determine the future.

Berta felt particularly passionate about these events. The prospect of so many young men from her community leaving for the dangers and uncertainty of war—as her brother, Lucius, had done just one month earlier—filled her with fear. The terrors that had been rousing her from sleep since his departure would, no doubt, intensify once her friend John Wootters also decamped for the war. She had come to know him as a kind and sensitive person; he seemed to lack the rough edges so prevalent in many young men of their area, and that filled her with concern about his ability to withstand a life of danger and hardship. His designation as First Sergeant of the company, however, suggested that his fellow soldiers and officers had seen in him a depth of character and leadership that would serve them all well.

The long summer days meant that the church service would begin in full afternoon sun, before the cool of evening. The Smith family took their places in the church sanctuary, along with the rest of the community. As the service progressed, Berta's eyes scanned the congregation. An observant young woman with a keen eye and an excellent memory, she could recognize many of them by the backs of their heads. In front of her to the right, sat a farmer named Abner who, as far as she knew, had never missed a service. He was easily identified by the deep furrows on the back of his neck as well as the mop of carefully trimmed hair that was, at other times, constrained by a well-worn hat. Abner and his wife, who seemed as tired as her husband's hat, had nearly enough children to fill an entire row. Berta was always impressed by their well-behaved brood and how they never seemed to move a muscle during services.

Near the front of the sanctuary sat the town physician, his shiny bald pate surrounded by a circle of white hair. He was flanked by his wife and an older son, whose main duty was to keep the aging doctor from falling out of the pew when he inevitably nodded off. Berta smiled to herself, recalling a Bible story about Eutychus, who not only went to sleep but fell out of a third-floor window during one of the apostle Paul's sermons in the ancient town of Troas. According to that story, Eutychus was miraculously restored to health by Paul, so Berta concluded that the sleepy doctor would likely be forgiven if he slid to the floor.[4]

Sitting in the front rows of the sanctuary were the soldiers being honored. She saw John Wootters sitting at the end of one pew and could only imagine what thoughts might be occupying his mind. She had never seen him in uniform

[4]   *The Holy Bible, New Testament, Acts 20:9-12.*

before. She was impressed by how well the suit fit him and how dashing he looked. Berta found herself becoming tearful as she asked God to afford him special protection. The prayer service went on and on with what seemed to be no end in sight. She hoped to personally give Wootters her best wishes; the next day would surely be too filled with activities and confusion to offer such an opportunity.

As the evening progressed, the atmosphere grew still and heavy, with only the ladies' hand-held fans stirring a warm breeze. The minister and countless deacons expounded at length on the biblical importance of warfare and called upon divine support for their cause.

On hearing this, Berta couldn't help but wonder whether congregations in Northern states were having similar prayer services and also calling on the same God for intervention on behalf of their troops. She didn't have a clear solution to this conundrum. But she was sure that all soldiers needed a full measure of divine assistance to carry out their mission with duty and honor, and she, as one who stayed behind, would only ask that their lives be preserved and that their hearts and minds be supplied with the assurance of God's love for them. When they were finally blessed with the last "Amen" of the evening, the congregation was released from the confines of the church into the cool of the evening.

Berta exited the church and spied John Wootters standing aside near the doorway. She could not take her eyes off him, in the gray tunic adorned with the braid of his First Sergeant rank. As their eyes met, Berta was overcome by feelings she didn't understand. Despite attempts to maintain her composure, her eyes filled with tears and her cheeks flushed red. She struggled to smile.

"Now, now, young lady, you should put on a joyful face," John said. "This is supposed to be a time of celebration and enthusiasm, not one of sadness. If for no other reason, you should rejoice that we can, at last, breathe some fresher air. I think the only person that didn't offer an oration or a prayer was your friend Hannah. Perhaps if she had, it would have had a positive effect."

Berta dabbed at her tears with a handkerchief, as she didn't want to seem silly to her elegant friend. Even so, as she approached him, she noted that his clean-shaven face made him look both innocent and years younger. Surprised, she stumbled slightly over her words.

"Mr. Wootters, I trust that is not a hint of sarcasm that I hear in your description of these services, but I do welcome the chance to breathe more freely," Berta said, pushing a wayward strand of hair from her face. "I recall from the Scriptures that our Lord preferred shorter, more private prayers, rather than such oratory. Nevertheless, I am sure that every utterance was made with heartfelt sincerity."

Wootters nodded as she noted that her prayers for his safe return—and that of all the Crockett Southrons—would accompany them on their journey.

"My gentle-hearted friend, I greatly appreciate your kind words," he said. "But I must say that I haven't sensed any fear in my comrades, and I am sure that we will meet our challenges without hesitation. Your prayers will be most welcome, and I can assure you that I will also pray for our safety as well as the will to carry out our duties."

Berta immediately regretted her words, thinking they were more childish than she would have liked. Following his gracious response, she was more confused: his face and smile suggested a softness to his nature, but his eyes revealed a steely determination that revealed very different traits. In the months that followed, she would try to remember her feelings at these moments but could only recall the sense of confusion that swirled in her head.

"Mr. Wootters, I know that I should act braver than I really am but I must admit to a great sense of fear about the departure of so many for a war whose cause is hard to understand," Berta said. "You seem so strong and determined, and I don't understand why I can't be braver than I am."

John smiled, acknowledging the sense of Berta's words. The difference between fear and uncertainty, he explained, lay in the fact that most people lived through uncertainty at some point in their lives; fear was born from a perceived lack of control. Moreover, people would always experience circumstances or situations that were beyond their ability to manage. It was during those times—those fearful, seemingly helpless times—that people should depend on their faith in God.

"He will be with us whatever the situation," John said. "We can only pray for our faith not to falter in these times of such challenge."

Buoyed by his words, Berta curtseyed her thank-you as John excused himself for the evening. The hour was late, and he was expected to speak at the ceremony the following day. "I will be thinking about you as I express our thanks for the flag."

On Wednesday morning, July 17, Berta awoke to a cloudless blue sky so typical of summertime in Texas. The bright sunlight reminded her that the day would be warm, and shady spots would be at a premium during the flag presentation ceremony scheduled for noontime. She met Hannah and her mother in the hotel lobby; her father had already gone to the town square to secure comfortable seats in the shade so that Anna Jane would be reasonably comfortable throughout the afternoon. The town was abuzz with activity as they made their way toward the square, where a podium had been erected in front of Mrs. Hall's Hotel. The structure was festooned with colorful red, white and blue bunting to represent the new Confederacy and its "Stars and Bars" flag.

As the band began playing, more people arrived. Berta and her party scanned the crowd for her father. On spotting him, Oscar and Hannah helped Anna Jane make her way to the seats he had reserved. Prone to fainting spells and exhaustion, she had never regained her full measure of stamina since Berta's birth. The severe hemorrhage that had complicated the delivery of her last child had nearly killed her. Although her mind and spirit were alert and energetic, her body could only endure a limited amount of physical activity.

Mercifully, the speeches were short. According to crowd gossip, Captain Currie was eager to begin the trek to Louisiana and did not want to linger any longer than necessary. The men—more than one hundred of them—would march on the Old San Antonio Road. Once they crossed the Sabine River and reached Natchitoches, they would head south toward Baton Rouge and New Orleans. Currie expected them to complete their journey within two weeks; importantly, it would be the first opportunity he and his officers would have to assess the fitness of the new volunteers. Enthusiasm notwithstanding, he felt certain they would meet his expectations.

This last public display of support was eagerly welcomed by the recruits. Currie understood that separation from friends and loved ones would be one of their greatest challenges in the coming months or years. This festive event was an opportunity to make the most of a final, if temporary, farewell. Once the dignitaries were introduced and prayers offered, the county judge welcomed Miss Sarah Jane Monroe to present the flag to the company.[5]

Sarah Jane was older than Berta, who watched with admiration as the young woman moved to the center of the podium. Berta thought she was dressed perfectly for the occasion: a long dress of red and blue with white lace on the bodice and generous petticoats, which made a striking contrast to the severe black suits of the men sitting behind her. They all stood as Sarah Jane moved to pick up the neatly folded flag from the low table. At the end of the row, First Sergeant John Wootters stood at attention. Once again Berta was surprised by his aura of authority and strength. He stood erect, motionless, as Sarah Jane began her presentation in a clear, confident voice.

She referred to the new flag as a glorious symbol of Southern independence and admonished the soldiers to never permit it to be dishonored. As she continued her speech, there was hardly a dry eye in the audience, although there was much clapping. At the conclusion of her remarks, Sarah Jane held up the flag. The crowd remained silent as John Wootters advanced to the stage and took the flag in his arms. In a calm voice, he spoke of the honor he felt in receiving the flag on behalf of his company and expressed his appreciation for this gift.

"As long as a heart pulsates and an arm is nerved, the banner will be protected," John said. "As long as one of us survives, the flag will never be sullied or dishonored by any act unworthy of a soldier or gentleman."

[5] *Appendix I. Item 5. Transcription of Crockett Argus newspaper report of The Flag Presentation, July 17, 1861.*

With these words, Berta fully grasped for the first time that this man who seemed to her larger than life might never return—and she began to weep. Her sobs were obscured by the applause and shouts of the crowd around her. As John Wootters rejoined his troops to the side of the podium, the banner of the Crockett Southrons was unfurled and raised high on a standard. With the flag-bearer leading them, the men marched quickly around the town square and turned east on the Old San Antonio Road toward Louisiana and the unknown dangers that lay ahead.

A gentle hug from her father reminded Berta that their return trip home would begin soon, as evening was approaching. Oscar had the carriage and horses waiting as they left the town square, where many of the Crockett residents continued to mingle. Some spoke with excitement in their voices, while others appeared more somber, reflecting the realization that their beloved Southland was embarking on what could be a dangerous and costly war.

Smiling, John Smith held Anna Jane's hand as she began nodding off. The strenuous day had taken its toll on her fragile body. Hannah, having established that her mistress was comfortable and the other riders were situated, took her place atop the carriage next to Oscar, who had been waiting patiently. The occasional whinny of the horses and the sound of their hooves scratching the ground were sure signs they were ready to go. With a soft whistle, Oscar prompted them into action. They made their way through the thinning crowd and headed north toward Smith Landing Plantation.

The carriage made its way down the road and out of town, and was soon engulfed by the lengthening shadows of the pine forest. Berta noticed that her mother was now asleep, and her father encircled his shoulder with his wife's other arm. While her parents seemed to be resting quietly, she kept going over what John Wootters had said to her the previous evening. Berta could not stop thinking, wondering whether it was God's will for her brother, Lucius, and her friend, John Wootters, to be leaving their homes for war. She was certain that the answers to her questions would be slow in coming and would remain a lingering problem in her mind. Anxious for a distraction, Berta remembered her promise to learn a new song on the piano, one that seemed so popular with the Houston County band and everyone at the celebration. Even though she had not written music, she thought she could remember enough to play the lively tune titled "I Wish I Was in Dixie's Land."

John Smith smiled contentedly, tightening his embrace of his wife, as the carriage proceeded the twenty miles to their home. Berta watched him, wondering what he was thinking as he periodically glanced at her and then at the passing forest. How could she know that he was recalling the day of her birth nearly fourteen years earlier, an event that had so profoundly affected his life?

III

SEPTEMBER 1847
BLADEN COUNTY, NORTH CAROLINA

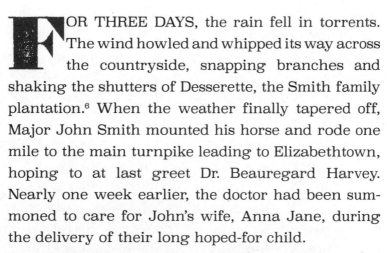

FOR THREE DAYS, the rain fell in torrents. The wind howled and whipped its way across the countryside, snapping branches and shaking the shutters of Desserette, the Smith family plantation.[6] When the weather finally tapered off, Major John Smith mounted his horse and rode one mile to the main turnpike leading to Elizabethtown, hoping to at last greet Dr. Beauregard Harvey. Nearly one week earlier, the doctor had been summoned to care for John's wife, Anna Jane, during the delivery of their long hoped-for child.

[6] *Appendix II. Item 3. Desserette–The Smith Plantation in Bladen County, North Carolina.*

Her labor, which had lasted more than a day and a night, and delivery had been fraught with problems from the beginning. Despite the assistance of Hannah, the household slave who had attended Anna Jane since before her marriage thirteen years earlier, the infant refused to enter the world until Dr. Harvey used his considerable skills to move her into the proper position. Anna Jane had rejoiced with her husband at the birth of their only daughter, her joy made even greater as the baby came fully crowned with a shock of red hair, clearly marking her as her mother's child. Major Smith, as John was known around Bladen County, North Carolina, was delighted at the prospect of another beautiful girl in his family, one who would surely be as bright and lively as his adored wife.

Their joy, however, was short-lived. By the second day, Anna Jane, who had been weakened by the prolonged labor and delivery, began hemorrhaging. Hannah tried every remedy she had learned from her mother and aunts in South Carolina, but the bleeding continued, with Anna Jane becoming more frail and pallid. By the second day, it was clear that her condition was deteriorating; the situation was made worse by her refusal to take food or water.

Both Hannah and Major Smith knew the situation was desperate. They also knew that for Anna Jane to survive, they would have to fetch Dr. Harvey. The river was swollen from the pounding rains; high water and a swift current made it impossible to navigate the twenty miles upstream to Elizabethtown. The only way to reach Desserette was by the turnpike road, which was more of a trail through the pine forest. It followed high ground on the west side of the Cape Fear River, but in most places it was a river of mud. Hannah suggested that Oscar could get through to Elizabethtown to find Dr. Harvey. Frantic with concern for Anna Jane, Major Smith agreed and dispatched him on this uncertain mission.

As the afternoon wore on and streaks of sunlight began to peek through the clouds, Major Smith left Hannah in charge and rode the mile to the main road to await Oscar's return and to view the storm and flood damage. Riding to wait for Oscar, Major Smith had time to size up the situation and to reflect on the events that had led to this day.

Oscar, he knew, held a very special place at Desserette as he was both responsible and very intelligent. He was also devoted to Hannah, whom he called his "special woman," and to the Smith family. Major Smith had designated him as overseer of the slaves who worked in the cotton fields, an increasing source of the family's prosperity. Oscar was respected, or at least feared, by the slaves who worked the fields, picked the cotton, removed the seeds, created the bales and stored them until their shipment downriver to the Port of Wilmington. Maintaining control of this workforce was essential, and Major Smith had learned over the years that having a slave serve as overseer was more effective than the harsher discipline used by many of his peers in Bladen County.

The possibility of unrest among the slaves was always a concern, and it was for this reason that the militia was such a constant presence. A leader of the local militia, Major Smith had a long tradition of military service in his family,[7] and he was highly regarded by the white population as a man of experience, skill and integrity. His own militia activities also meant that he was intimately familiar with that area of the Carolinas between the Cape Fear and Pee Dee Rivers and the counties to the south. It was there, further south, that he met Anna Jane Pouncey.

[7] *Appendix II. Item 4. The American Revolution in North Carolina, the Battle of Elizabethtown and the family of Major Smith.*

Following a period of intense courtship, he married Anna Jane and persuaded her to leave her beloved Cheraw area of South Carolina and reestablish her life in Bladen County, North Carolina. Once established in her new home, the young Mrs. Smith had quickly become a welcome and gracious addition to genteel society. She was widely regarded in the area surrounding Elizabethtown as a person of faith, wisdom and style.

In their thirteen years of marriage, Anna Jane had given birth three times before the arrival of this new baby girl. Two children had died in infancy, but a son, Lucius, had survived and was now an active, intelligent five-year-old. Since the birth of Lucius, Major Smith and Anna Jane had wondered why they had been unable to conceive again—and then came the joyful news that Anna Jane was pregnant. It seemed like an answer to their prayers. But now, her sudden physical decline following the birth cast a pall over the happy house. It seemed unlikely that Anna Jane could live without a miracle, which also brought the infant's survival into question.

As Major Smith rode toward the banks of the Cape Fear River, he was amazed at the sight of the usually placid waterway between the plantation and the city of Wilmington. For now, in the storm's aftermath, the water was rushing downstream faster than he could have imagined. The sheer power of the river, engorged by the rains of the previous days, was a stark reminder of how he and his family existed through the whims of nature. Everything they did on the plantation depended on the weather and the abundance of the soil. Had these rains arrived one month earlier, they would have wiped out a year's worth of cotton production. Fortunately, however, most of the crop had already been picked and placed in storage barns to dry. The work of ginning the cotton to remove the seeds and prepare bales would be done over the next several months. In years past, this particular stage in the process had severely restricted the amount of cotton they could produce, as it was slow and tedious. But the invention of the cotton gin by Eli Whitney had revolutionized cotton production.

Desserette and its counterparts across the South were able to meet the demands of cotton mills in Great Britain, which enriched planters in Carolina and throughout the Southland. Their ability to continue meeting this demand was limited only by the productivity of the land. Cotton, like tobacco two generations before, was highly profitable; however, the crop also quickly depleted the soil of its ability to sustain abundant production. The only remedy was to allow large tracts of land to lie fallow for two or more years before resuming production. The availability of suitable land was becoming a problem, so much so that some Bladen County neighbors had moved west in search of acreage to areas in Alabama, Mississippi and Texas.

Access to routes for delivering the cotton to a shipping point was also essential. The Cape Fear River was a key route for Desserette, and it was nearly always navigable by the barges that carried their crop to Wilmington. Major Smith and his fellow cotton growers often wondered how long it would be before steam-powered boats fully replaced the water current and mule-team assisted transport. Given that the SS Savannah had crossed the Atlantic more than thirty years earlier, there was little doubt that boats would soon appear that were capable of navigating the Cape Fear and other rivers to deliver cotton to the ports and the markets of the world.

One of Major Smith's great concerns was the growing need for more labor to work the expanding acreage devoted to cotton and prepare the crop for market. Cotton, while highly profitable, required even more labor than the naval stores industry. And while the plantation had enough slaves on site to do the work, he worried about the increasing cost and difficulty in managing the labor. The price of an able-bodied male slave was rising and, as the land became less productive, it was clear that the plantation's future profitability was in doubt. Already planters in more northerly states, such as Maryland, Delaware, even Virginia, were reducing their slave numbers and selling them to the expanding plantations in Mississippi and Louisiana. New slave imports into the United States were illegal which had been signed into law by President Thomas Jefferson forty years earlier.

As for Major Smith's own opinion and perception of slavery and individual slaves, these had changed since his marriage to Anna Jane. In 1834, after their wedding, her parents, Major James and Ann Kolb Pouncey, presented Anna Jane with two families of slaves whose ancestors had been owned by the Kolb and Pouncey families for a century. The respect that Anna Jane showed these individuals and the diligence with which they served her family had helped to tweak Major Smith's perspective. In particular, Hannah and Oscar, who had assumed responsibilities of the highest level of importance at Desserette, proved to be more like family than slave labor.

Never had this been more true than at the present moment, when the survival of his adored wife depended on Hannah's care and on Oscar's success in finding—and returning with—Dr. Harvey. As the day wore on and the shadows lengthened, Major Smith realized that if Oscar didn't bring the doctor soon, it might be too late. He prayed for Anna Jane's life to be spared. Indeed, Major Smith had learned much about faith from Anna Jane, who brought an awareness of Christian spirituality to their marriage. As a child, he had attended church services, but it was only in recent years that he had begun to understand and share Anna Jane's appreciation of God's daily presence their lives.

Not surprisingly, Major Smith's increased understanding of faith and spirituality also affected his evolving view of slavery. Anna Jane's family had arrived in the New World one hundred and fifty years earlier in search of religious freedom. Those moving to South Carolina from Pennsylvania had founded the Welsh Neck Baptist Church in an area known as the Old Cheraw District. While many generations had passed since anyone in their area was familiar with the language of Wales, the virtues of loyalty, moderation and sincerity that often defined the Welsh character remained strong. These traits were based on a deep religious conviction and the Baptist faith, which Major Smith gradually made his own.

Membership at the Smith's church was not taken lightly. Not only were members expected to have a significant understanding of their beliefs but they were also expected to demonstrate a level of spiritual maturity and behavior consistent with expectations in the New Testament gospels.[8] Moreover, all believers had equal standing in spiritual matters and were individually responsible for their own relationship with God and their salvation.

Major Smith had known few, if any, individuals who reflected the values of Christian love more than Hannah and Oscar. He admired their devotion to each other and to their children, especially their youngest who was clearly impaired and would likely never function independently. They were

---

[8] *Appendix II. Item 5. History of the Welsh Neck Baptist Church.*

loyal and trustworthy, and it was with complete confidence that he left Anna Jane in Hannah's capable hands.

Major Smith was roused from his ruminations by the appearance of a buggy with Oscar at the reins. A glimmer of hope reawakened in him as he prayed that the help Anna Jane so desperately needed was inside the carriage.

"Greetings to you my friend," came the familiar voice of Dr. Beauregard Harvey. "Surely your man, Oscar, is the most skillful of drivers. We could have never made this trip were it not for his ability to find alternate trails."

A short, middle-aged man with graying hair stepped out of the carriage. Dr. Harvey's usual proper dress—a black waist-coat and necktie—was rumpled after the arduous trip, but his warm smile set Major Smith at ease.

"Doctor Harvey, you can't imagine how grateful I am that you are here," Major Smith said, trembling. "My precious Anna Jane seems at the very brink of departing this life."

"John, please call me Beauregard, as my mother did," Dr. Harvey said, shaking the other man's hand. "Now, let's put aside pleasantries and get to the house without any further delay."

Bladen County was fortunate to count Dr. Harvey as a physician-in-residence. A native of Virginia, he had pursued his medical education in Philadelphia, but, as he would often comment, the cold winters and city life were not for him. So he eventually made Bladen County his home. A well-known and respected member of the Baptist Church, Dr. Harvey treated slaves as readily as he did their masters and was, as a result, regarded fondly by all.

During his rounds to the area's plantations, he had also become familiar with the remedies used by slave women, many of whom had extensive knowledge of herbs and potions that were carefully passed from one generation to the next.

On arriving at the main plantation house, the men were greeted by Hannah, who took the doctor's top coat and held the large front door open as he entered the dimly lit hallway.

"Thanks to the Lord you have come, Doctor," she said. "We have been praying for your safe arrival, and we hope you can help Miz Anna. She has had a really hard time of it."

"Well, I know she has had the best nurse in Bladen County helping her," Dr. Harvey smiled. "So tell me what has happened since I was here last."

Hannah described Anna Jane's initial recovery and subsequent lapse. First came two days of bleeding, more blood than Hannah thought could be in a human body. When the flow finally waned, Hannah went to wash her mistress and found something she hadn't expected.

"I couldn't tell what it was, and then I saw it was a piece of flesh," Hannah explained. "The flesh came loose, and I saved it for you to see. The bleeding stopped after that and there has not been any for at least an hour."

After studying the tissue Hannah had saved, Dr. Harvey told her that she had likely saved Anna Jane's life. The flesh was a part of the afterbirth, which didn't completely pass after the baby came, causing Anna Jane to lose blood until it did pass or Hannah removed it. At this point, Dr. Harvey turned his attention to the patient, noting that she could be roused but was clearly too weak to respond coherently or to move about without help. Her pallor seemed greater against the intense red of her hair; even the occasional freckle paled to the point of disappearing. Nevertheless, Dr. Harvey concluded that Anna Jane was making progress.

"And how is the baby, Hannah?" he asked.

"Oh, Dr. Harvey, little Abigail is just fine. Since Miz Anna wasn't able to nurse her, I took it on myself," Hannah smiled. "That child does have an appetite. She's hungry all the time except when she's sleeping."

John, whose attention was focused on his wife, heard that the baby was called Abigail and that Hannah was nursing her, and realized with some alarm that he had not stopped to consider whether his infant daughter was receiving nourishment, much less had been given a name.

"I didn't know you were still in a nursing way, but you must still be nursing your little one," Dr. Harvey said.

"I am," Hannah nodded. "I'm hoping little Ossie gets stronger, and some days he does seem more like he should be."

Hannah had borne many children, but from the moment of his birth she knew that her last baby was not like the others. He lacked the strength and alertness of her previous children, and his face and eyes looked slightly different. Knowing how distressed she was about her youngest, Dr. Harvey had been able to offer Hannah some words of comfort, but no diagnosis. In the three years since Ossie's birth, he had not discovered either an explanation of the illness or an effective treatment. Although he could sit up and crawl a bit, Ossie was not as active or vocal as other children his age. His sweet nature, however, compensated for any shortcomings. And while Hannah did worry about her son, she was convinced that things happen for a reason, that God had a plan. She liked to say that God wanted her to have Ossie, so she would have to do for him as best she could.

It occurred to Dr. Harvey to tell Hannah about a visit he was planning to Philadelphia in the spring. Once there, he said, he would consult with other doctors about Ossie's condition. The boy had such definite features that it was possible one of his medical colleagues may have examined other children like him and would know what could be done to help."[9]

By this time, Anna Jane began to stir, asking for some broth and tea, and the ever-watchful Hannah promptly left to fulfill the request. Major Smith, while elated by his wife's improvement, was confused about the care of the new baby; he knew that Hannah was nursing her, but he regretted not being more aware of her immediate needs. All of his attention and thought had been focused on Anna Jane for the past days. He took advantage of Hannah's brief absence to express to Dr. Harvey his trepidation about the slave nursing his daughter.

Dr. Harvey reassured him that, when it came to nourishment, there was no difference between African and Anglo-Saxon milk. "I can't imagine a better wet nurse for baby Abigail," he told the anxious father. "And from the sounds coming from the next room, the baby is strong enough to fully make use of her substantial lung power."

Even as the doctor spoke, the cries increased in volume and frequency. Right on cue, Hannah came in with the tray, but rather than serving Anna Jane first, she went straight to the cradle. A pair of loving arms and a few gentle words worked wonders to still the infant's distress, and Hannah took advantage of the quiet to present Abigail to the gathered admirers. Anna Jane held her baby and wept.

"Oh John, she really is a beautiful baby," she whispered. "I am so thankful to God for giving her to us."

While those few words left her breathless, she went on to tell her husband that she wanted to name her only daughter Philomena Berta Smith.

"Yes, Anna, I have heard you mention those names, but Hannah is already calling her Abigail," Major Smith said. "At

[9] *Although there is no definite evidence it is possible from the descriptions that this child had Down's Syndrome.*

some point in her life, this baby may decide to name herself something entirely different."

Anna Jane mustered a slight smile. "Where in creation did Hannah come up with such a name for this beautiful baby?" she said in a subdued voice. "It is an interesting name but not as classically elegant as befits such a tiny noble figure."

Hannah, having taken the baby in her arms, turned to offer her mistress some more broth. Anna Jane seized the moment to ask how she had thought of the name Abigail.

"Oh, Miz Anna, Abigail was one of the wisest and prettiest women in the Bible," Hannah answered. "The preacher at church told us about how Abigail tried to save her man from the devil's rum, which had got hold of him something hard. She saved him from being killed by King David's men, but the rum got him anyway. Because she was so smart and beautiful, she became King David's wife."[10]

At this moment, the baby began to wail again, and Hannah went off to feed her. Major Smith, who had heard Hannah's explanation marveled at how much she knew about the world without ever having left the Carolinas. Taking his wife's hand, he reiterated his concern for her health and reminded her that all would be well as long as she was well.

"Whatever the baby is called, she will always be a blessing to her family," he said. "Now you let Hannah care for the baby, and you eat and rest. We all need you to recover."

Anna Jane put on a brave face for Major Smith's sake. In the back of her mind, however, she knew that her recovery would be a long, slow journey. Already she was overwhelmed with a weakness that felt insurmountable. As sleep began to overtake her, she prayed to God to let her live to see her

---

[10] *The Holy Bible, Old Testament, 1Samuel 25:14–42.*

precious new baby grown and to face the future, whatever it might hold, with her dearest John. And so she slept, her faith a constant reassurance through the night.

SPRING 1857
BLADEN COUNTY, NORTH CAROLINA

BERTA RAN INTO THE COOKING HOUSE and was greeted by a wave of heat and a medley of mouth-watering smells. But she was much too excited to be distracted by the aroma of baking bread.

"Come quickly, Hannah, and see what is happening to the old possum!" she cried, tugging on the slave's apron. "The one you feed and worry about so much is in the smokehouse, and something is going on."

The kitchen at Desserette was Hannah's fiefdom, and there was little doubt as to who was in charge. With a fire usually going in the long fireplace, she would move the glowing coals to the end, where she worked her magic over the skillet or cauldron. Baked sweets. Spicy concoctions. Savory stews. There was always something delicious brewing in the cooking house.

Today, Hannah frowned her disapproval at the girl's outburst, even as Ossie squealed with delight. He stopped shelling peas long enough to acknowledge Berta, then quickly returned to the job at hand. Hannah smiled while trying to appear indignant at the sudden intrusion of a hollering white child into her domain.

"Miss Abigail, you be careful," she scolded. "You are so riled up, you may faint away." Hannah was especially fond of the nine-year-old, whom she had taken care of since her birth. Anna Jane's ongoing debilitated state meant that Berta often sought Hannah's company and counsel so as not to disturb her mother.

Ossie was several years older than Berta, but had never developed normally; his speech and mind were like that of a three-year-old child, not one who was already thirteen. While his limitations were many, he was content to spend hours shelling peas at a small table in the cooking house under his mother's watchful eye. When not occupied with this task, he would use charcoal fragments to create designs on wooden shingles. These artworks received Ossie's intense devotion, and only he knew what they meant. One thing was certain: he prized them and fiercely protected his stable of art projects. Even with his limited speech skills, he had no difficulty expressing his intentions or desires, and was fully capable of showing affection for Hannah and his father, Oscar. He was also fond of Berta and always greeted her with genuine affection, although he would refer to her at various times as either his "mudder" or his "sisser."

Caring for Ossie was a high priority for Hannah, and she was thankful that her mistress, Anna Jane, and Major Smith had promised to provide for him and for her as long as the child needed care. The family physician, Dr. Harvey, had not been able to explain the child's lack of development; even a discussion with medical colleagues had failed to enlighten the situation. Other physicians had cared for similarly affected children, but no remedy or explanation had ever been found. What they did find was that affected children usually did not live to maturity; indeed, Ossie had already surpassed most expectations.

"Old possum seems to do just fine," Hannah said, wiping her hands. "Now if you will let go of my apron, I will come with you to see what is such a worry. You finish your work, Ossie, while I find out what the commotion is all about."

Age had slowed Hannah somewhat, but her curiosity and alertness remained sharp. She was about ten years older than her mistress, and had spent most of her life helping to care for Anna Jane and her family. Her own parents had been slaves in the South Carolina household of Anna Jane's parents. As she followed Berta out to the smokehouse, she wondered what could upset the child so.

"Look, Hannah! Look in the window and you can see the old possum," Berta pointed. "What in heaven's name is happening to her?"

"I don't see anything happening to her. She's likely scared enough to jump out of her hide, so she's pretending she's dead. She's just playing possum."

"She does look dead now, but a minute ago she was lying on her back and seemed to have little bugs crawling on her stomach," Berta said. "I don't see any little bugs now so maybe they killed her! What could be the trouble, Hannah?"

"Miss Abigail, those weren't bugs," Hannah chuckled. "Those were her babies being born and crawling into her pouch, where they will be warm and can nurse until they get big enough to look like little possums and come out in the daylight. I knew she was expecting babies as she was getting bigger. She probably climbed in the shed to have the babies cause she still thinks that old tree is hers, even though it has been cut into firewood."

"That old possum sure is brave to lie there with her babies instead of running away like she usually does," Berta said.

"I don't doubt that she is a brave possum, but as soon as she thinks you're gone, she will be out of the shed or hiding somewhere in the wood pile as fast as you can blink your eyes," Hannah said. "We'll let her be now. She's had enough excitement for one day."

Berta climbed down from her perch by the smokehouse window, reluctant to leave the wondrous sight of the possum and her babies. As they neared the kitchen structure, she chewed her bottom lip thoughtfully. Hannah could tell that something was on the child's mind, but she waited patiently until Berta was ready to talk. It took only a few minutes for Berta to ask her question.

"I know that Mother tells me to do what's right, but sometimes it's hard to do just as she says and then to have to tell her what I did anyway," she frowned. "How do I know what's the right thing to do, and how do I make myself not want something else?"

"Miss Abigail, when you're young you haven't had as many chances to know what happens when you make choices. That's why you need to do what your Momma tells you to do as long as you are a child," Hannah said. "Even though people know what's right they sometimes act like they don't, so God gave us commandments to help guide us. An animal like old possum does what their nature tells them to do: run away, stay and fight, or play possum. God has put the nature that best suits the animal inside them so they don't need to think about anything. People are different. They have to find out what's right and then be brave enough to do it."

"I knew you would know the answer!" Berta said as they walked to the cook house. "You know so much."

Pleased, but preoccupied with thoughts of preparing dinner, Hannah gave the little girl a hug and shooed her back to the main house. Berta skipped through the entry parlor to the back sitting room where her mother preferred to rest during the day near a fireplace that was nearly always in operation. Cold weather or any chill in the air made Anna Jane uncomfortable. She had not been the same since her last pregnancy. Her monthly menstruation had stopped altogether, and she had never been able to nurse her new baby. Hannah had continued to nurse Berta, who had grown into a healthy, active child. Anna Jane and John regretted not being able to have more children, but they were thankful for the son and daughter they did have.

As was the situation for many children of plantation owners in Bladen County, itinerant tutors would come to their home for several days at a time and add to the education that was provided by the parents. Berta had become an avid reader with an insatiable curiosity. Her questions were constant, her energy boundless. Anna Jane was also pleased to note that Berta was musically inclined, indeed talented. She had learned to play familiar tunes on the harpsichord that had been brought from South Carolina years earlier. Then one year, her music tutor mentioned that a modern forte-piano was for sale in Charleston; Major Smith had had it shipped to Wilmington and eventually to Desserette. When the instrument was found to be in good working order, he bought it for the price of eighteen bales of cotton.[11]

The arrival of the piano at the plantation was an event that none in attendance would ever forget. It was an upright piano of grand proportions, at least nine feet tall and weighing nearly a thousand pounds. Oscar and five other able men struggled to move it from the dock to a wagon and then into the main house. The piano had apparently been created by a craftsman named George Traegser from Covington, Kentucky. A small silver plaque on the piano stated that it was registered as Patent No. 28, but no other information about its history was available. It was not clear to either the Smith family or to local musicians why it was patented, but they assumed that a louvered front panel operated by foot pedals that modulated the piano's tones and the fact that it had only eighty-six keys were likely its unique characteristics.

The piano soon became a cherished part of their home and a great source of pleasure for the entire family. Berta, in particular, came to consider the piano a close friend as entertainment for a young child on the plantation was limited. She saw white children of her age only when they gathered in Elizabethtown for shopping or church services, or during occasional visits to neighboring plantations. She had read more than once all the books from their library that she could master, and her mother did not permit her to wander about the plantation out of sight of the main house or Hannah. She spent hours playing etudes of varying difficulty provided by her tutor. As he also brought the music for their church services in Elizabethtown, much of Berta's repertoire consisted of religious music.

[11] *Personal communication from Frances Wootters Denman, daughter of Berta Smith and granddaughter of Anna Jane and Major John Smith.*

"Berta, I am so glad you have come into the house as I was wondering what adventure you had been up to," Anna Jane greeted her daughter.

"You won't believe what I have just seen," Berta said. "If it hadn't been for Hannah, it would have been terribly frightening."

"Indeed, what could have caused such concern for so intrepid an explorer as my little girl?"

Berta spent several minutes regaling her mother with the story of the old possum, the babies and the insight Hannah had given her into human and animal nature. Anna Jane listened intently, smiling and marveling at the morning's events. Berta's joy made her own physical limitations seem less important.

"Truly, the Lord has given you an inquiring mind and a gentle heart, and I know that you will grow into a very brave person who is also thoughtful and kind," Anna Jane said. "I do not believe you can teach a person to be brave, but you can certainly learn how to control your fears."

At the moment, Anna Jane was controlling her concern about her husband and son, who were down in Texas, and praying for their safe return. Once a part of Mexico and then briefly an independent country, Texas seemed very foreign and far away to this Southern-bred girl. Major Smith had taken both Oscar and Lucius with him on this adventure. Rumor had it that the vast state had fertile acreage as far as the eye could see and a pleasant climate, too. Anna Jane's greatest fear was that the increasing population and scarcity of arable land in the South would propel her husband to move the family to Texas, a world away from Bladen County and her family in the Cheraw District. She also worried whether she would survive the trip if they did move.

Berta had her own private concerns, namely whether or not they would be able to take the piano. Given how large and heavy it was, she had her doubts. But she pressed her mother, pointing out that she would never feel lonely as long as she had her parents and her beloved instrument nearby.

"I am certain that your father would find a way to keep you and the piano together," Anna Jane laughed. "He is very proud of you for learning to play it so well and continuing to improve your skills. Why don't you play some tunes while I take a rest?"

A letter had arrived from Major Smith several days earlier with news of his return from Texas and indicated that the ship should land at Wilmington by the end of that week. He wrote that he and Oscar would waste no time in returning to Desserette, as he had obtained horses for the last leg of the journey; their baggage would arrive later. In the meantime, Lucius would remain in Texas with their new overseer, Elijah Chadwick, to take care of some business that had not been concluded. Brimming with enthusiasm and optimism, Major Smith's letter confirmed the bright economic prospects in this new state.

While he didn't say it outright, it seemed to Anna Jane that a move to Texas was now inevitable—and soon. In earlier letters, Major Smith had mentioned how much their son had grown and matured into a competent youth, capable of managing affairs and making thoughtful decisions. Both parents were proud of how Lucius was turning out; as a young boy, he had been more interested in riding horses and exploring the hills and forests of Bladen County. His tutors had initially recommended that he continue his education at the new Roanoke College in Virginia. They believed that its ties to the Christian faith would benefit both his educational and spiritual growth; Lucius, however, had never been partial to either scholarship or religion.

Anna Jane was startled from her reverie by shouts from the garden. Much to her surprise, John burst into the room moments later; his most recent letter still lay in her lap. Overwhelmed by joy and relief, Anna Jane felt a surge of strength from the emotion of the moment, a strength that propelled her from her chair and into John's outstretched arms. As she collapsed against his chest, she knew that whatever the future held for them, she would be a part of it.

"Oh, John, I am so thankful that God has returned you to me safely," she said, hugging him. "We have all missed you terribly, but it looks like the trip to Texas has certainly agreed with you."

Anna Jane sat back down and invited Major Smith to share the details of his trip, of how Lucius was faring and what was keeping him from coming home. Any thoughts Berta had of practicing the piano fled at the sight of her father. Eager to hear about the place that might be their new home, she climbed up into his lap. The dust from his long ride would have to settle later. The ladies wanted news, and they would not wait.

A tall man with broad shoulders and an air of authority, Major Smith possessed a naturally gentle expression and an ever-present slight smile. His hair was thinning, but he sported a well-trimmed beard; his remarkable blue eyes, surrounded by fine lines, lent him a certain air of wisdom. Hannah appeared then with a pot of warm tea and some cakes, along with a glass of sweet milk for Berta.

"The only things more beautiful than the blessed land of Texas are sitting in this room with me," Major Smith said. "I am so grateful to be able to return home to be with you."

Insisting that Hannah also serve generous portions of cake and tea to Oscar, he told the three women that not only could he not have made the trip without him, but he could only have left for such an extended period knowing that Hannah was there to care for his wife and daughter. For her part, Hannah informed him that Miz Abigail had diligently practiced her piano and that Oscar was already recounting their adventures in Texas—and how much he liked it.

"Texas is really a special land," Major Smith said, turning his attention back to Berta and Anna Jane "I think what makes it so special is the attitude of the people who live there, although the climate and soil are so blessed that God has surely had a special hand in it."

The best route to this promised land, he said, would be overland to Mobile, Alabama or to New Orleans, and then by ship to Galveston, at that time the largest city in Texas. Calling it very busy and progressive, Major Smith noted that Galveston was much newer than Charleston and also lacked the long-established residents that could sometimes be hostile to newcomers. Texas, on the other hand, was an open place, ripe with opportunity. It was a place where hard work and honesty were rewarded generously and where everyone was welcomed.

Galveston, in addition to being the state's largest metropolis, was a growing port on the Gulf of Mexico. It boasted an active cotton market and, Major Smith noted, bankers who appreciated the value of that product. The city was also prosperous enough to attract musical groups and artists, especially architects. At least three rivers fed into Galveston Bay, the largest of which was the Trinity River. During their visit, Major Smith, Oscar and Lucius took a packet steamer up the Trinity to explore the countryside. It was a ten-day journey that changed the course of their lives.

Not only did the landscape—gentle hills covered with stately pine trees—look very much like Bladen County, but they passed acre after acre that had never been touched by a plow. Major Smith anticipated that cotton would thrive in this environment; indeed, as they ventured further upriver, they saw that some planters were already producing a fine crop. And then there was the climate: warmer than the Carolinas, with mild winters and enough rainfall. The most promising area he'd seen was in Houston County on the Trinity River, whose main city, Crockett, was named for Davy Crockett, who fought and died at the Alamo.

Houston County was not to be confused with the city of Houston, Major Smith pointed out. That city was also named for a Texas hero, Sam Houston, the first president of the Republic of Texas. But instead of rolling hills and crisp pines, it featured a lush, flat, humid landscape situated on the banks of Buffalo Bayou.

Major Smith spoke with the passion of a religious zealot. He had learned much about this new state and all it had to offer, and he was clearly eager to go. Anna Jane knew the decision was all but made.

"I can see that you are in love with Texas," she told her husband. "The only matter not resolved in your mind is when we should move, not whether!"

"It does offer good prospects for our plantation and our family," Major Smith agreed. "If we ever want to expand our property in this part of the world, some move will be necessary."

Anna Jane nodded, not wanting to reveal how heavy her heart was at the thought of leaving family and friends and everything familiar. Rather, she hoped that Major Smith's enthusiasm was contagious, and that his joy would become hers.

Having prayed for guidance, she hoped now that this move would bring blessing and happiness to all in her household.

"Well, my dear, if the climate really is as warm as you suggest, I may be able to survive without a fire in the hearth and a shawl around my shoulders," Anna Jane said with a twinkle in her eye. "I think I might enjoy that circumstance."

"Father, will we be able to take the piano with us to Texas?" asked Berta from the comfort of his lap. "It's so big that I can't imagine a wagon large enough to carry it."

Major Smith reassured her that the massive instrument would have a place in their new home. He had, in fact, already secured passage for it and all their furnishings on a ship that would sail from Wilmington to Galveston. As the sea voyage was long and subject to weather delays, he planned for his family and the slave families to take the household goods and travel overland through Atlanta to Montgomery, Alabama and finally to the port of Mobile. From there, they would sail to Galveston, with a stop in New Orleans, arrive in Texas on practically the same day as their furnishings.

During his Texas tour, Major Smith had purchased a new property in Houston County, including four sections of some of the finest farmland he'd ever seen. Lucius had stayed behind to help Mr. Chadwick with the supervision of the new property and to ensure that there were enough slaves to clear the ground and plant a crop of cotton before the spring rains cleared out. The Smith family would also have a new house; by year's end, they would be living in a home on a high bluff overlooking the Trinity River. As Major Smith elaborated on their route and plans, Anna Jane ticked off a mental list of people to visit on their way down to Mobile, including friends in Georgia and a close cousin in Marengo County, Alabama, people she'd thought never to see again.

Surely this was a sign of happy times ahead.

"I know that you have always wanted Lucius and Berta to attend college in Virginia, but I have learned of a university with a reliable reputation that is promoted by the Baptist convention" Major Smith's voice broke interrupted her day-dream. "And thinking of Berta's musical talent, I have also been told there are tutors who should be able to visit our new home to help her with her studies and musical training. I expect to provide every opportunity for Berta whether it is in Texas, the eastern states or the music centers of Europe."

Berta's ears perked up at the mention of her name. "I will be happy to go to Texas as long as I'm with you and Mother and Hannah and the piano," she said. "I will pray to God to make me brave enough to overcome any fears. If the old pos-sum can overcome her fears, then I can, too."

A puzzled Major Smith ruffled his daughter's hair and requested that she entertain them with a lively tune on the piano. Noting that Hannah was waiting outside the parlor, no doubt listening to his description of their future home, he then mused aloud about more tea, and about wanting Hannah to hear about their new home.

Minutes later, as if by magic, Hannah entered, holding a steaming pot of tea.

"Would you be needing some more tea, Major Smith?"

"Yes, that would be most welcome," he said. "Please make sure Oscar tells you all about our trip, Hannah."

"Well, he told me he didn't see bears or wild Indians, but I'm still wondering about what's there," she said. "And I'm wondering who's going with you to Texas and who's staying here."

Major Smith knew this would come up, and he had a ready answer.

"I can't take everyone to Texas, but as I have told you before, you, Oscar and your relatives will always be with us," he said. "No one knows what the future holds, but I am sure that it will be better for all of us in this new land. I will make good on the promises that I have made in the past."

He then turned to his daughter and said, "Indeed, Berta, we will take your piano to Texas. Now, can you play my favorite song "Standing on Jordan's Stormy Banks?""

"Oh, yes! I will be glad to play it for you," she clapped her hands and jumped down off his lap. "We could even change the words if you and Mother will sing it."

Together, they joined in this new version of the song:

> *On Cape Fear's stormy banks I stand,*
>   *and cast a wishful eye,*
> *To Texas' fair and happy lands where my*
>   *possessions lie.*
> *I am bound for the promised land, I am bound for*
>   *Texas land.*
> *Who will come and go with me, I am bound for*
>   *the promised land.*

The clearest voice of all was Hannah's, which floated out the windows and up in the bright afternoon sky.

CHRISTMASTIME 1857
HOUSTON COUNTY, TEXAS

IN DECEMBER, darkness came early to East Texas, and the dense forests further muted the effects of the fading sunlight. On this night, the moon was nearly full and reflecting off the pale roadway as the Smith family's carriage rumbled toward a new home in Texas. This was the final leg of their journey, one that had begun in Bladen County, North Carolina and taken more than two months to complete.

The first weeks were very tiring for Anna Jane as the group traveled through Georgia and Alabama. Stops in Atlanta and Montgomery had allowed her some respite, and a visit to her cousin's plantation in Marengo County, Alabama had boosted her mood and energy level.

The remainder of the trip had been by water: down the Tombigbee River to Mobile and then by ship to New Orleans. A fair breeze had filled the sails from New Orleans to Galveston, where they remained for a week while Anna Jane and Major Smith made arrangements for their arrival in Houston County. When the day of departure finally arrived, the entire party was eager to see the new plantation and settle down. The autumn rains had been gentle, and the current of the Trinity River did not unduly prolong their trip to Crockett.

No one was more excited to land in Houston County than Anna Jane, whose desire to see her son after nearly a year gave her an energy and strength she hadn't had for years. Lucius had been awaiting their arrival for several days and would meet them near Crockett at the Trinity River landing known as Hall's Bluff. He would have a carriage for the family, wagons for their luggage and several of the slaves who had been with them since leaving North Carolina. They would go by roadway through Crockett to their new home; the boat would continue upriver with their furnishings, including Berta's piano, to the landing at their new plantation, which was as far as the river was navigable. That landing would serve as a future loading point for the cotton produced on their land and at surrounding plantations for shipment back to Galveston.

In the time that he had been away from home, Lucius, now sixteen years old, had grown into a tall, handsome young man with a full head of dark-brown hair. He had also developed physically, thanks to his work on the land and the new home. On spotting him in the gathered crowd, Anna Jane recognized a younger, taller, perhaps even more attractive, version of his father, and her eyes welled up with tears of joy.

As the riverboat docked, Lucius immediately took charge, directing the unloading of the cargo and passengers. Both Major Smith and Anna Jane would later comment on how mature and confident their son seemed as he took control of their disembarkation.

With the luggage secured and the passengers in place, the Smiths proceeded on their journey from the landing to the town of Crockett, where they would spend the rest of that day and the night becoming familiar with their new hometown. Anna Jane and Berta visited the Baptist church and the mercantile store, while Major Smith called at the Masonic Lodge with Lucius where he renewed his acquaintance with friends made on his earlier visit. By late afternoon the following day, it was time to leave and head north, as it would take several hours to get to the new house.

The evening shadows had already begun to lengthen as Lucius took the reins to guide the carriage. Elijah Chadwick, the overseer, had preceded them with the wagons, luggage and household slaves. Major Smith joined his son atop the carriage, eager to hear what progress had been made on the building and the land in his absence.

"I think you will be pleased," Lucius told him. "There are only a few minor details to be finished in the house over the next few weeks, and Elijah's crew has cleared land for planting cotton, although next year's crop will be smaller than in the future."

He went on to confirm his father's suspicions that the soil was, indeed, very fertile, and announced that a small garden planted just a few months earlier had already provided a good crop of late corn.

Inside the carriage, Berta fidgeted with anticipation, chattering as the carriage rumbled through the night. She was delighted at the prospect of a new home, new surroundings, new friends—and particularly pleased that her piano, which she'd glimpsed as it was unloaded in Galveston, had survived the long trip seemingly unscathed. During their brief stay in Crockett, she had also met Mr. Rogerson, a piano teacher from Galveston, who played music she'd never heard before—compositions by Beethoven and Chopin that seemed much more complicated than the church hymns she'd grown up playing. He had high expectations, she confided to her mother, so she would need to practice quite a bit to prepare for her lessons.

"He thinks that you are blessed with talent, and he wants to help you use it well," Anna Jane smiled at her daughter's excitement. "Your piano and its companions from Bladen County will be in their new home very soon, as will you."

"And I am sure that I will love it there, Mother!"

Watching her daughter speak with animation and conviction, Anna Jane realized that she had a very independent head on her shoulders and would soon become a young woman. Although Anna Jane had often prayed for greater physical strength, this had never been fully granted, and she was reminded daily of her limited stamina and dependence on her family for so many things. She was thankful that her spirit and mind were unaffected and thankful to have survived long enough to witness Berta develop a keen mind of her own, an insatiable curiosity, spiritual awareness and a significant, though untested, musical talent.

Indeed, listening to Berta's animated discourse during their two-month journey made her worry somewhat about the child's future prospects in this new land. She and Major Smith had already discussed educational opportunities, and they would continue her schooling at home as they had in Bladen County. While in Galveston, they had secured the services of two tutors: one whose skill was in mathematics and science, and another who could instruct Berta in Latin, history and literary matters. They would visit for several days every month for instruction and to help the Smiths acquire new volumes for their library. As for Berta's musical education, Anna Jane had no doubt that it would be well maintained and challenged by her third tutor, Mr. Rogerson.

Anna Jane had always assumed that Berta would be able to continue her studies in Virginia, at such a place as the newly created Hollins College. But that now seemed very far away, perhaps too far. Nevertheless, Major Smith had assured her that when the time came, he would send an appropriate member of Hannah and Oscar's family to accompany and look after their daughter.

Like other members of Anna Jane's family, Berta's most striking feature was her red hair and fair complexion, which was highlighted by constantly pink cheeks and an occasional freckle. These features had been passed down to Anna Jane from her grandmother, Sara James Kolb, and her mother, Ann Kolb Pouncey. If she could have changed anything, it would have been to give Berta some curl to her red locks, which, although lustrous and thick, knew only to hang in a straight line. Consequently, the child had worn her hair in braids or pigtails for most of her life.

Berta was also unusually kind and patient, especially for someone her age. Perhaps she had learned this by witnessing her own mother's limitations, or by having spent so much time with Ossie, Hannah's son, whose limited mental and physical abilities meant that he needed constant care and supervision. Whatever the reason, Anna Jane was, once again, grateful for her daughter's good nature. Her brief reverie was interrupted by Berta's continuing commentary.

"The trip has been a long one, but it was very exciting, especially the sailing from Mobile to Galveston. I had never seen so large a schooner and had never expected to really sail on one," Berta said as the carriage bounced along the rutted roadway. " Although after this trip, I am not sure I will ever be able to leave our new home in Texas. It seems that we have gone halfway around the world, and we still have a few more miles to travel."

In the interest of distracting her, Anna Jane steered Berta to the subject of Lucius and how much he had changed in such a short time.

"Lucius seems to be a grown man," Berta agreed. "I don't remember him being so handsome, either."

"Indeed he is," her mother smiled at Hannah, who nodded. "And only last year, he was still a boy."

And so the conversation went from topic to topic—from the paddle-wheeler trip up the Trinity River to the perils of sandbars as described by the riverboat captain. Berta worried aloud that their new home might be too isolated, but her mother quickly dispelled the notion, pointing out that Crocket was not only close enough, but that it also boasted a comfortable hotel, a welcoming church and a well-stocked mercantile store, which was owned by Col. John Long and Mr. Lodwick Downes. In a happy coincidence, Mr. Downes' wife, Harriet, was also from North Carolina, so she and Anna Jane had much to talk about in their first meeting.

As it happened, Mr. Downes' nephew, James Wootters, helped his uncle in the mercantile store. A native of Maryland, James had finished a college course in Maryland after both of his parents died. He hoped that his younger siblings, including a brother named John, would eventually leave the eastern shore of Maryland and join him in Texas, where he said, there were greater fortunes to be made.

By the time the Smiths reached their new home, night had fallen. The short days of winter made the trip seem longer than it really was, and as they approached the house, the candlelight from the windows was a welcome sight for the weary travelers. Even though Houston County was warm at Christmastime, at least by Carolina standards, a blazing fire in the entry parlor fireplace made for a cheerful reception.

Even more cheerful than the warm fireplace was the broad smile on Oscar's face. He had been waiting for them at the entrance that led from the roadway to the plantation. The main house, which was close to the Trinity River landing site, was still several miles from the turn-in off the main road. The carriage path to the plantation house, while newer, was an improvement over the muddy, rut-filled thoroughfare. The principal north-south roadway through Houston County continued northward, from Crockett to the town of Palestine. In Crockett, it crossed the long-established El Camino Real roadway, known as the Old San Antonio Road, which had been built by the first European settlers in Texas in the 1690s.[12] While the older road was in good condition despite its age, the north-south route remained a tedious and unpredictable route, despite increasing numbers of travelers.[13]

The new homes for the Smith family and the slaves that accompanied them from North Carolina, while incomplete, were enough to ensure their comfort and safety until Oscar

[12] "Old San Antonio Road", Handbook of Texas Online.
[13] Bishop, E. Houston County, Handbook of Texas Online.

and his crew could finish building them. The spring planting would demand their efforts soon enough.

Anna Jane and Berta were delighted to see some of their familiar furnishings already in their new home, including the oversized piano which had a special room of its own off the entry parlor. Oscar had arrived at the plantation with their household goods and a complement of able-bodied men to move the furnishings from the dock to the home. The task had been accomplished and added to the sense of familiarity and welcome felt by Berta, her mother and Hannah.

"I know the piano will need to be tuned," Anna Jane said to her daughter. "But I believe you have some of the written music that we brought from North Carolina. This has been a fatiguing day, and I would like nothing better than to sit with your father in the new parlor and listen to you try out your instrument. Songs of the Christmas season, perhaps?"

Berta hurried off to find her music among the various crates in the entry hall, glad to have a job to do. Her parents' relief was palpable as they savored the silence, the warm fire and the end of the journey they had undertaken.

"I am so thankful that we are at last home again," Anna Jane said, embracing her husband. "I hope we will never be apart for such a long time again."

"Darling Anna, your presence and love warms my life better than any fireplace ever could," Major Smith said. "No one could be as happy as I am that we are finally here."

He would not have any reason to be away, he said, except for occasional trips to Galveston to look after their financial affairs. There was a great deal of work yet to be done to make the plantation productive and prosperous, and he planned to be there every step of the way. Those words were music to Anna Jane's ears. Nothing mattered to her more than family, which led her to broach a subject she had been turning over in her mind since leaving Bladen County.

It was about Hannah, Oscar and their relatives. While Anna Jane's greatest regret was her lack of strength and stamina, she found herself tonight sitting in front of a fire with her husband in Texas. The journey, previously unthinkable, had been made possible because of Hannah's efforts and devotion. Since the day Berta was born, Anna Jane had depended on Hannah, as a helper and a trusted friend. After all, Hannah, Oscar and Ossie were God's children, just as she, Berta, Lucius and Major Smith were; God, she reminded her husband, was color-blind and did not distinguish between black and white, slave or master. Anna Jane's thoughts on slavery struck a slight note of discord in an otherwise very happy marriage. It was a pity, Major Smith pointed out, that the country had not been able to resolve the problem of slavery, all the more so because he could not envision a peaceful solution to this contentious issue that had divided families, communities and states.

Eager to avoid an unpleasant discussion, Anna Jane applauded loudly when Berta finished her first piece.

"Just listen to her play, John!" she said. "I am so fortunate that you are here to share this blessing with me. Now tell me all about what you, Lucius and Oscar have done to provide us with such a welcoming new home."

As it turned out, there was much tell. His first trip to Texas and subsequent meetings in Galveston had led to the property opportunities in Houston County. Through his affiliation with the Masons, he met Samuel May Williams,[14] whose introductions led to Houston County. After he traveled the Trinity River with Lucius, Oscar and Elijah Chadwick

---

[14] *Appendix II, Item 6. Samuel May Williams of Galveston, Texas.*

for a first-hand look at the area, it was clear that the delivery of cotton to the port would be both swift and efficient. Moreover, much of the land had never been cultivated, which was good for planting but also meant that clearing it would be a challenge. The pine forests provided enough timber for any construction needs, with enough left over to sell to help meet the growing demand for new buildings in Galveston and the expanding town of Houston.

Crockett proved to be a progressive town. Col. Long, an owner of both the hotel and the mercantile store, had played an important role in persuading the Texas and Red River Telegraph Company to bring its service to Crocket several year earlier. Barring any storms, which could interrupt the lines, the telegraph allowed them to communicate with cotton brokers and financial contacts in a matter of hours, rather than days. It also connected Crockett to Galveston and cities to the east, such as Shreveport, New Orleans and Natchez, thereby enhacing its own importance.

By the time he returned to North Carolina to arrange for the family's passage to Galveston, the building process was underway, and Elijah Chadwick and Lucius had the job well in hand. Major Smith was especially impressed with his son's efforts and didn't hesitate to say so.

"I am certain that Lucius will be able to contribute to the direction that our property will need in the future," he said. "He has matured in the past year and is showing qualities of which we can both be proud."

"Indeed, he seems very confident in his abilities," Anna Jane said.

"There is still much for you to see," Major Smith said. "Now I want you to rest and recover strength. I will show you the property tomorrow in the daylight."

Berta, having finished playing the carols, entered the parlor to inquire about dinner first, and then whether she could play Christmas melodies all year long. Her parents laughed.

"Sweet Berta, you can play them every day if you wish," Anna Jane said.

"It's just that they remind me why Hannah told me on the ship that we don't need to be afraid," the child said, frowning with concentration. "It's because God is with us."

"As you grow older, you will understand even more how God's presence in your life will help you overcome your fears," her mother nodded. "I am thankful that Hannah has told you those things and she is very correct in doing so. But now we should see what Lucius and Mr. Chadwick have provided for our first meal in our new home!"

On entering the new dining room, a generous banquet awaited them. Berta hopped from one foot to another in anticipation of the meal. There was venison, sweet corn and an abundance of freshly baked bread and tarts. The corn, Lucius pointed out proudly, was from the first harvest of their very own garden.

"We aren't the best of cooks, but Elijah and I hope the meal is an adequate welcome," Lucius said. "We have had more practice with the cook-fire since being away from Hannah! We have many reasons to welcome your arrival."

"Well, you must be getting enough to eat as you seem to have grown a foot since I last saw," his mother said. "I am just so thankful to see you looking so well that I can scarcely keep a dry eye. And this delicious meal is an extra gift."

Over dinner, Lucius brought them up to date on how he had been spending his time in Houston County. Constructing the house and other buildings had been his principle task, one that could not have been done without the help of their new neighbors, the Wallings. Their son, Hosea, had become a real friend. On the few days that Lucius didn't work on the property, Hosea had taken him to nearby fishing and hunting areas. Hosea's older brother, Robert, was a skilled craftsman who had also helped with the construction. The Wallings lived nearby on the road to Crockett in a small community called Daly's.

"I am delighted that we have such pleasant neighbors, and I look forward to meeting Mrs. Walling," Anna Jane said. "Your father and I are very proud of what you have accomplished, Lucius."

Berta, in the meantime, was looking at her brother in a new light. During the day that she and Lucius had been together for the first time in nearly a year, she had been astonished at his growth and newly acquired manliness. She realized that the brother that seemed near her age had now moved to the adult world.

"Well, I must say that I am certainly glad to see our property so productive," Anna Jane said, shaking out her napkin before putting it in her lap. "But I want you to remind all of you to use your knife and fork when eating the corn-on-the-cob, as we don't want our children to eat with their hands like savages!"

A proper Southern lady, Anna Jane always insisted on good manners and high standards, no matter the levity of the occasion.

"Indeed, my dear Anna Jane, we will expect only the highest degree of decorum at the Smith Landing Plantation," Major Smith smiled broadly. "Especially when enjoying an outstanding meal of corn and venison."

And with that, the reunited Smith family joined hands to express their thanks to God for bringing them all safely to their new home.

VI

AUTUMN 1860
HOUSTON COUNTY, TEXAS

IN THE THREE YEARS since moving his family to Texas, Major Smith had frequently traveled to Galveston, as that city was the center of banking, commerce and trade on which his expanding plantation depended. He used those visits, as during this particularly warm week in late autumn, to attend to his cotton shipments and other business matters. In his opinion, the move to Texas had been the right one to make: this season's cotton harvest had been the most abundant in his memory. Enough rainfall and the labor of more than ninety slaves had yielded a bumper crop, more than anyone had expected.

Lucius, who was assuming more of the daily management of the plantation, had accompanied his father on this trip, and Major Smith was pleased to have the company. He appreciated the extended time available to visit with his son, knowing that opportunities for such conversations were becoming less and less frequent.

Perhaps more important than the cotton was the change in Anna Jane. Over the past three years, she had become much stronger, an improvement she attributed to the warmer climate. Berta, too, had grown remarkably and exhibited a significant talent for playing the oversized piano that was such a prominent presence in their home. Although still maturing, Berta bore an uncanny resemblance to her mother, not only physically, but also in her intelligence and sensitive spirit. Moreover, she was blossoming into a beautiful and talented young woman.

During his Galveston visits, Major Smith would also come with a list of requests from Anna Jane and Berta for items of clothing, decorations for their home and books for their expanding library. On this trip, he was especially interested in acquiring the final installments of the serial publication of Charles Dickens' novel, *A Tale of Two Cities*. Over the past year, these chapters had gradually made their way to the book dealer in Galveston, and the return trip up the Trinity River to Smith Landing would give him an opportunity to read this fascinating book.

The description of that particular era as "the best and worst of times" and by its characterization of "wisdom or foolishness, and belief or incredulity" struck a chord with Major Smith. He could not help but feel that these contrasts reflected what he was witnessing in Texas. The United States had recently come through the most intense and divisive presidential nomination effort in its history. People were angry, even more than Major Smith had imagined,[15] and there was an undercurrent of uncertainty rippling through the population. Despite the rosy outlook for his plantation and his family, he was not at all positive that things would turn out so well for the country.

Having finished breakfast on the first morning of their return trip, Major Smith and Lucius were enjoying a view of the marshlands from their deck chairs. The packet steamers that made the trip from Galveston to the towns and plantations along the Trinity River were shallow draft boats; they were able to cross Galveston Bay to the deeper waters of the river and avoid the changing locations of sandbars. During the first day on the river, they passed through swamps before reaching the piney woods further upstream. Once in the piney woodlands, they would see more settlements, towns and plantations, where the trees had been cut and the land planted in cotton and other crops.

Despite his optimism about their own situation, Major Smith was anxious about the political climate he had just observed in Galveston. It was obvious that the voters of Texas had already made up their minds about the upcoming presidential election on November 6, and he sensed that the possible results of the election would bring about, in Dickens' words, a "winter of despair." On the one hand, there were those determined to impose their will on a nation regardless of the outcome of the election; on the other side were those calling for dissolution of the union if their interests were not preserved. The two groups appeared to be on a collision course as surely as if they were steam engines barreling toward each other on the same track. Lucius, noting

[15] *Appendix II. Item 7. The Presidential Nomination and Election of 1860.*

his father's somber expression, decided to lighten the mood.

"It would appear that every bird in the land has migrated to this swampy marshland in Texas," he laughed. "When the birds arise together, it's like a cloud dark enough to blot out sunlight. Their sounds drown out our voices!"

Major Smith looked at his son, who was often described as a younger version of himself, and smiled. He could see the physical similarities—Lucius shared his father's dark hair and tall stature. But his mind and thoughts were more akin to his mother's gentle, contemplative nature.

"Indeed, Lucius, the wonders of nature are greater than our minds can comprehend. More creatures of every sort all sharing a small part of the Earth and living at peace with each other!" his father replied. "I only wish we humans could live with each other in such harmony, despite our differences. I have to say that I am very glad you have made this trip with me, and I want to hear your thoughts about what we've seen."

Lucius seized on that comment to bring up something that had been bothering him since their departure from Galveston.

"Actually, I have more questions than thoughts," he said. "I was very surprised to overhear so many conversations critical of Governor Sam Houston. I have always heard of him referred to as the "Father of Texas" and thought he was held in high regard. I don't understand what has caused some to dislike him so intensely."

Major Smith paused in his reply, knowing that Lucius and members of his generation would be among the most affected by the turmoil brewing in their midst.

"Here's the thing: the problem that has led to such anger is one that has plagued our nation since before its independence," his father said, choosing his words carefully. "That problem is the institution of slavery."

"I don't understand why we, as a nation, haven't been able to deal with this in a peaceful and civilized manner."

"The answers to these questions are beyond our complete understanding," Major Smith said. "I do know that early generations of slave owners assumed that Africans were intellectually and spiritually inferior, simply because they looked, acted or thought differently. Of course, now we know that is utter nonsense, and yet slavery continues to be the law of the land."

"Truly, I know Oscar to be a man of great capacity and spiritual strength," Lucius declared. "We have spent time together building our homes and hunting in the forests, and he is clearly a person of excellent character and ability."

His father nodded his agreement. He and Anna Jane had gone back and forth discussing the best possible solutions for their slaves but had yet to come up with a satisfactory answer. They had repeatedly assured Oscar and Hannah that they would always have a home with the Smiths and that they would never have to worry about providing for Ossie. Freeing them was the logical choice, but it did not always work. Major Smith had heard that the Wallings had sought to grant freedom to a family of slaves, but Texas laws prohibited them from doing so. In fact, many political leaders throughout the southern states were insisting that the only possible solution was secession from the United States. Governor Houston vigorously opposed that idea, which made him unpopular in some quarters.

"I have heard many in Daly's and in Crockett talk with enthusiasm about the Southland leaving the union," Lucius said. "What do you think would happen then?"

Major Smith shrugged. Predicting how the federal government would respond to such a movement was no easy feat. The election in November would determine everything. The Democratic Party, which had until then supported the Southern agrarian interests, had been unable to agree on a candidate. At its convention in Charleston, it split into two smaller groups, which would seem to have no chance of success in the national election. The northern Democrats nominated Stephen Douglas, who favored giving residents of the new western territories the ability to vote on the issue of slavery. But the southern delegates loudly opposed this and refused to support any restrictions on slavery. Many of them, including the delegates from Texas, quit the Democratic convention and later nominated John Breckenridge of Kentucky as their candidate. Secession from the union seemingly was preferable to any compromise on slavery.

"Father, I often heard in Galveston that most of the men dislike the Republican candidate, Lincoln, even more than they do the other candidates," Lucius said.

"That's true. It is unlikely that Lincoln will receive a single vote in Texas or the rest of the Southland," his father nodded. "With the voices of moderation so badly divided among the other candidates, it is possible that he will be the next President. He has vowed to oppose secession at any cost. That could result in war. And only a mad man or one who had never experienced warfare would want that to be the outcome."

Major Smith had also heard whispers of secession in inns and business establishments across Galveston. He was afraid that the call for careful deliberation would be drowned out amid the shouts calling for war. Lucius, sensing that a shadow had once again moved into their conversation, got up.

"I know you would like to read your new book, so I'll stroll around the deck and take in the view."

As Lucius walked away, Major Smith, unable to focus his thoughts, fixed his gaze on the river bank. The riverside terrain abruptly changed from the coastal marshland; the raucous cry of a raven roused him from his reverie. Suddenly, Major Smith was afraid. He could not explain it, but in the pit of his stomach was the fear that his only son would likely be one of those who would respond to a call to arms. After a brief moment, he realized that he was gripping the Dickens manuscript as if his life depended on it.

After an uneventful trip upriver, the packet steamer was at last nearing its destination at the landing in Houston County. This location, twelve miles west of Crockett, was the principle stopping point for steamboats near the main town. The vessel blew its whistle to alert the dock hands of its arrival. Crockett was the last major stop for the boat, although it often continued to Smith Landing when cargo needed to bc loaded. On this occasion, Major Smith could see two red-haired companions on the dock, but was surprised by their glum expressions. He was equally surprised by the absence of Hannah, who had accompanied them on every previous trip to Crockett. Lucius was in the stern of the boat supervising the proper unloading of their goods as Major Smith descended the gang plank to his waiting ladies.

"What is it that makes my sweet girls so gloomy on this otherwise fine day?" he asked.

"Oh, Father," said a tearful Berta throwing herself into his arms. "Little Ossie has died!"

"Dear Lord in Heaven, whatever happened to the child? When did he pass away?" her stunned father exclaimed.

"We don't know," Berta sobbed. "He didn't seem ill the day before and the next morning Hannah found him without any sign of life."

"My darling child, I am so very sorry," Major Smith said, comforting her. "You have never experienced the loss of someone you knew and loved so well. It is perfectly natural to cry. Anna Jane, please tell me what happened."

Distressed herself, Anna Jane told him that Ossie had seemed quite himself until three days ago, when he began struggling somewhat for breath. But he did not seem ill otherwise. Then the day before yesterday Hannah had gone to wake him and found that the life had gone out of him during the night. There was nothing to be done as he had died quietly during his sleep.

"Hannah and Oscar both are as stoic as ever," Anna Jane said. "But I know that she feels her soul deeply grieved by this loss."

"My dear Berta," Major Smith said, gently embracing his daughter, "I know you and Hannah are very sad that Little Ossie is gone, but you know that he is now with the Lord. From his earliest days we had been told that he would not live for very long. He has now completed his earthly life and God has taken him home to a much better one."

Berta nodded, not fully believing that Ossie would think it was better to be separated from his parents but trusting her father's words. She told herself that she would miss seeing Ossie in his usual place, shelling peas or working on his art, but she would not be afraid for him. Hannah and Oscar, Anna Jane told them, were having a service today. They had chosen a burial site near where the slaves' church building would be built. Ossie would be the church graveyard's first occupant.

"Now, my precious girls, let's see if Lucius has gotten our luggage in the carriage and we can return home unless you have other things we need to do in Crockett," Major Smith said. "If you need to stop by the Long and Downes store, Lucius needs a strap for his saddle, and I would like to have a brief conversation with Lodwick."

"Wonderful idea," Anna Jane said. "Berta needs some new ribbons for her hair, and I'm sure Mr. Downes has a good supply."

The previous year had seen the unexpected death of Col. John Long, and his widow had recently married Mr. James Wootters.[16] As the new couple was on a trip to Galveston, the Smith family would need to wait for another opportunity to congratulate them on their marriage. Earlier in the summer, James Wootters' brother and sister had moved to Crockett from Queen Anne's County, Maryland. They were presently living with the Downes family, and the younger brother, John Wootters, was working at the mercantile store.

The Long and Downes Mercantile Store contained a vast collection of supplies, but the emphasis was on equipment parts, hardware and saddlery that was sold both to the plantation owners and farmers with smaller acreage who lived throughout Houston County. There were entire rooms filled with grain and other commodities as well as medicines—at times questionable—for almost any ailment. Ladies' clothing was not their specialty; the styles on offer were mainly of interest to those who worked outdoors. The more fashionable attire was often bought from traveling vendors, whose visits

[16] *Miller, A.S. Wootters, James C., Handbook of Texas Online.*

to the larger towns were widely advertised and eagerly anticipated. Families would also plan periodic visits to more urban locations, such as Galveston. On this occasion, however, Berta and her mother were more interested in diverting their thoughts from the recent tragedy and in giving John Smith a chance to visit with his friend.

They were examining the selection of ribbons when John Wootters, Lodwick Downes' nephew and one of the store's principal workers, appeared and offered his assistance. Berta thought it amusing that this young man would have a useful opinion concerning ribbon colors, but she politely welcomed his suggestions. He introduced himself even though they had already met at church.

"Of course I know your name," she said. "I recall that you and your family prefer that it be spelled with two 't's. Indeed, Mr. Wootters, I would certainly value your opinion of these ribbons and which one would best keep my hair from blowing in the wind and match my new dresses. I didn't realize you were an expert on fashion matters."

"I am no expert on such matters, Miss Smith, but almost anyone would know that any type of ornament would be made more attractive by your own beauty," the young Wootters said. "I'm no musical expert either, but I certainly admired your piano playing last Sunday. I had no idea you could play so well or that you had such an extensive repertoire."

"Mr. Wootters, two such agreeable compliments would be welcome under any circumstances, but on this day, they are especially pleasant," Berta said. "The Smith family is bereaved by the unexpected death of our household servant's youngest child."

"I am very sorry to hear of your loss," he said.

"My father thought a bit of shopping would ease the pain a bit," Berta said, showing a bit of a smile. "At least, it keeps our minds occupied while he visits with Mr. Downes."

"I heard that you learn from Mr. Rogerson of Galveston, who comes by our store occasionally when he visits your home for your tutorials," he said. "He also has commented that you seem to have more talent that he usually finds in other students."

John Wootters had heard Mr. Rogerson perform in Galveston several months earlier during a trip to take delivery of some merchandise. The music was very pleasant, he noted. A new music style—something called German Romantic—that was currently very popular in Europe. Berta was surprised—and pleased—to hear that this young man had such musical interests as well as such an agreeable manner.

After half an hour of examining various ribbon sizes and colors, Berta chose four ribbons. "One spool of each should keep my mother's and my own wind-blown hair nicely controlled."

While Anna Jane and Berta pored over merchandise, Major Smith was visiting with his friend Lodwick Downes to share his impression of his trip to Galveston. Downes expressed no surprise over the secessionist rumblings in the state's largest city; he was aware of similar feelings in even the smallest villages of Houston County. He agreed with Major Smith that the outcome of the presidential election was inevitable in Texas, and assumed that the results would be the same throughout the South.

Sam Houston had never held much enthusiasm for slavery, he reminded Major Smith, and although he was an owner, he never depended on slaves for his major business activities.

Houston's principal efforts had always been to bring Texas into the Union, and the threat of dissolution was too great for him to consider. It was Lodwick Downes' opinion that Texas would overwhelmingly vote for secession and that Houston County might be unanimous in its assent.

What neither man could predict with certainty was the extent or the outcome of secession. States that had abandoned the Democratic Party at the Charleston convention would surely join in leaving the Union. But they couldn't predict how the remaining states or the federal government would react. They also wondered if towns and cities in the Northern states would concern themselves with the departure of distant Southern states from the Union. Following a brief discussion, Major Smith and Lodwick Downes concluded that the federal government would be the most likely to object and that, without widespread popular support, secession could possibly proceed without great opposition. But this outcome wasn't certain. An alternative course—the abrupt emancipation of the slave population—was even more distasteful and unacceptable to many across the Southland.

As the Smith family returned home, the warm sunshine of the autumn day made the trip a pleasant one. However, concern continued to gnaw at Major Smith's core. Despite his prayer for guidance, he continued to wonder if whatever the future held was destined to be the worst of times.

As he agitated over the state of Texas and the nation, he was somewhat surprised at how much happier Berta seemed. He could not imagine how something as insignificant as hair ribbons could have such an effect on what had earlier seemed to be a very somber mood. Anna Jane also smiled, although more inwardly, as she could not help having overheard the conversation between Berta and John Wootters. And she had to agree that Mr. Wootters was a very charming young man.

LATE MARCH 1861
CROCKETT, TEXAS

SPRINGTIME HAD BEEN DELAYED by the lingering cold of winter, but when it arrived, the once dormant flowering trees of the Texas piney woods seemed more exuberant in their blooms than in previous years. The dogwoods and redbud trees seemed to light up the forest, and the magnolia trees with their dark, waxy green leaves showed the promise of flowers yet to come. Everywhere the light green glow of emerging leaves indicated that spring was on the way.

These signs of nature's rebirth were especially meaningful to the Smith family as they were traveling to Crockett for Easter services. Berta planned to help with the piano music for the church services, and the family would be staying at Mrs. Hall's Hotel. Having once served as a boarding house, it was now the best inn in the town. Sadly, the Long Hotel had been destroyed in a fire the previous winter.

Oscar was guiding the team of horses and would return to the plantation that afternoon as Major Smith and Anna Jane had agreed that his presence would be needed at the Sunday church service for the slaves on the plantation. New clothing had been ordered from Galveston for Berta and her mother, who would use the day to make the necessary alterations in time for the Easter celebration.

In the meantime, Major Smith and Lucius would make arrangements for Oscar to pick up supplies from the mercantile store. If time permitted, Major Smith would also take his son to the Masonic Lodge and make introductions all around. He was pleased that Lucius had expressed interest in continuing their family tradition of associating with this organization. As the carriage followed the road through the quiet forest, each of them understood that the future of the Southland would likely be anything but quiet. The secession of Texas and the threat of war was the topic of every conversation.

Anna Jane was in a particularly somber mood. She spent the ride gazing at the passing forest, while Berta tried to read a book despite the frequent bouncing of the carriage. Major Smith was sitting in his usual place, next to his wife and facing his son, who was wearing his Sunday-best jacket and pressed shirt. Lucius studied this father who was riding quietly, apparently lost in thought.

"I am very pleased with the progress we have made with the new mare you brought to our stable last month," he said finally. "She is very spirited, but she seems willing and able to learn."

"I am glad to hear you say so, Lucius," Major Smith said. "I thought she was a good horse and worth the bale of cotton I paid for her. I am, however, a little concerned about her stamina when the weather gets warmer. Nevertheless, she may provide us with colts that could be very useful on the plantation."

"Do you think she would be suitable for a mounted military group?" Lucius said. "Hosea told me just the other day that he heard one was to be formed soon, and if that is the case, he and I will be interested in joining."

That declaration woke Anna Jane from her reverie. She sat forward with a sharp gasp.

"Surely you aren't considering joining an army unit!" she said, her voice wavering. "I know you are now a man and can make your own decisions, but I am still your mother and have a right to an opinion about your plans."

"Mother, please don't become tearful as I have not made any plans and would only do so if such joining became a duty and a necessity."

Anna Jane blanched, her skin even paler than usual. She could not prevent the tears the began coursing a delicate path down her powdered cheeks.

"John, please tell Lucius that we need him at home and not in some army that likely will not have any need to form," she said.

"Anna Jane, none of us knows what the future holds," he answered. "But all of the information we've heard cannot be reassuring for a peaceful future."

A grave stillness fell over the carriage. Scarcely a month had passed since Texas had voted overwhelmingly to join the other cotton states in seceding from the Union; federal troops in Texas didn't hesitate to peacefully leave their fortifications and supplies to the state government. Whatever happened next depended on the actions of the new president, Abraham Lincoln, as he had the power to order military force to prevent secession from proceeding. And the latest news to reach Houston County involved South Carolina men firing on a federal government ship trying to deliver supplies to a Union-held fort in Charleston Bay.

"Is there no way for reasonable people to resolve their problems without the threat of war?" Anna Jane asked.

"Unfortunately, the voices of reason are too easily obscured by the strident cries for secession on one hand and the abrupt abolition of slavery on the other," Major Smith shook his head. "The Peace Convention failed; Texas and other cotton states did not even send delegates. I believe the enthusiasm for secession is too great for the small, quiet voice of reason to be heard."

"Surely, the new president will not send troops into battle against his own citizens!" Anna Jane said, trembling.

"That is why there is much talk about forming companies of troops across the south," Lucius chimed in. "We must be ready to respond and defend our constitutionally protected rights. Perhaps the northern states will be less likely to engage in a war that doesn't greatly benefit their way of life if they understand that we will stand strongly for our rights."

"At this point, we can only pray that such will not be the result of human stubbornness," said his father, whose expression showed no evidence of optimism.

It was unlikely, Major Smith thought to himself, that the new self-proclaimed Confederate States of America, with Jefferson Davis as its president, would succeed unless North

Carolina, Virginia and Tennessee joined the secessionist states in breaking away from the Union. President Lincoln had stated in his inaugural speech that he had no plan to change the status of any slave; he had also flatly rejected the idea of secession. Tensions were running high in the North and South, as the political stand-off mushroomed into something more consequential and far-reaching.

Berta, who had been listening to the conversations, was aware that there was much that she did not understand about the circumstances. She wondered if her family could, indeed, be affected by this war. She looked at her brother, whom she adored and looked up to, unable to imagine him marching off to the dangers of war.

"Lucius, I do not want you to join the army," she said, her voice unsteady. "Please tell me that such is not going to happen."

He smiled at her fondly and took her hands in his.

"These are times, Berta, when men must be prepared to face danger to defend their homes and their freedom," he said. "If war comes to this country, I would feel obligated to defend our homeland."

Berta couldn't respond. Up to this moment, she had not realized the degree to which her brother had become a man, one who was clearly aware of his responsibilities. Her understanding of his role in the family would have to change. The remaining distance to Crockett passed with Berta quietly dwelling on this new reality and wondering how her role in their family might evolve. Was she prepared to leave behind the amusements provided by her piano and her books? The prospect of accepting more responsibility for herself and how that might occur occupied her mind until their arrival at the hotel.

As their luggage was unloaded from the carriage, Anna Jane and Berta were informed that packages had arrived for them from Galveston. This news seemed to cheer up both Smith women, as new clothes were a far cry from the image of a battlefield.

"Will the seamstress really be able to fit the new clothes in such a short time?" Berta asked. "I don't know how anyone can do such a thing!"

It was a matter of skill, her mother informed her, a skill that the seamstress practiced daily, just as Berta practiced her piano. Sewing was an art that could be acquired and developed with practice. On their return home, Anna Jane promised to teach her daughter how to better use a needle and thread, perhaps even how to knit, as a lady could only benefit from such practical skills.

As Major Smith, Lucius and Oscar left for the mercantile store, the ladies excused themselves to attend to their fittings. Once that was done, they would proceed to the church building, where Berta would practice the music she was to play at Easter services.

On arriving at the store, the Smiths and Oscar were informed that their supplies were there and ready for loading. Major Smith thanked Lodwick Downes for ensuring the prompt delivery of their shipment, as his plans for clearing additional acreage for planting depended on those supplies arriving before the springtime rains.

A portly man with a jolly demeanor, Lodwick Downes always wore a smile and was on a first-name basis with nearly everyone in Houston County.

"It is a privilege to be of service, John," he said. "I am thankful that there is such great demand for your cotton product and that you and your peers can meet that demand. I only wish that I could be as content in my mind about our future, considering the turmoil pervading our land."

For the past two years, business had been brisk and profits abundant, Downes noted. Any disruption would be unwelcome, if not catastrophic. He could not imagine having to import equipment from a foreign country, especially if that foreign country were New England. With the ever present talk of war and secession trickling into the conversation, Downes invited Major Smith to join him for a spot of better-than-average bourbon whiskey.

"Lucius has certainly grown up," the proprietor said, pouring two glasses and setting them down on the counter.

"He certainly has, right before my eyes," Major Smith agreed, taking a long pull of bourbon. "But I can't help being anxious about his zeal for defending the new Confederate nation. I'm sure he will waste no time in volunteering."

"You seem to know about what is happening in ways that I have not heard or read," Downes said. "Please tell me what you have learned."

Major Smith brought him up to date on what Lincoln had said in his inaugural speech. With the Republicans controlling the Presidency and both houses of Congress, he added, there was no chance that the Peace Commission and its recommendations could have reversed the secession process. Moreover, Lincoln would not hesitate to prevent the success of the Confederacy with whatever means necessary.

Downes' normally jovial expression fell. "I suppose this means war is a certainty. "

Major Smith put an arm around his friend's now-slumped shoulders and nodded in defeat. While much would depend on the Northern states' willingness to support a fight, it did seem that war was inevitable. Without saying it, both men feared the outcome: that the United States of America would cease to exist.

"It is difficult to swallow, as my own father and his father served and suffered in the revolution that gave birth to the United States," Major Smith said. "But the rule of law and personal liberty require all of us to stand firm in our beliefs and to support our states, our communities and our freedom to the fullest extent."

Downes, noting that John Wootters had come into the room, turned toward his nephew and attempted to take a lighter tone.

"Has the shipment for the Smith Landing Plantation been accounted for and made ready for delivery?" he asked.

"Yes sir, and Lucius has seen that it is stowed on the carriage for transport," John Wootters replied. He paused for a moment and then continued. "Major Smith, I couldn't help but overhear what you were saying, and I value your thoughts on these matters. It concerns me that many think this war will be fought to protect the institution of slavery. Slavery may have been the spark that started the fire, but many of us have other reasons for going to war."

"Young man, I appreciate what you are saying," Major Smith said, taking Wootters' offered hand. "I also pray that you and your comrades will stand firm for the homes and freedoms we hold dear and that God will protect you all."

John Wootters thanked Major Smith for his kind words and relayed the news that Lucius had spoken to him about joining up. A Mr. Redding Pridgen was organizing a company with a mounted unit and had recruited Lucius to serve. Somewhat surprised that Wootters knew his son's plans before he did, Major Smith confessed that Lucius had only confirmed his intentions that very morning. Sensing a potentially uncomfortable moment, the younger man changed topics altogether.

"Lucius also told me that Miss Smith will be providing piano music for the church services on Sunday," Wootters said.

"Berta's music is an important part of her activity," Major Smith said. "I believe she is practicing her music there now, that is if she and her mother have finished with their wardrobe fittings. They have ordered new Easter dresses from Galveston."

"Since your ladies bear such a resemblance to each other, do they have matching outfits?" Wootters smiled.

Major Smith chuckled. "I confess I do not know, but blue and green seem to be their usual preferences."

With the carriage packed up, the Smiths and Oscar made ready to leave. Oscar would return to the plantation, while Major Smith and Lucius proceeded to the Masonic Lodge for the planned visit.

"We hope to see you on Sunday and trust that Berta will be playing in the proper key!" Major Smith said to Wootters as he left.

"I am certain she will perform perfectly," Wootters said. "I will look forward to hearing her play."

As soon as the Smiths had left, Wootters asked his uncle if he could leave early. He had a mind, he said, to stop by the church and welcome Miss Smith to Crockett. Downes waved the young man out the door.

"I see no reason for you to stay any longer on this fine afternoon, John," he said with a sly grin. "I am pleased that you are developing such an interest in religious matters."

As the afternoon shadows lengthened and the heat of the day gave way to cooler evening temperatures, John Wootters quietly took a seat in the back row of the church. Berta Smith was playing passionately, seated to face the choir and unaware of her new audience. As she completed one of the pieces, Wootters surprised her with applause from the back of the room. She gave a brief cry of alarm as she turned to see him standing and clapping.

"Bravo!" Wootters said, smiling broadly. "A beautiful presentation of one of my favorite songs, Miss Smith."

"Indeed, Mr. Wootters, are you in the habit of surprising people so?" Berta asked "If you have been listening for very long you know that I missed some notes in my previous attempts. Hopefully I won't miss too many on Sunday."

"I would say that your playing is good enough for a concert in Vienna." Carrying a burlap bag, he walked to the front of the church to join the smiling Berta.

"I doubt that I will be going to Vienna or anywhere else, especially if the packet boat stops running and we really do have a war," Berta frowned.

"I wish you wouldn't let these prospects weigh so heavily on your mind, Miss Smith," Wootters teased. "Your father told me that you and your mother have new dresses for Easter service this Sunday. I don't know the exact colors, but we had a supply of blue and green ribbons in the store so I thought I would bring you some choices."

"You have brought a smile to my face, Mr. Wootters," Berta said, pushing stray strands of hair out of her eyes. "I am very pleased to have such choices. A ribbon will surely help me keep my hair under control!"

"I am sure that any of these choices will help with that," Wootters said. He seemed taller than Berta remembered and even more handsome.

"I suspect that these are an attempt to make me more cheerful than I was on our ride from the plantation this morning," she continued. "My father probably told you that we were rather taken aback by the news that Lucius is considering joining an army unit. It is still a shock to me."

Wootters nodded. "Your father did tell me, but I hope you won't let it detract from your joyful Easter celebration," he said. "Indeed, Berta, a smile on your face will be a welcome accompaniment to your pleasant music. I hope I am not being rude by addressing you by your given name, am I? Although I would almost prefer calling you Abigail as it has a somewhat more lyrical quality."

"How do you know that I am called by that quaint name?" said Berta. "The only person who ever uses it is Hannah, although my mother will when she is more exasperated than usual."

"I wouldn't know that special name of yours, except that Hannah told me about it when she was in the store recently," Wootters confessed. "I hope my attempts at cheering you up don't seem too clumsy, but I really do not want you grieving over something you cannot control."

Berta said nothing for a minute, and then nodded at him. "You may call me Berta or Abigail, whichever you prefer."

"Your father mentioned that your mother's grandfather had lost his life during the American Revolution," Wootters said. "I am very sorry for that loss. I know that the memory of those stories can remain with us for generations."

Berta, now sitting in a pew, ran the ribbons through her fingers making knots with them but her thoughts were clearly elsewhere. She didn't know all the facts, but she did know that Anna Jane's grandfather, Col. Abel Kolb, had been a leader of the patriotic Whig forces in the upper Peedee River area of South Carolina.[17] One day, she recalled the story, he was confronted by Tory troops while on a visit to his home. In defending his home and his family, including Berta's grandmother who was a child at the time, he gave himself up, only to be murdered in the sight of his wife and children. Had it not been for the loyalty of the small group of slaves, who stayed behind when they could have fled, the family would have been in desperate straits.

"Oscar, who helped load our carriage today, and Hannah, the household slave who cares for my mother, are descendants of those slaves," Berta told him.

"They must be very special people, and they deserve special respect," he said. "Now, Miss Smith, we have had enough of these burdensome thoughts for one day. Please share the ribbons with your mother, if they aren't all tied into small knots!"

Berta thanked him for the ribbons and for his kindness. But the day had grown dark, and it was time to find her family. Wootters offered to escort her to the hotel. His words of encouragement lifted her mood.

"I know that your music will be perfect for the Easter service," he said. "I will be listening carefully if my attention isn't too distracted by your presence."

[17] *Appendix II. Item 8. Col. Abel Kolb and the American Revolution in South Carolina.*

VIII

LATE JUNE 1861
SMITH LANDING PLANTATION,
HOUSTON COUNTY

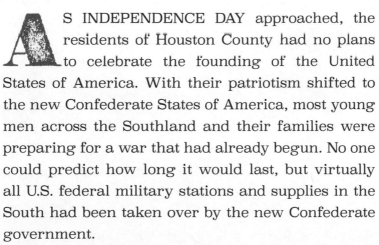

A
S INDEPENDENCE DAY approached, the residents of Houston County had no plans to celebrate the founding of the United States of America. With their patriotism shifted to the new Confederate States of America, most young men across the Southland and their families were preparing for a war that had already begun. No one could predict how long it would last, but virtually all U.S. federal military stations and supplies in the South had been taken over by the new Confederate government.

The call for men to serve had gone out to the people of Texas, and the response was impassioned.

Already, there were units forming in communities through-out the state. Men who were highly regarded in their coun-ties—many of whom were also military veterans –recruited for units that they themselves would command; young men often joined units with friends or family members.

Redding S. Pridgen, a planter well known to the Smiths, lived in northern Houston County and was recruiting mount-ed riflemen. Born in Alabama in 1822, he came to Texas with his parents in 1840. During the Mexican War in 1846-1847, Pridgen served with First Mounted Texas Riflemen in McCowan's Company.[18] Redding and his wife, Elizabeth, now owned a plantation in the Elkhart area. During the first weeks of summer 1861, rumors of recruitment for Sibley's brigade were widespread in Texas; those rumors were confirmed as Pridgen began recruiting mounted rifleman in June. Robert Walling, overseer on the Pridgen plantation, enlisted and was appointed third sergeant.[19] Elijah Chadwick, overseer at the Smith Landing Plantation, also joined, followed by Hosea Walling and Lucius Smith, who enlisted as privates.

Lucius had already told his father of his intention to join this unit, and they both agreed to wait before telling Anna Jane. Major Smith thought it would be better for her physical and emotional health if Anna Jane were to receive the infor-mation gradually, rather than as a sudden revelation.

On this warm afternoon at the end of June, Anna Jane and Major Smith were sitting on the front veranda gazing at the languid Trinity River as it flowed past their high riverbank. The field sloping toward the river was awash in a blanket of yellow flowers and punctuated by the constant hum of hon-ey bees from Hannah's own hives. The pastoral scene belied the momentous occasion: Lucius, who was indoors packing,

[18] *Redding Scott Pridgen, www.findagrave.com*
[19] *Appendix II. Item 9. The Wallings of Houston County, Texas.*

would be leaving to join his army unit in just a few hours. Hannah, now slightly stooped and her hair streaked with gray, emerged to offer tea while they waited for their son.

"Indeed, Hannah, some tea would be appreciated, and it may help to calm my grieving heart," Anna Jane said. She had done her best over the past few days to maintain a cheerful and optimistic demeanor, but on this day she dropped all pretense. As Hannah withdrew, Anna Jane turned to Major Smith, her eyes brimming with tears.

"If I didn't know that Lucius was going to be in the company of capable friends, I believe my mind would dissolve with grief."

"It is truly a blessing that he will have someone close to share his army life, but I have the greatest of confidence in his own strength of character and ability," Major Smith said. "He has truly become a man of determination and integrity. All we can do now is to support his decision and assure him of our approval and love."

Anna Jane nodded, not trusting herself to speak. She understood the truth of what her husband was saying, but she found it nearly impossible to say such things when she had no idea where her son was going or when—or if—he might return. Lucius had told them that Captain Pridgen planned to move the company to San Antonio, where they would join other groups under the direction of Col. Tom Green, a Travis County lawyer and clerk to the Texas Supreme Court. Having commanded a company in the First Texas Regiment of Mounted Riflemen in the Battle of Monterrey during the Mexican War, Green was generally thought to be one of the state's most experienced military leaders.[20] It was not clear, however, where the company would go once it left San

[20] *Alwyn Barr, "Green, Thomas," Handbook of Texas Online.*

Antonio, and that uncertainty worried Anna Jane more than anything. A few minutes later, Oscar approached his owners and quietly cleared his throat to announce his presence.

"Oscar, have you made sure that Lucius has the equipment and mounts I asked you to provide for him?" Major Smith said, turning to his trusted slave.

"Yes sir, I've made sure he has the guns and both of the horses. He didn't want to take your Magnus, but I told him that you wouldn't have it any other way," Oscar said. He said he wanted to leave his usual horse for you and Miss Berta to ride and he would take one of the other horses to carry his bags. Believe me, Lucius will have the best horse in the army and as good guns as anyone."

"Thank you for helping Lucius with his packing," Major Smith said. "I will count on you and Hannah keeping him in your prayers."

"I am praying for him already," Oscar nodded. "There he comes now. Don't he look like a fine soldier?"

And there he was, looking like more of a man than he had even that morning. Major Smith beamed with pride, despite a nagging anxiety, as his son led the prize stallion down the pathway to the front of the veranda.

"I can't believe you would insist on having me take Magnus as my mount!" Lucius exclaimed. "He is the finest horse in Houston County."

"Giving you the best mount and weapons I have is the least I can do to support your decision to join Pridgen's company," his father said. "As much as your mother and I want you here with us, we understand your commitment to the cause of the Confederacy. Please know that with you go our love and admiration, and our prayers for your safe return."

With those words, even Lucius was perilously close to giving in to the emotion of the moment. His mother, understanding as only a mother could, stepped up to say her own good-bye.

"I want you to remain well and safe wherever you may travel, Lucius," Anna Jane said, her voice faltering. "Please give me a hug and one more for Berta. She will be very sorry not have to have arrived from Crockett in time to see you off."

"It's likely that we may pass Berta on the way to Crockett," Lucius said, mounting his horse. "If we do, I will give her a proper farewell. If I miss seeing her, ask her to say a special prayer for me and my friends."

As he rode away from the plantation home, Lucius felt only anticipation. Any inkling of hardship or danger was obscured by the excitement of joining his friends in what would be the greatest adventure of their lives. As he disappeared from view, a fog of gloom settled over the Smith Landing Plantation. Anna Jane, having put on a brave face for her son's sake, gave in to tears and despair.

"Surely giving our son to the Confederate cause is enough torment for our family," she said, once her tears had subsided. "I trust that you will not be leaving me during this time."

"Anna Jane, I have thought about my responsibilities and what would be the best path to follow during these very difficult days," Major Smith said. "Even though I have some experience in the Carolina militia, my best service will be here."

He confirmed that the Smith Landing Plantation would continue planting and producing cotton, with the understanding that any profits would go to support the Confederate cause. Without Lucius to manage and supervise operations, Oscar's help as an overseer of other slaves would be more critical than ever.

Worrying about her son was at the top of Anna Jane's list, but other concerns abounded as well. Her many relatives and friends back in Bladen County were much closer to the battlefields than anybody in Texas. Since Virginia and North Carolina had seceded—and been the last states to do so—the Confederacy's seat of government had moved from Montgomery, Alabama to Richmond, Virginia—bringing Jefferson Davis' government much nearer to the front lines.

"There is no way to predict what is in men's minds and hearts, but the best outcome for the Confederacy will be quick and decisive victories," Major Smith said, as if reading his wife's mind. "The longer and more extensive the conflict, the less likely that the South will be able to prevail, as the size of the northern population and their manufacturing resources are much larger than ours."

Although he did not say it aloud, he also wondered how the people of the Northern states felt about this war, whether they were willing to support a long, costly and perhaps bloody conflict. In the years since America's independence from Great Britain, many other Europeans had emigrated to the northern part of the country. Whether or not they were willing to take up arms for their adopted homeland was still in question. And it was a big question, particular since it seemed that much of the fighting was likely to occur in the Eastern seaboard states. Texas and other states would rally to their cause and enhance the chances of success.

"Did you know that Dr. Edward Currie is organizing a company in Crockett?" Major Smith said. "I understand his company will join the First Texas Infantry, which has been formed in Virginia."

"I know Dr. Currie is highly regarded as a physician," Anna Jane said, a note of skepticism in her voice. "I was not aware that he had any military experience."

As it turned out, the doctor, originally from Mississippi, had served under Jefferson Davis during the Mexican War. Once that conflict had ended, he settled in Texas to practice medicine.[21] According to Major Smith, a number of young men from Crockett were signing on with Dr. Currie, among them John Wootters, whose uncle, Lodwick Downes, owned the mercantile store. At an official presentation in Crockett, Wootters would receive the flag on behalf of his fellow infantrymen.

"You remember Wootters, Anna Jane?" her husband asked. "I believe you and Berta have met him during one of your shopping trips to Crockett."

At last, Anna Jane had something to smile about on this somber day.

"My darling John, how can you be so insightful concerning issues of our country and state and so effective in managing the affairs of our property and yet be so blind to what is happening under your nose?" she laughed. "I believe that our Berta has more than a cordial interest in Mr. Wootters; in fact, Hannah has confirmed it. I also think Berta would attend the flag ceremony even if it meant she had to walk to town in her bare feet!"

Major Smith was speechless. Berta was just a little girl, a child really, and Wootters was a man. An older man. Surely his wife was mistaken. Their daughter would never have noticed Wootters if it weren't for the fact that he attended their church and waited on them at his uncle's store. Anna Jane laughed and shook her head as her husband gave voice to his thoughts.

[21] *History of Houston County, Texas. p. 312.*

"Let me remind you that the age difference between this young man and our young Berta is no greater than the advantage you had over me when I lived a protected life on Pouncey Plantation," she said. "And yet I noticed you and did not discourage your interest. Unless your vision has dimmed, you might have noticed that our daughter has become a beautiful young lady!"

When she and Berta were at the mercantile store, she told him, John Wootters never overlooked an opportunity to inquire about her needs or to comment on her musical talents. But she asked Major Smith to keep this information to himself, as Berta hadn't yet expressed her feelings about John Wootters to her parents. Anna Jane did not want to cause her any embarrassment, particularly since affection at a young age often did not stay its course. In light of the news that Wootters was going to war only reinforced the idea that they should not interfere, especially since they knew how upset she would be at having missed Lucius' departure.

It wasn't long before the carriage arrived from Crockett. Hannah and Berta came into the entrance hall with a more somber air than usual.

"Oh, Mother, I am so glad to be back home, but I am very sorry to have not been here when Lucius left, " Berta said on entering the parlor and finding Anna Jane. "I didn't know this would be his last day at home before joining the company. Thankfully, Hannah and I passed their troop just outside Crockett, and I had a chance to visit with him briefly. I noticed that he was riding Magnus, and when I asked him why, he told me that he and I would both have new horses. I don't know what he meant by that, but he seemed very excited, and said that he would write us a letter when they reached San Antonio."

At that moment, Major Smith came in. "I heard the sound of your voice, Berta, from upstairs," he said, enfolding his daughter in a tight hug. "We are glad you are home. I hope your visit in Crockett was a good one, but I know you and Lucius will regret not having a chance to say good-bye."

"Had I known he would be leaving today, I would have found some other time to visit the church pianist," Berta said. "But I did see him and his troop on the roadway and was able to give him a farewell kiss. He seemed too excited for any longer conversation."

Anna Jane, who seemed more pallid than usual, sighed. "It has been an exhausting day, but I am relieved by your presence, Berta," she patted the seat next to hers. "Please come sit by me and tell me all about your visit in Crockett and with Lucius. Also, you must ask your father what Lucius was referring to about the horses."

John, who had assumed his usual place in the over-stuffed great chair that faced Anna Jane's favorite divan, informed Berta that Lucius had joined a mounted company and would be facing many, possibly arduous, treks. He told her about insisting that her brother take Magnus, as he was one of the strongest, most fearless mounts Major Smith had ever owned. In the stallion's absence, Lucius wanted us wanted us to ride Betsy, his own good-natured, dependable mare.

"She is a wonderful horse and gentle enough for me to ride comfortably," Berta said. "I am also glad she will be here with us as she is very fond of Lucius. I will think of him every time I ride her. I will miss him greatly."

"Did you and Hannah go to the store or have any other visits in town?" Anna Jane asked her daughter.

"We did, that is Hannah did," Berta nodded with great

animation. "Hannah went to the mercantile store for some sugar and flour, and she must have mentioned that I was practicing piano at the church because Mr. John Wootters walked over to visit as I was finishing my session. He commented on how much he enjoyed the Beethoven sonata I was playing."

The picture suddenly became very clear to Major Smith. What his wife had told him was absolutely true. John Wootters had caught his daughter's fancy; he could see it in her eyes and the way she spoke his name.

"Your mother and I were just discussing plans to be in Crockett in the next several weeks for the flag presentation to the Currie Company, which will soon be leaving for New Orleans," he said. "I expect that you and Hannah will attend with us if you would like to. It should be a memorable ceremony and a suitable substitute for a patriotic display that in past years would have occurred on the Fourth of July.

"Oh yes, I want very much to attend!" Berta said. "Hannah has already told me that she wishes to be there. She holds Mr. Wootters in very high regard, and he has been chosen to receive the flag and offer a response on behalf of the company."

"I am sure that all participants in the ceremony will be pleased to have a large and enthusiastic crowd in attendance," Major Smith said, the corners of his mouth twitching. "But how has Hannah come to have such a good opinion of him?"

Berta was a bit surprised by the question, but she pointed out that Wootters often helped them during their visits to the mercantile store. He was, she noted, very polite and accommodating. Hannah had even told him about how she called Berta by a special name, Abigail, and the significance of that name.

"She even told him that she thought 'Abigail' was more in keeping with my nature than my proper name," Berta said. "I don't know why she would think that, but I told Mr. Wootters that he could use whichever name he preferred."

"Well, Berta, since you are on a first-name basis with the young man, it's only appropriate that he and I share the same name," her father smiled. "I have always been proud to share the name John with both the prophet and apostle of the Bible."

"Father, I believe you are teasing me," Berta smiled back. "I only refer to him as Mr. Wootters. He is very kind and interested in our welfare, but I know him best from our church meetings. We should all go to Crockett for the presentation to show our support and appreciation to all the young men who will be leaving their homes to defend our freedoms."

As always, Berta's maturity and insights surprised and impressed her parents. They would definitely be going, Major Smith thought to himself. For the company from Houston County and especially for the young man named John Wootters.

IX

NOVEMBER 1861
CROCKETT, TEXAS

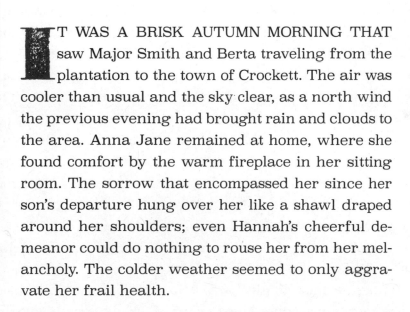

IT WAS A BRISK AUTUMN MORNING THAT saw Major Smith and Berta traveling from the plantation to the town of Crockett. The air was cooler than usual and the sky clear, as a north wind the previous evening had brought rain and clouds to the area. Anna Jane remained at home, where she found comfort by the warm fireplace in her sitting room. The sorrow that encompassed her since her son's departure hung over her like a shawl draped around her shoulders; even Hannah's cheerful demeanor could do nothing to rouse her from her melancholy. The colder weather seemed to only aggravate her frail health.

Despite obtaining the best medical advice in Houston County, the Smiths had received no satisfactory explanation—nor any possible remedy—for Anna Jane's physical decline. They had traveled to Galveston to consult with the most experienced physicians in Texas. Major Smith had even suggested that she go to New Orleans in search of answers. As a much larger city, it would naturally be home to a broader range of doctors with experience treating a variety of illnesses and conditions. But Anna Jane knew that her lack of strength would make such a trip too difficult. Instead, she followed the suggestions of various advisors—an easily digestible diet with additional salt, rest and a warm environment—and stayed put at Smith Landing plantation.

On her better days and despite her physical limitations, Anna Jane continued to take an active interest in her family and their lives. However, with Lucius gone to serve in the Confederate army, her usually cheerful mood had turned darker. Frequently overcome by a sense of hopelessness and the belief that her death was imminent, she prayed daily that she would survive to see Lucius and his friends, the Walling brothers, return safely. She also prayed that John Wootters would return from Virginia and that she would also be fortunate enough to see Berta with an established future.

As the carriage made its way toward Crockett, Berta noticed that with the recent frost and winds, most of the hardwood trees across the low-lying terrain had shed their foliage. The gray limbs reached skyward in stark contrast to the green pines silhouetted against a bright blue sky. She felt a sense of loneliness descend as she reflected on the passing countryside.

"Father, I must admit that it is hard for me not to feel sad these past few months," Berta said, after a period of silence.

"I miss Lucius and the joy he brings to our household. The winter woodlands are so barren, they only add to my feelings of emptiness."

"I share your feelings of sadness," her father said. "I find myself thinking of your brother often and with some regret that I did not try to dissuade him from enlisting so soon."

Despite his misgivings, Major Smith found some measure of comfort knowing that Lucius was, at least, with his trusted, capable friends, Hosea and Robert Walling, and under the command of the experienced Redding Pridgen. He knew that they would face many hardships; that was the price of war. But he was also certain they would look out for each other. Just recently, he and Anna Jane had gotten word that Lucius' unit was leaving San Antonio and heading to New Mexico to secure that area for the Confederacy. The soldiers would trek across the western part of the state toward the town of El Paso del Norte, which had a substantial Army base and plentiful supplies, and cross into New Mexico from there. It was a long journey—much of it across an area scarce with water—to make in winter. Once again, Major Smith offered up a silent prayer for his son's safety.

"I also pray that John Wootters is well and safe," Berta said. "I have heard they are having a very cold winter in the East."

In fact, everything had changed with the change of season. Both Lucius and John Wootters were gone to war, along with so many other young men from the area, and those events had taken their toll on her mother's emotional and physical state. Moreover, since late July, the Union Navy had very effectively blockaded the Port of Galveston. With the threat of Union soldiers coming ashore, her piano tutor was unable to make the trip from that city. In fact, none of her tutors, musical or academic, had been to Smith Landing in several months. And given the tenuous situation, there was no telling when the packet boats would again be able to make regular trips up the Trinity River. Indeed, life as it had been just one year earlier would be unlikely to resume as long as the war continued.

On this particular trip to Crockett, Berta would be going directly to the Baptist church to meet with the woman who played piano there. Since Berta's tutor could not come, she had kindly offered to step in and help with her musical education. Major Smith, on the other hand, was intent on finding out the fate of a cotton shipment that had been delivered to Galveston. This year's crop had been among the largest in memory, but the Union Navy's blockade meant that the packet boats that usually delivered the cotton were only able to escape the port occasionally.

There was some hope among the planters that a few boats had managed to slip out and reach Mexico or Havana, where the cotton could be loaded onto other boats sailing under foreign flags. If not, then the warehouses in Galveston would soon be over-filled with cotton, and river traffic to Crockett would come to a complete standstill. Perhaps more importantly, the Confederacy was dependent on revenue from cotton sales to the mills in Europe. That money bought weapons and equipment the Confederate Army desperately needed, and without it, they would be at a serious disadvantage.

"I know you have been very busy with the harvest and delivery of the cotton to the gin," Berta said, as if reading her father's thoughts. "What will happen if the ships cannot sail?"

"Our plantation and others across the Southland have pledged the revenues from these crops to the cause of our new country," Major Smith said. "The problem is that our states have, in past years, been so occupied with agriculture that little effort has been directed toward manufacturing. We will need to import war material if we are to defend our homeland."

As their carriage continued through the forest, Berta was reminded that the roadways had been much improved since their first journey from Crockett four years earlier. She wondered aloud if other roads had been improved and whether it would be possible to deliver the cotton to Galveston over land, by wagon. Major Smith smiled, impressed by his daughter's keen intelligence and foresight.

"You are quite right; the roads have benefited from the efforts of the plantation owners who are required to maintain them," he said, also noting that the trip to Crockett was substantially shorter now with the improved roadway. "It's possible that some of the crop could be sent to Mexico by land. I will be meeting with Andrew Gossett about that during our visit. On these matters, he is the most knowledgeable person in Crockett."

Andrew Gossett's father, Elijah, was originally from Tennessee and had been a boyhood friend of the celebrated Davy Crockett.[22] The younger Gossett and his brother moved to the area with their father before the War for Texas Independence. When Crockett and his men came to Texas to fight the Mexican army, they stopped for a night or two at Elijah Gossett's homestead on the way to San Antonio and, eventually, the Alamo. The town was named Crockett in honor of that fallen hero. Andrew Gossett, who donated the land that was now the town square, had since served as sheriff and judge for the county and was one of its most respected citizens.

[22] Long, C. "Elijah Gossett", Handbook of Texas Online.

With Berta practicing piano at the church, Major Smith meeting with business and government leaders and Oscar loading supplies at the mercantile store, it would be a busy visit to Crockett. Major Smith agreed that, after his meeting with Andrew Gossett, he would first stop by the Masonic Lodge and then head to the church to collect Berta. Together, they would meet Oscar at the mercantile store.

"If I finish earlier I will meet you at the store, as it's very near the church, and I can amuse myself by looking at what they consider the latest fashions," Berta said impishly. "I'm sure I can find some new music at the church, but I don't expect Mr. Downes to have any new, stylish clothes."

The grand piano, which played such an important role in their household, continued to be a source of pleasure for Berta and her parents. She practiced often and diligently, and her skills had improved tremendously as a result. Indeed, Anna Jane had expressed concern about future opportunity for her child's musical talent. While the effects of the war throughout the South were still uncertain, she realized that their plan to send Berta back to Virginia or another Eastern location for school would not be possible for quite some time.

On arriving at the town square, Major Smith disembarked from the carriage and entered the building that housed Andrew Gossett's office. Oscar would drop Berta at the church before returning to the store. As Major Smith approached the door to Gossett's office, he was welcomed by a thunderous voice.

"Major Smith, I could see through the window that you were heading in this direction," Judge Gossett boomed. "Come in here, warm your hands and sit for a spell."

With the post office and telegraph station next door, Gossett was able to monitor the affairs of the state and the

Confederacy in a more timely manner; the weekly newspaper, the Crockett Argus, could only provide limited current information. Rumor was that, if the Galveston port blockade went on for much longer, the paper might cease publication as all of its newsprint and printing paper arrived through that port. Major Smith entered the spacious, sparsely furnished office, and the two men settled into broad wood chairs in front of the hearth.

"Judge Gossett, this fire is much appreciated as the carriage could hardly keep out the cold north wind," he said. "My only comfort on that chilly ride has been a warm conversation with my daughter Berta, who is growing up too quickly. While I would like for you to meet her some time, my primary purpose in being here is to talk business. In your opinion, what is the outlook for commercial activity in Galveston and in Texas? And what do you see as alternatives for inland planters and our crop?"

Gossett shook his head, knowing that the news was bad and the outlook bleak. Galveston was in a state of panic. The port was virtually shut down, and military leaders did not think the city could be defended in the event of an invasion, which seemed increasingly probable. At least half of the population has already fled inland seeking refuge with family and friends. In the past four months, the town of Houston, unprepared for an overwhelming influx of new residents, had almost doubled in population. Planters in Houston County had also seen the arrival of friends and relatives eager to find a safe haven until the situation changed.

"I am in a quandary about the prospects for our cotton crop," Major Smith told his friend. "It is abundant, as you know, but I'm concerned about being able to sell it and provide that value to the Confederacy."

"You're right to be concerned," Gossett said. "If the crops from our cotton states can be exchanged for armaments and supplies, our Southland may be able to withstand prolonged hostilities. I have been told that no rifle has ever been manufactured in Texas, and that lack of industry across the region has us at a disadvantage."

Nodding his agreement, Major Smith asked the judge about the possibility of getting the cotton crop out from another port. The Texas coastline was vast, and it seemed unlikely that any Union naval force could secure every mile of it. He also mentioned the idea of transporting the cotton overland to Mexico and then transferring to ships flying under European flags.

"Although there are a number of ports along the Texas coast, the problems of delivering the cotton and securing its safe passage at sea are daunting," Gossett said. "Just outside this window is a part of the Old San Antonio Road, which could be a way to deliver the cotton to the Mexican border. It is a long and hazardous journey, but one that has been undertaken by travelers for many years."

While the road was well-established all the way from Crockett to San Antonio, the journey grew more uncertain as one traveled further south. A trek to the towns of Laredo or Villa de Dolores on the Rio Grande River would traverse remote and barren terrain, much of it home to hostile Indian tribes. With the U.S. Army no longer in place to deter their raids, it was a brave, well-armed soul who traveled through that area.

"I am familiar with the local unit of our militia and I believe that, with appropriate assistance, they could manage such a venture," Major Smith said. "Adequate wagons and mules should be something that we Texans can produce, even if our foundry capabilities are limited. Wagons loaded with cotton bales would provide protection for armed troops as a bale could hardly be penetrated by any light firearm."

"I expect that by this time next year, our militia unit could be deployed in such a capacity," Gossett replied. "But, absent the troops, I know there would be concern about possible slave unrest."

Discontent, even rebellion, among the slaves was always a concern; Major Smith knew that. But his plantation was blessed with a population that was very loyal to his family and to each other. While newly acquired slaves could be unpredictable in responding to their circumstances, he was not at all worried about his own. That prompted his friend to issue a well-meant warning.

"I have overheard complaints from some of our local residents that your good treatment of your slaves may affect their attitude toward other white people, that it may not be respectful enough," Gossett said. "It has never been a problem for me, but you should be aware that some folks resent the situation."

Caught off guard, Major Smith expressed his surprise and concern. He knew that hard feelings could lead to unpleasant confrontations; he would mention the problem to Oscar and ask him to relay the message to the other slaves that they could all be in danger from some of the white population's rougher elements. They should take extra care to mind their manners when in town.

"I have found that those who do not own slaves often resent black people who show abilities and skills that they themselves do not have," Gossett said. "One never knows how this hostility may manifest; avoiding such problems is always the best solution."

The judge made his way to the fireplace, stoked the now dying embers and threw a new log on the fire. As the room grew warmer, the two men caught up on news of their respective families. Gossett noted that there was much talk about town and admiration for Berta's skill on the piano. He also asked after Lucius and offered a prayer for his success and safety.

"I appreciate those words, my friend," Major Smith stood up to go. "As the day is getting by, I must retrieve Berta and get back home before supper. Many thanks for your advice, prayers and friendship."

Following a brief visit to the Masonic Lodge, Major Smith passed by the church and learned that Berta had finished her session and would meet him at the mercantile store. He set off in that direction, his eyes searching the town square for her trademark red hair. Not immediately seeing her, he glanced toward their carriage and saw Oscar waving to him to come aboard. As he approached, he saw Berta already seated inside.

"I didn't expect you to be finished with your meeting so soon," her father said, reaching to open the carriage door. "I hope all went well for you and the church pianist."

It was then he noticed Berta trembling, huddled in the corner of the front seat.

"Whatever is the matter, child?" he exclaimed. "You are shaking like a leaf."

"Oh, Father! I have had a terrible experience, and I just want to go home as quickly as we can," Berta moaned as the carriage lurched to a start.

"Tell me, what has you so upset?" asked her father, his fists clenched in a surge of protective instinct.

As her eyes filled with tears, the words seemed to lodge in her throat. But, amid the whispered mutters, her father heard her say, "that old man Jencks really frightened me, and he must be the meanest person on this earth." Major Smith could not recall ever seeing his daughter in such a state of distress.

"What has that derelict Jencks done to cause you such unhappiness?"

"He said some really threatening things to me, and I was just walking down the street in front of the mercantile store," she sobbed. "He appeared out of nowhere and started accusing me of trying to teach Oscar to read and telling me that I was only going to make trouble for all of us if I kept doing that."

"What did you say to him? Where was Oscar when all of this was happening?"

"Oscar was in the store getting ready to load the carriage, and he came out when he heard Jencks yelling at me," Berta said, now looking more angry than tearful. "I'm sure Oscar did nothing to anger the old devil; I certainly didn't say anything to him. I was so surprised by his presence that I don't think I uttered a single word in his direction. When Oscar came through the door, Jencks turned around and walked away."

Major Smith wished for a moment that Anna Jane or even Hannah was present as one of them would likely know how to react more appropriately to an angry young woman who was probably not of a mind to be placated. He was angry himself, indeed furious that such a man as Jencks would speak to Berta in that fashion. Jencks was said to love his whisky, and people around town said that the sheriff often locked him up after a drinking binge, just to keep the peace.

"Now, Berta, please try to calm yourself," he finally said. "Tell me what you think caused him to act as he did."

"I don't know what he meant," she answered. "I have only one or twice answered a question he asked about a particular word and its spelling, and I have helped Hannah read Bible verses. Anyway, I don't see anything wrong with them knowing what a written sign might mean or being able to read."

"My dear, you have not been around people like Jencks," her father said. "Our life on the plantation, in our church and with your tutors has only exposed you to the more genteel segments of our society. I'm afraid that you need to learn about such individuals and how you should respond to what they might say. You must also be aware that you are becoming a young woman, and the way you behave around men, especially those of dubious character, must change as you do."

While he had every confidence that Berta's instincts would eventually guide her in these situations, he was grateful to have Anna Jane waiting at home. She would surely know what and how to teach their daughter in matters of proper behavior. Berta's outgoing nature could easily be misinterpreted by some men, particularly those who weren't gentlemen, as being something other than sociable and charitable. That and her beauty could, in the wrong situation, be a dangerous combination.

"I know you to be a brave young lady, but bravery should never be a substitute for good common sense and caution," her father warned. "Perhaps the best advice I can give you is to avoid being alone outside of our home and limiting your interactions with individuals of the cruder classes whenever possible."

As the carriage rumbled on, Major Smith thought about what Berta had told him. Perhaps Jencks' suspicion that Oscar could read, even to a limited extent, reminded him of his own illiteracy. Too many people assumed that members of the black race were unable to learn and assume responsibilities and were therefore of a low class. But Major Smith knew that was a fallacy: the only thing Oscar and other slaves lacked was the opportunity to improve their status. Awareness of his own deficiencies fueled Jencks' rage, so he took aim at the only available target: Berta. The man likely did not want to confront Oscar directly as doing so would reveal his own lack of bravery; the slave was taller and as strong as anyone in town.

Berta, whose tears had dried, listened intently to her father. He had enjoyed a life rich with experience thus far, and she knew he had a great deal of wisdom to share.

"I suspect that you were surprised at being criticized without cause, and it made you very angry," he said. "Be careful with that kind of anger, Berta. It can make you react in ways you later regret. Don't worry about your tears; they were tears of anger. I have heard that is a common reaction among women." Major Smith smiled at his daughter, adding, "I am fortunate not to have been the cause of such a reaction in you or your mother."

Berta permitted a glimmer of a smile in response to her father's attempt to lighten the conversation. "Thank you, Father," she said. "I don't understand what would make a person be so hateful and cruel!"

How could he explain to this sunny soul the existence of blighted ones like Jencks? Many would point to whiskey as the cause of his problems, but his type often revealed its true colors when fueled by liquor. He had seen Jencks' pitiful wife and their herd of ragged-looking children along the roadway, homesteading a piece of property not far from Daly's. They seemed to be underfed and lacking in proper clothing. Major Smith suspected that they frequently bore the brunt of the other man's mean spirit, and it made him sad to the bone. What children learned from life with their families often stayed with them forever.

After an interval of calm, Major Smith spoke again. "I don't think we need to alarm your mother with all that has happened today," he said. "But asking her some of these questions may help you with your own answers. She has many thoughtful insights into such matters."

He decided right then that he would also caution Oscar about showing proper humility when dealing with people in Crockett. Recalling his conversation with Judge Gossett, Major Smith understood that they certainly had enough problems without creating unnecessary new ones. Berta, in the meantime, had moved to more pleasant thoughts about her piano and the new music the woman at church had let her borrow. A composer named Stephen Foster had written most of them, and they were very popular. New songs would be just the thing to get her mind off people like Jencks.

FEBRUARY 1862
SMITH LANDING PLANTATION, HOUSTON COUNTY

EBRUARY WAS A TIME of transition in Houston County as the chill of winter waned and the promise of nature's rebirth slowly emerged. The winter months of early 1862, however, had been an unusually harsh time in southeastern Texas and throughout many of the Southern states.

News of the hardships endured by Texans serving in the Confederate Army in distant Virginia gradually made its way back to their homes by the postal service, which could only be described as erratic. Letters, when available, were shared by friends and relatives. On this particular day in early February, the winter doldrums were underscored by leaden skies and a constant drizzle.

Anna Jane rested on the divan in her parlor, watching as the flames swept over the new logs. Normally, a roaring fire would cheer her, but today she saw the flames as the consuming ravages of war, reducing everything in their path to ash. The somber calm of this scene was disrupted by the approaching sounds of a happy Berta, who bounded into the parlor closely followed by a breathless, but smiling, Hannah. "Oh, Mother, you won't believe what the postmaster from the store at Daly's just brought!" she exclaimed, waving an envelope. "A letter from Mr. John Wootters. I can't believe it!"

Berta was surprised that Wootters had written, but Anna Jane was not surprised in the least. Nevertheless, she clapped her hands and invited her daughter to share the young man's news. "Hannah, you come in too," she said. "I know you will want to hear what he has to say."

Hannah nodded and went to fetch hot tea as Berta opened the letter and began reading to herself. By the time she returned, Berta was weeping.

"I sure hope that Sergeant Wootters is doing better than you, child," Hannah said, setting down the tea tray. "Tell us what he's written that's making you worry so."

"Please tell us what he has written," her mother agreed. "Surely it's not a secret."

"His letter certainly is not a cause of worry," Berta said, regaining her composure. "In fact, the most he seems to be suffering from is a bit of boredom. There are no secrets, Mother, but I am not certain that Mr. Wootters is accurately describing his military life. He says that he has written other letters, but I haven't received them. I wonder if the letters I wrote were ever delivered since he doesn't mention having gotten any."

"Now, Berta, if you are so inclined, please share some of this information with your attentive audience," her mother said.

"He writes that they have had false alarms of impending battle, but they have yet to catch more than a fleeting glimpse of the Union troops. Their assignment has been a ten-mile sector of the Potomac River bank. Although the enemy can be seen on the other shore, they have shown no inclination for a fight. It seems that the main concern has been the lack of entertainment and that he misses hearing me play the piano."

As she continued reading, Berta again found herself on the verge of tears.

"Several of the company members have musical instruments and perform occasionally for our amusement," she read. Again, she paused.

"Just what is it about this letter that you don't believe?" Anna Jane asked.

"He describes their living quarters as mere shacks with 'gaps between the boards large enough for birds to fly through,'" she read. "I presume that he is making an attempt at light-heartedness. He maintains that he didn't know that the sky contained as much snow as has fallen on them and that some of his fellow soldiers have been ill.[23] He also mentions that Col. McLeod took pneumonia and has gone to be with the Lord, which he says 'must be an improvement over the quarters of the First Texas.' I think life must be much harder for the troops than he wants me to believe."

[23] Polley, JB. "Hood's Texas Brigade," 1910.

"Thank the Lord that he is alive and seems well," Hannah said.

"Hannah is right; he does seem to be well," Anna Jane said. "We have all heard about the terrible battle at Bull Run, when the Federals seemed no match for the Virginia infantry.[24] Maybe the Union troops' enthusiasm for the fight is not as great as we had feared."

Berta, who was still trembling slightly, felt emotionally spent. Imagining John Wootters in a shack in the snow with Union troops just across the river was too much for her. She excused herself and went upstairs to lie down. As she climbed the stairs, Hannah noted that Berta had placed the letter in her blouse—next to her heart.

———

Major Smith had not ridden the mare, Betsy, to Crockett that day as she was expected to give birth at any time. For this trip, which was primarily to learn what he could about the new Confederate government's activities and news about either the Sibley Brigade or the troops in Virginia, he had taken another mount. His obligations at the plantation were less pressing than usual; the fields had been prepared for the spring planting, and he had decided to not clear more land as the ability to deliver the crop to buyers remained doubtful. In the meantime, the plantation slaves were occupied with providing a continuous supply of firewood for both their master's home and their own settlement, known as Cedar Branch.

On his return to Smith Landing that evening, he learned of the letter from John Wootters. He agreed with his daughter that the young man's optimistic tone was very deliberate;

[24] Foote, S. The Civil War, Vol. 1, p. 71–84.

clearly, he did not want to upset Berta. Major Smith had already learned from other sources that the regiment had suffered a high number of casualties due to illness and that the death of Col. McLeod was considered a great loss to the entire brigade.[25] McLeod had assumed command of the First Texas Regiment after Col. Wigfall had been promoted Brigadier General to command the recently designated Texas Brigade. Considered a hero by many in Texas, McLeod had served in the War of Texas Independence and led the ill-fated Santa Fe Expedition twenty years earlier.[26]

All the news wasn't bad, however. Lodwick Downes told Major Smith that John Wootters had been elected to the position of Third Lieutenant by his company, demonstrating their confidence in his character and leadership.[27] Major Smith agreed with his family that this was an appropriate recognition of their friend's good qualities and ability.

He had been hoping for some information about Sibley's Brigade, which had left San Antonio in October for the long and dangerous trek to El Paso and the invasion of New Mexico.[28] There had been no recent word of the Brigade's whereabouts or activities, which only caused Anna Jane more anxiety.

Hannah and Berta's best efforts to provide comfort, companionship and musical entertainment had little effect. Anna Jane remained listless and uninterested in activities that she once embraced. The only thing that could engage her was news about their son. As the sun set on this winter day, the seemingly good news about John Wootters was the only glimmer of hope available. Hannah noted that Berta had not

[25] Cutrer, T. "McLeod, Hugh," Handbook of Texas Online.

[26] Carroll, H. Bailey, "Texas Santa Fe Expedition." Handbook of Texas Online

[27] Appendix I. Item 6. Register–J.H. Wootters elected 2nd Jr. Lt., Co I, 1Reg't. Inf. Texas Volunteers, Confed. Arch. Chap. 1, File No 76, p. 524.

[28] Taylor, J. Bloody Valverde: A Civil War Battle on the Rio Grande, February 21, 1862, p. 17.

offered the letter to her parents to read; to her knowledge, the young woman continued to keep it on her person.

Later that month, Betsy the mare gave birth to a male foal that Oscar confirmed had been sired by Magnus, the stallion given to Lucius for his service in Captain Pridgen's Horse Cavalry Company. Major Smith hoped that this new animal, like its sire, would have the strength and endurance necessary to fulfill his role at the plantation. The Smith family had not received any communications from Lucius since October, when he wrote of the company's imminent departure for El Paso. Their goal was to secure the territory of New Mexico for the Confederacy, and Lucius had been in high spirits about this mission.[29]

Major Smith was confident that Captain Pridgen would provide the company with competent leadership; he was also impressed with Col. Tom Green, commander of their Fifth Regiment.

With the departure of both Lucius and Elijah Chadwick, the plantation's former overseer, John had assumed their responsibilities for the daily management of the plantation. He had supervised the preparation of the fields for the next planting season which, despite the freezing days of February, were on the horizon for March. The preparation of the seeds and the fields was a high priority, but they would not expand the area being cultivated. While it was true that the future remained tenuous, idleness was not an option. Revenues from the cotton crop would be critical to the Confederate war effort.

Although the expected Union occupation of Galveston had not happened, shipping from the port was at a virtual standstill due to the naval blockade. Major Smith and other planters in Houston County were planning to send their crops

[29] *Ibid. p. 12.*

of the 1862 season to Mexico under militia protection, and preparations for this planting season had fully occupied the ninety slaves in Major Smith's charge.

Other than planting and harvesting the cotton crop, the plantation provided food for its community of slaves and the Smith family. Beef production, other than a small herd of milk cows, had never become a major focus. As many other plantation owners had discovered, cattle did not seem to thrive in the warm, humid climate.[30] Anna Jane often related a family story about her ancestor, Johannes Kolb, who had emigrated from Pennsylvania to South Carolina, and brought with him a herd of fine cattle, expecting them to prosper in the absence of harsh winters. Much to his dismay, his cows steadily lost weight and produced less milk in the southern environment. He eventually abandoned this endeavor in favor of a grist mill, which he built and operated at his property on the Pee Dee River.

Hogs and chickens did not suffer from the ailments that affected cattle. Those, along with crops of corn, various greens and other vegetables would provide for most of their needs. These agricultural activities were overseen by Oscar. Hannah, as usual, was devoted to caring for Anna Jane, even as Berta, who seemed to be more of a young woman every day, had increasingly become her mother's constant companion. Major Smith thanked God for having such loyal and loving women to take care of his wife, as his duties often took him away from home for the entire day.

Berta readily accepted her role as advocate of optimism and cheer for her mother, whose bouts of melancholy were

[30] Boles, JB. *The South Through Time–Volume II. p. 524.*

punctuated by periods of contentment. She was aware that her role in the family involved something other than her own amusement, and the absence of Lucius increased the opportunities for her to interact and converse with her parents. Hannah always made sure that Anna Jane's personal needs were taken care of, helping her to care for and maintain her appearance.

One afternoon, Berta found her mother sitting peacefully in her great chair before the fireplace, reading from the family Bible, which was so large it required a special stand. Anna Jane's red hair, now showing signs of graying, was combed and secured with a ribbon. She was wearing a pressed white blouse and was wrapped in a light shawl to further protect her from the occasional chill that moved through the room. The familiar strains of *"Für Elise"* drifted in from the music parlor, filling the room. Anna Jane stopped reading as Hannah entered the room.

"Miz Smith, would you want some tea and cornbread?" she asked. "I made a fresh batch, and it should be good with honey."

"Thank you, that would be delicious, Hannah," Anna Jane smiled. "My appetite seems to be improved. Please bring some for Berta as well. I know she'll want to have a bite when she finishes her practicing."

"Yes, ma'am," Hannah said. "That child sure does play that piano."

As Berta completed her playing and came in to the parlor, her mother gave gentle applause.

"Berta, I enjoy your playing so much, and your mastery of those pieces seems to be quite good," Anna Jane said, motioning for her daughter to join her. "I think your presence and your music help to lighten the burdens on my mind."

Berta took this opportunity to mention to her mother the concerns that had been weighing on her since the frightful experience with Mr. Jencks.

"I know you are very worried about Lucius, as am I," Berta said. "I am only reassured when I realize that he is a grown man with strong convictions. He told me that his faith in God's love and presence would always give him the strength to overcome his fear. I only wish my faith was so strong."

"I can only overcome my grief over Lucius' departure with help from our heavenly Father," her mother said. "I realize that my worry cannot be of any use to Lucius and that our Lord will always be with him, no matter what happens, and I certainly don't want these matters to cause you more distress."

"Mother, I think I am coming to terms with Lucius being away and this terrible war," Berta frowned. "But I have a much harder time understanding something that occurred on a trip to Crockett about a month before Christmas."

As Anna Jane sipped her tea, Berta recounted the experience at the mercantile store, sparing her no details about what Jencks said and how he had aimed a veiled threat at her entire family, all because he thought she was teaching Oscar to read.

"Darling, please don't let this upset you so," Anna Jane said, putting an arm around Berta, who was unable to stop herself from crying as she recalled the episode. "Some people feel personally threatened when slaves achieve a level of education, especially if that level exceeds their own. Those kinds of people often seek out others of an even lower status just to feel superior, and they consider slaves to be a culture of lower status. They don't realize that what slaves lack is opportunity, not ability."

Anna Jane knew full well that many slaves would benefit from education if it were made available to them. It was unfortunate, even wrong, she thought, that slavery was assumed to be a permanent status and did not allow for those with ability to better themselves. Freedom was not within their reach, except in rare cases where it was granted by their owners—and that was not permitted in Texas. Personally, Anna Jane thought that those with the will and capacity to elevate themselves to full citizenship through hard work and education should be able to do so. But she realized that the South, with its often narrow mindset, would likely always have two cultures, one black and one white. Even within those cultures, there were different classes of individuals based on a variety of factors and circumstances.

"What do you mean by a person's class?" asked Berta, who had been listening to her mother. "That sounds like something you'd find in European countries or in India, where they have a caste system, but not in America."

"That's right, in some European and Asian countries, a person's class is determined by birth," her mother explained. "They inherit the so-called class of their parents and generally aren't able to change that status during their lifetime, except in rare exceptions."

She went on to explain that a society in which one's efforts and personal qualities, no matter how worthy, could not result in personal advancement or recognition went against the fabric of American culture. In America, she said, hard work and good character were rewarded, no matter one's class. As she so often did, Anna Jane crafted her explanation from a Biblical perspective.

The Bible, she pointed out, taught people to respect and honor God and to treat others as they themselves would want to be treated. To follow these commandments one was expected to respect and show kindness to all people, and to recognize that they also had to live by the standards set for everyone. Honesty, trustworthiness, loyalty, bravery and tolerance of the beliefs of others—all these were characteristics found in a higher class of individual.

"But Hannah and Oscar have these characteristics," Berta said. "Yet that awful Mr. Jencks, who seems to lack all of those traits, would wish to look down on them."

"Indeed, my sweet girl, Hannah and Oscar and many others possess these qualities and are considered among the highest class of individuals in their culture," Anna Jane said. "That Jencks man, on the other hand, is a mean-spirited person, and those like him are best avoided. I don't know much about him or his wife, but I feel very sorry for anyone who cannot avoid being around them."

It was a pity, she noted, that their children with no educational opportunities, would likely not enjoy a better future than their parents. Perhaps someday there would be schools and organizations to help such children.

"Perhaps that's what I will do," Berta said, sitting up tall. "Someday, I may want to have a school to help educate children who lack those opportunities. It is very sad, indeed, that the Jencks children may be destined to grow up to be like their father. It seems very unfair that such a horrible man should determine what kind of life they'll experience."

Anna Jane marveled at what a thoughtful and strong-minded person her daughter was. She had no doubt that Berta would be a blessing to their family and to others, and she prayed for God to guide her in these matters as she grew to adulthood. Major Smith had mentioned the unfortunate incident to Anna Jane, but it seemed that Berta had grown stronger because of it. Yes, her daughter was innocent, per-haps sheltered, but she was not foolish. Thinking of Berta brought Lucius to mind again, and she felt a shadow cast its gloom. Rather than give in to the despair that would follow, she quickly asked Berta to play some of the new songs she had brought back from Crockett. So it was that the tunes of Stephen Foster once again rang through the Smith home.

XI

SUMMER 1862
SMITH LANDING PLANTATION

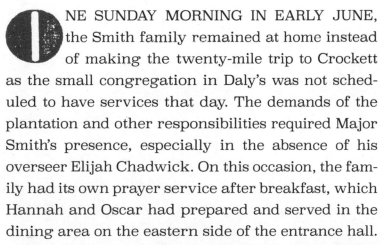

ONE SUNDAY MORNING IN EARLY JUNE, the Smith family remained at home instead of making the twenty-mile trip to Crockett as the small congregation in Daly's was not scheduled to have services that day. The demands of the plantation and other responsibilities required Major Smith's presence, especially in the absence of his overseer Elijah Chadwick. On this occasion, the family had its own prayer service after breakfast, which Hannah and Oscar had prepared and served in the dining area on the eastern side of the entrance hall.

The dining room had views of the Trinity River and of Hannah's special garden. From her chair in the parlor, Anna Jane had a view of the garden, which gave her great pleasure. On those days when she was feeling particularly weak, she would sit near the window and marvel at the garden's abundance. Hannah, who had an unusually green thumb, harvested seeds from a wide variety of flowering plants as well as edible greens and melons, always making certain that there was enough and enough variety to feed her charges.

That morning, as they were finishing their last cup of tea, Oscar appeared at the entrance of the room, looking somber.

"What is it, Oscar?" Major Smith asked.

"Major Smith, sir, we have visitors," Oscar said. "It's the postmaster from Crockett, and he has the preacher from the church with him."

A sudden gripping in his chest propelled Major Smith up from his chair, so sudden that he had to hold onto the back of the chair to keep from falling, and a dark veil clouded his vision. At that moment, a cloud must have passed over the face of the sun, for when he regained his vision, the room had noticeably darkened. In his heart, Major Smith knew why the visitors were there, and he sank back into his chair.

As a former military commander, he had also been responsible for notifying families when one of their loved ones died in the line of duty. Anna Jane and Berta remained transfixed, motionless at the table; they could hear Hannah sobbing in the entrance hall. The Baptist minister went directly to Anna Jane and Berta and embraced them together, while the postmaster extended his hand to Major Smith. The only audible sound was Hannah's crying.

The hush that had engulfed the room was interrupted by the sound of Major Smith opening the letter from Captain Redding S. Pridgen, Company H, Fifth Regiment, Texas

Mounted Volunteers. Major Smith stared out the window, oblivious to the garden or the pine forests in the distance; he focused instead on infinity as he realized, just then, that life would never again be the same for his family. With an unexpected surge of energy, Anna Jane rose from her chair and came toward him, collapsing into his embrace, their combined grief keeping them tightly in its grip. Hannah had hugged Berta, who, convulsed with sobs, kept murmuring with disbelief that her brother was gone forever.

"Oh, John," Anna Jane whispered. "I have feared that such a message would arrive every day since Lucius rode away nearly a year ago. Now my worst nightmares have come true. If ever the Lord were to give us strength and peace, now is the time of our greatest need. How will I ever survive this day?"

"I have no words," her husband said. "I have also had such fears, but I pushed them to the back of my mind."

In a trembling voice, Hannah spoke up from the back corner and asked Major Smith to read the letter. He nodded, opened it and began to read with a grief stricken voice.

> To my esteemed friends, Major John Smith and Mrs. Anna J. Smith.
>
> It is with great sadness and regret that I must relate to you the loss of your son Lucius in the noble defense of our beloved Southland and our freedoms.

John was unable to continue as tears filled his eyes, and he could no longer focus on the pages in his hands. After a few moments, he collected himself and continued reading:

Lucius was wounded during an attack, in which he demonstrated great bravery and gallantry. This occurred on the afternoon of February 21 at Valverde, a crossing of the Rio Grande del Norte, as our brigade engaged our foes near their Fort Craig. Our Company H had been directed by Colonel Green to capture a Federal artillery battery and was among those who faced intense fire as they succeeded in overcoming the enemy and seizing the weapons. Sadly, our losses were great and none nearer to my heart than my friend and companion, Lucius.

During their success on the field, Lucius was wounded. His companions helped him to our camp, where he was attended by Powhatan Jordan, the captain of Company A and an able physician from San Antonio. By the next morning Lucius lost his gallant struggle and, surrounded by his fellow troopers, his spirit was summoned by our Maker.

Major Smith paused here, took a breath and again focused on reading the letter. The silence in the room was interrupted only by the morning breeze ruffling the branches of a shade tree outside the window.

On February 22nd, he and the other Texans lost in the great victory were laid to rest with full military honors in a Christian service surrounded by the survivors of the battle. I regret the delay in writing to you, but we have only now returned to San Antonio. Although our mission was not the success we had hoped for, Lucius and the other gallant troops of our Company H captured the cannons, which have been returned to Texas where they will continue to aid our quest for freedom and independence. Again, please accept my deepest sympathies and be assured of my highest regard for your son and his valiant service. May our Heavenly Father receive him and his fallen companions into eternal rest and peace.

With highest regards and sincerest sympathy,

Redding S. Pridgen, Captain, Company H, Fifth Regiment, Texas Mounted Volunteers, Confederate States of America.

As John finished reading, he could hear an insect buzzing softly through the open window and the call of a bird somewhere in the distance. Nature went on, ignorant of the grief that held this family in its clenched fist.

The minister rose and asked all present to join hands, offering to lead them in prayer. Anna motioned to Hannah and Oscar to join the circle and Hannah's large black hand engulfed Berta's delicate fingers in a gentle clasp.

"Almighty God, never has your flock, gathered here today, been more in need of your presence. In this time of great sadness, we long for You to restore our souls. We are confident in Your promise to welcome Lucius into Your everlasting presence and to have him dwell in Your house forever. Pour out Your blessings and comfort on each person gathered here as we pray in the name of Christ. Amen."

Only a mockingbird's song interrupted the silence that followed. The minister told them that he would hasten back to Crockett for the Sunday service, and he would also inform the congregation what had occurred. He assured the Smith family that the entire flock would share their grief, uphold their spirits to God and pray for them to receive divine comfort.

With a supply of cornbread and ham on hand for the return trip, the minister and post master departed. Hannah and Oscar accompanied them down the entrance road. The Smith family, meanwhile, remained seated at the dining table. Nobody said anything, each of them in the world of their own minds and their own grief.

"John, I have suspected in my heart that Lucius had passed from this life some months ago, and I have been inwardly grieving about this for too long a time," Anna Jane said, finally breaking the silence. "Now that I know it's certain, I can ask God to heal the empty space in my heart. Perhaps this dark tunnel through which I have been passing is finally coming to an end."

"I have not had such premonitions, and I am stunned by this message," Major Smith said. "I have never had thoughts other than that Lucius was safe. It may take more than this letter to convince me."

Berta, who had been sitting quietly, again began sobbing. She stood and excused herself, fleeing for the refuge of her own room.

After an hour, Hannah knocked on the door to the parlor where Anna Jane and Major Smith were talking to ask if they wanted any fresh tea or a midday meal. Noticing that her eyes were swollen and red from crying, they replied that some food would be welcome but first they wanted Hannah to sit down and tell them of her feelings about what had happened that morning. Hannah, who had spent very little time sitting in the parlor and conversing with white people, came more fully into the room but continued to stand.

"Oh, Miz Anna, I had suspected that Lucius had gone to be with the Lord, but I sometimes didn't believe those feelings," Hannah said. "It don't seem real. I know that somehow we will get past this, but I also know I will always miss him, just like I do my little Ossie. It's been near two years that my boy has been gone, and I still catch myself looking over to where he used to sit to see what he's up to. What I do know is that they are both now with the Lord in a better place than any of us has ever been. I feel sorry for myself, but I know I should not feel sorry for them."

Anna Jane nodded. She knew Hannah's words to be true and hoped that someday she, too, could accept her son's departure from this world. Sooner would be better for her family, especially Berta. Anna Jane did not think that her own delicate health would allow her many more days on this earth. The time she did have left would be best spent not plagued with grief. Concerned about Berta, she asked the slave to check on her before preparing their meal.

After regaining her own composure, Hannah knocked on the door to Berta's bedroom. When there was no response to her first knock, she gently pushed the door open and inquired within.

"Missy Abigail, is there anything I can get for you that would help you to feel better?"

"Oh! Hannah, please come in and tell me what I can do to stop crying and feeling so hopeless," Berta said. "You haven't called me Abigail in quite some time."

"Sometimes tears just have to flow until your eyes are empty, and then they quit on their own," Hannah said, smoothing the young girl's hair. " I called you Abigail because what you need is to act like that woman in the Bible. She was not only beautiful and smart but also very brave. Your brother won't be coming to this home again, but he would want you to be brave and not grieve for him."

This sent Berta into another fit of sobs. It didn't seem possible that her brother would never again walk into their house or gallop down the road on his horse, that she would never again hear the tales of his hunting expeditions or other adventures or that she would never be able to tell him how proud she was to have him as a brother.

"I never really told Lucius how much I loved him and how important he was to me," Berta cried into Hannah's lap. "I wish I could ask him to forgive me for not being thoughtful enough to tell him those things."

"Miss Abigail, you can't ask Lucius those things," Hannah shook her head. "But you can always ask our Lord for forgiveness. He promises us that we will be granted what we want and need. Since you know that Lucius is with the Lord, he will likely know of your prayers, and since the Lord forgives you, surely Lucius will also." With that, she persuaded Berta to put on a good face and come back downstairs. Her mother and father were also suffering, she said, and would be happy to see her in a more cheerful state.

"I will do my best, Hannah, and thank you for being so kind," Berta said, managing a weak smile.

When Berta reentered the parlor, her parents were drinking tea and discussing their circumstances. Her father was arranging a visit to San Antonio; he thought a talk with some of the men from Lucius' company would bring him some peace of mind. The trip wouldn't take more than two weeks.

"Indeed, my dearest John, I want you to go," Anna Jane said. "Please remember every word that is said about our dear son and return quickly."

Seeing Berta at the door, Anna Jane invited her to join them.

"I am so glad that you seem to be more composed," she said to her daughter. "We have much to do to carry on with our lives."

Six weeks after the news of his son's death, Major Smith traveled to San Antonio to meet with those who had survived the trek back from their ill-fated expedition.[31] Summer evenings at the Smith Landing Plantation were the only respite from the oppressive heat. Two weeks after Major Smith's departure, Anna Jane and Berta were sitting on the veranda of their home hoping for a cooling breeze. The sounds of the impending night were rising—katydids buzzing, frogs croaking and the whippoorwills plaintively calling—in a mounting crescendo. In the nearly two months since the visitors from Crockett had delivered their devastating news, Anna Jane had noticed a marked improvement in her own mood. The initial shock and grief had seemingly given way to a sense of acceptance and healing.

Berta continued to struggle with a sense of guilt over not telling Lucius how much she loved and admired him before he left for his final adventure. It seemed that her prayers for forgiveness were slow in being answered. As she sat with her mother, she marveled at the nighttime sounds and the melancholy effect they had on her. This music surely must be the same song that nature had offered since creation.

A person's life, unlike these vibrant rhythms, was only a brief audience for that symphony. As conductor of this musical masterpiece, God would ultimately bring it to a perfect conclusion. Going forward, she determined that she would no longer be as thoughtless as she had seemed to be toward

[31] *Appendix II. Item 10. Sibley's Brigade and the War in the West.*

her brother. Instead, she would ask God to help her express her feelings for her loved ones more fully.

The ladies' reverie was interrupted by the sounds of a carriage coming up the entrance road from the other side of the home and the calls of the driver to Hannah heralding the return of Major Smith from San Antonio. Major Smith had been accompanied on this journey by Oscar's son, Edgar, so that Oscar could remain at the plantation.

Major Smith greeted his admiring ladies and joined them on the veranda, while Oscar and his son took care of the carriage, the horses and his luggage.

"Oh John, we are glad that you are home safely!" Anna Jane said. "Please come and tell us all about your journey."

"It feels good to sit on a chair that isn't trying to bounce you into a ditch, but I must say that young Edgar is an excellent driver like his father," he smiled, settling into a comfortable chair. "The trip was as good as one could expect. San Antonio is a tedious distance away, and I was reminded that our cotton crop will be following the same path after the harvest in the fall."

Major Smith stretched his long legs, propping his feet on a stool. Once in San Antonio, he found accommodations at the Menger Inn, which was located next door to what was left of the Alamo. Passing by that site every day, he told them, reminded him of a previous generation of brave young men willing to make the ultimate sacrifice for freedom, just like Lucius and his comrades.

He had not been able to find Dr. Powhatan Jordan, who cared for our Lucius in his final hours. According to Captain Pridgen, he had not seen Dr. Jordan since the Sibley Brigade's return to Texas and the doctor's whereabouts remained a mystery. However, a few members of Company H of the Fifth Texas Mounted Regiment were still in San Antonio, and Major Smith was able to meet with Elijah Chadwick, who had ridden into battle with Lucius on that fateful day.

"Elijah has returned safely," Anna Jane said. "That is something to be grateful for."

"Indeed, he has but he had more sad news to relate. Not only did we lose Lucius in the battle at Valverde, but his friend, Hosea Walling, was also killed."

But the tragic tale didn't end there. As Hosea died, so did his older brother, Robert, who was wounded and died of pneumonia a short time after the battle. The Walling family had lost both of its sons in the same battle. It was more than Berta could stand.

"Oh, my God in Heaven!" she cried out. "How many more losses will we all be asked to bear?"

"Truly, grief will cover our land," Anna Jane said. "We will go tomorrow to pay the Wallings a visit."

"Elijah had much to say about our son," Major Smith went on. His eyes filled with tears and his voice faltered.

Apparently, Lucius had shown exceptional bravery in his final battle. In some way, one that he could not express aloud to his wife and daughter, he was proud that his son's life, if it had to end now, had ended on a note of bravery and honor. He hoped that Lucius would be remembered in such a way by those who served with him. He knew that any soldier or true man, in the best sense of those words, would want to depart this life known as a gentleman of integrity who faced death with a determined spirit and a clear conscience.

After hearing the details of the battle and how Lucius spent his last hours, Berta had had enough. Once again, she fled to the safety of her bedroom.

After a sleepless night, the Smith family rose early the next morning and gathered for breakfast. Hannah served the meal as Major Smith asked what the ladies had done in his absence. The list was filled with war-related activities. They'd been asked by the ladies at church to help knit one hundred pairs of socks and some sweaters to send to the Crockett Southrons in time for winter. Anna Jane admitted that the handiwork had been good for her spirits.

"I seem to be less aware of the foreboding melancholy that oppressed me in recent months," she said. "Perhaps knowing that Lucius is now with the Lord and my worry can no longer be of any use to anyone eases my mind."

Perhaps the best news they had received was a letter from John Wootters. He had written a long one to his uncle, Lodwick Downes, who had been kind enough to share it with the Smith ladies. Lieutenant Wootters had also written to Berta in late April, but it had arrived only in the past two weeks. In March, his brigade had been ordered to move back from a position at the Potomac River. They were in the area of Fredericksburg when he wrote, and they were not pleased with the move as it seemed like a retreat. Their new defense line was the Rappahannock River, and they had not engaged the enemy since their move. Berta did not understand why the brigade wanted to be closer to the fighting. Wouldn't they want to be further from the battlefield and out of harm's way?

"No, dear girl, I would expect that eagerness for engagement," her father said. "Especially of troops that have not truly been tested in battle. Did Lieutenant Wootters have anything else to report?"

Berta shook her head. Although she had written him several letters, she had received only one in return over the past six months. In that missive, he told her about the unseasonably cold weather and a snowstorm they had endured earlier in the month. Heavy rains followed, turning the roads into rivers of mud. He mentioned wanting to hear Berta play some tunes on the piano, and he seemed especially concerned about the safety of Gus, the pet pig that lived in the side-yard of the Downes & Long store. In Virginia, he said, Gus would likely have become bacon and ham as that, along with corn, was their main food. His letter, she said, was filled with news and musings, not feelings.

"Recall that the letter was written before the First Infantry had been engaged in any serious combat, and soldiers under almost any circumstances will continue to minimize the seriousness of their situation," Major Smith reminded her. "You do not need to chasten him for his lightheartedness; I expect that letters written by him after the battles of May and June will be much more serious."

Berta saw the sense in her father's words. She had followed his advice and written to John Wootters about the loss of Lucius and its devastating effects. She had not, however, told him of her own grief in failing to tell her brother of her love and pride in him. But, having vowed not to make that mistake again, she did tell Wootters how proud she was of his brave actions and how fervently the family prayed for his safe return to Texas and his home.

"I cannot imagine any person that would not appreciate and be strengthened by such sincere sentiment," her mother said. "I would encourage you to continue reminding him of those thoughts."

In an attempt to lighten the somber mood around the table, Major Smith changed the subject altogether. He reminded the ladies that, war notwithstanding, life went on, and should not be persistently plagued by melancholy. For the past year, he observed, Berta's formal education had been interrupted. And while he was pleased that she had continued musical studies with the pianist in Crockett, her academic and social development were also important. He and Anna Jane were concerned about the lack of other young ladies her age in the area. Berta should form friendships and feed her intellectual spirit. Unfortunately, with so much fighting in Virginia, continuing her education in that state would not be an option. So her parents decided that a solution much closer to our home would be ideal.

"God has blessed you with a keen mind as well as a loving heart," Major Smith told her. "To ignore your need for further education would be poor stewardship of the talents you have been given."

He had heard that the Masonic Lodge in Fairfield in Freestone County has opened a new school for young women known as the Fairfield Female College. It was just across the Trinity River, about a half a day's journey from Smith Landing plantation. The school has close affiliations with the Baptist church and its president, Henry Lee Graves, a Mason from North Carolina, had an excellent academic reputation. Graves had served as president of Baylor University in Independence since its founding. There was also a separate Baylor Female College in Independence. Major Smith suggested that they visit these and other schools where Berta might want to pursue her studies in the future.[32]

"We should consider a visit to the schools in the next few months," Anna Jane said. "Selfishly, I would not want you to leave us for at least a year, and I do not want you very far away."

Berta was overwhelmed by her parents' thoughtfulness and generosity, especially in the wake of their loss. As much as she wanted to pursue schooling, she also knew it would take her at least a year to be ready to live away from home. That was something she'd never done, and it would be a difficult change for her. Perhaps in a year they would all be more comfortable with that plan. Until then, they would take the time to heal.

[32] *Shields, D.R. Fairfield Female College, Handbook of Texas Online*

XII

1862-63
HOUSTON COUNTY, TEXAS

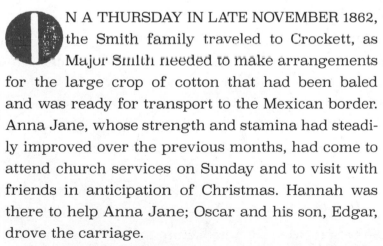

N A THURSDAY IN LATE NOVEMBER 1862, the Smith family traveled to Crockett, as Major Smith needed to make arrangements for the large crop of cotton that had been baled and was ready for transport to the Mexican border. Anna Jane, whose strength and stamina had steadily improved over the previous months, had come to attend church services on Sunday and to visit with friends in anticipation of Christmas. Hannah was there to help Anna Jane; Oscar and his son, Edgar, drove the carriage.

Berta had been looking forward to the visit. She was eager for information about John Wootters, and she also hoped to deliver some Christmas gifts that she had knitted when she and her mother were making winter clothing for the troops in Virginia. While Anna Jane's mood had seemed to lighten, Berta's had remained darker than usual. Her parents concluded that a major factor was the absence of her tutors from the Smith plantation.

Travel by paddlewheel boat on the Trinity River had ceased with the Federal threat to Galveston. Berta's tutors had most likely enlisted or been called to serve in some capacity, so she was without their regular instruction. While the blockade had been in effect for one year, the presence of a Union army force had not been evident until October, when a squadron of eight Federal ships had taken control of the harbor. With the island city considered indefensible, the heavy artillery protecting it had been removed by the Confederate commander. Business and commerce were now nonexistent, and most of the citizenry had relocated to inland sites.[33]

Concern about her education led Major Smith and Anna Jane to travel with Berta to Freestone County to visit the Fairfield Female College. The roads leading to the town of Fairfield were reached by the ferry at the Smith Landing Plantation. The road linking the communities of Augusta and Daly's in Houston County to the river continued across the ferry to Fairfield, which was accessible except after prolonged rainfall. The Smith family would visit the college, which had two twenty-week sessions yearly with the next one beginning in early January. They felt that Berta was mature enough to attend the school as a boarding student, and that she would benefit from the intellectual and social stimulation.

Hannah thought that Berta's melancholy was also due to the lack of any recent letter from John Wootters. The Downes

[33] Cotham, E.T., *Battle on the Bay: The Civil War Struggle for Galveston.*

family in Crockett had received a letter in October, which they had shared. Major Smith had told Berta that Wootters had received one of her letters and written several back, but had not received any reply. Berta was dismayed by this as she had written often. She knew that mail delivery was, at best, erratic; it was apparent that only a few of her letters were reaching John Wootters.

As they traveled to Crockett, she gazed through the carriage windows at the wintertime scene. Although this area was generally known as the piney woods, a wide variety of trees grew throughout the forests. Whereas the land near the streams and low-lying areas was populated by hardwoods, the gentle hills were covered with thick stands of evergreen trees that seemed to reach far into the sky blocking direct sunlight. Rays beaming through this canopy gave the appearance of an ancient cathedral with towering arches and high windows casting illumination on penitent worshipers.

Berta thought about John Wootters, praying that he be spared to return to his home in Texas. Her recent letters to him had implored him to be careful and encouraged him to ask God for protection. Berta had never really discussed her faith with him, suspecting that it would offer little comfort to one facing such grave dangers. But she wanted him to seek divine help and to remind him that God's ultimate grace and love were the only protection that could really meet all of their needs.

His last letter had been full of optimism and described how the Texans had enhanced their reputation of being among the best fighting troops in the Army of Northern Virginia. But Berta and everyone knew that when the letter was written, the Crockett Southrons and their comrades had no idea what lay ahead of them. All of the Smith family members hoped to find out more about the fate of Wootters' company on this visit to Crockett.

Worrying about John Wootters interfered with Berta's ability to focus on other areas of her life, especially her desire to be a comfort to her parents. She had mixed feelings about the possibility of attending Fairfield Female College but realized that some change in her daily activities would be helpful. And while living away from home seemed a daunting prospect, she reminded herself that she would not be that far from home. She secretly hoped that her parents would insist she attend the college.

As they were passing through Daly's near the homestead of the unpleasant Mr. Jencks, Berta saw several children that she suspected were his playing near the roadway. "Father, would you please have Oscar stop the carriage?"

Major Smith had no idea why his daughter would make such a request, but without further question, he called to Oscar to pull up the team. As the horses came to a stop, the group of disheveled children scattered to the side of the road, where they stared at the well-dressed travelers with bewilderment and suspicion. The older children had drawn back furthest from the carriage, leaving only the smallest child nearby. Berta spoke softly to the little girl.

"Little Missy, are you and your brothers and sisters part of the Jencks family?" The child did not speak, but nodded as her brothers and sisters looked on.

"I want to be your friend," Berta said, opening the carriage door and stepping out to the side of the road. "I have some things I made for you and your brothers and sisters." She took a package from Hannah and presented it to the speechless child.

The older children whispered nervously to each other but did not come closer to investigate the package or the visitor.

"I hope you can find a use for these woolens I have knitted," Berta said. "It is certain to be a cold winter. Please take them to your mother and share them with your brothers and sisters." Even as Berta left the package on the ground and turned back to the carriage, she could hear a small thank you from the little girl.

Once Berta had resumed her seat and said good bye to the children, Major Smith told Oscar to proceed without further delay. The carriage lurched forward. Looking back out the window, Berta saw the older children pulling at the package. She watched until the figures grew smaller and smaller and finally faded from sight.

"Anna Jane, I hope you and Berta have carefully considered this apparent act of kindness," Major Smith said. "While I am sure the children and their mother will be pleased with the gifts, I am uncertain how old Jencks will react. It will likely depend on his sobriety at the time. Hopefully they can avoid discussing where the wraps came from."

"Berta has become quite adept at knitting and I didn't see any harm in trying to extend a hand of charity to these children," Anna Jane scolded her husband. "From the looks of them, they will certainly be able to use whatever clothing we can give them."

Major Smith could see little benefit in discussing the potential ramifications of this act of charity, so they continued riding into the town without further conversation. Hannah did note that during the remainder of their journey, Berta had a smile on her face. She did not need to say anything to show how satisfied she was with her accomplishment.

On arriving in Crockett, the Smiths went straight to the new hotel in town to situate Anna Jane and Berta. Major Smith then walked over to the Masonic Lodge, where he expected to obtain information about the status of the Texas Brigade and plans for delivery of the cotton crop, which was now in storage. Lodwick Downes, Andrew Gossett and others had much to tell him, as news of the First Texas Regiment had filtered back to their community from the occasional letters and by telegraph. They confirmed that the only way to move the cotton was over land to the Rio Grande River in southern Texas, where it could be loaded through Mexican merchants on ships sailing under European flags. A militia group would be leaving with the first shipment of product within the month.

Lodwick Downes, who seemed to have aged greatly in the past year, greeted Smith warmly on his arrival at the lodge. The store owner had noticeably slowed his pace and seemed more stooped than in previous months, which Smith attributed to burdens resulting from the lack of commercial activity in town. These cares, reflected on his lined face, seemed to ebb somewhat as he clasped Major Smith's hand.

"John, my friend, It is so good to see you again," Downes said. "I have much news to share with you from my nephew, John Wootters. I also hope your family has come with you on this visit as I have a message to deliver to your daughter."

"Anna Jane and Berta are at the hotel, and we will be in town through Sunday," Smith responded. "I know that Berta will be anxious to see you and hear about the word from your nephew. She received a letter from him some time ago, but that was before the intense action the First Texas Regiment has had in more recent months. Tell me what you have learned about our Crockett Southrons and the war in the East."

Downes told him that a wire had come into Crockett two days ago containing news about the Confederates in Maryland and a terrible battle at a town called Sharpsburg. The letter from John Wootters to his uncle had been written after their brigade had fought a battle in August near Manassas, Virginia. It was about the second battle at that location, and it had been written before Robert E. Lee led his army north of the Potomac River into Maryland and the recent disaster.[34]

After the great victory at Manassas, Lee determined to move the army across the Potomac and into Union territory. This move was viewed with concern by many Southerners, as it was a distinct change from the more defensive strategy that Confederate President Jefferson Davis had discussed. This war was not a design of conquest, he noted, but rather an attempt to force the Federals to let the Southland go in peace. Instead, Abraham Lincoln had then declared all slaves to be free in his Emancipation Proclamation as well as his intention to enforce that proclamation in all territory under Federal control. Not surprisingly, it angered and motivated many who previously had been less enthusiastic about going to war.[35]

The only good news Downes had to report was that Wootters had, thus far, survived; many of his friends and fellow soldiers would never return home. At least seven of their company had been killed, including the commander,

[34] *Appendix II. Item 11. The 1st Texas Reg't, Hood's Brigade–1862. The Peninsula Campaign, Second Manassas and the Maryland Campaign.*
[35] *Foote, S. The Civil War: A Narrative, Volume One, pp. 687–700.*

Captain R. W. Cotton,[36] while many others, Wootters' friend Gus Aldrich included, were wounded. The First Texas Regiment commander, Lieutenant Col. Philip Work, reported losing 186 of 226 men in this single battle. Overall, more than 550 out of 850 were killed or wounded. Fortunately, Lee was able to withdraw back across the Potomac River, or the entire army might have been lost. And while further information had yet to trickle in, the results of the battle at Shiloh in April[37] and more recently at Sharpsburg made things look grim for the Confederacy. Wootters was promoted to senior second lieutenant the day following the battle at Sharpsburg and was now the commander of their company.[38]

Major Smith was stunned into silence. He could not imagine so many losses to a single group of men. It sounded as though the survival of any had been a miracle, and he was thankful that Wootters had been one of the fortunate few. He thought Wootters must have fought with great valor to have been given command of the company. He also hoped Downes had more encouraging news to share and said so.

"The pall of grief that has beset Anna Jane since the loss of Lucius has only recently begun to recede," Major Smith said. "Such terrible news could likely have a dampening effect on her."

Downes reassured his friend that the letter's contents were more optimistic than what he'd just heard. He would send it with Major Smith so that both Berta and Anna Jane could read it, and then retrieve it from them on Sunday after church. Major Smith then shared with him the possibility of Berta going away to the young women's college in Fairfield

---

[36] *Mainer, T. Houston County in the Civil War, p. 17-19.*

[37] *Appendix II. Item 12. General Albert Sidney Johnston and the Battle of Shiloh.*

[38] *Appendix I. Item 6. Regimental Return of the 1st Reg't Texas Vols. for the month of October 1862: JH Wooters(sic). Promoted from 2 Jr to 2 Sr Lieut Co I, 1st Reg't Texas Vols. September 30/62.*

and how he would visit with Judge Gossett on the subject during this visit. He confessed that he and Anna Jane both thought it would benefit Berta to occupy her mind and to be around girls her own age, as she, too, was becoming all too familiar with melancholy.

Major Smith was settled into a comfortable chair at the Masonic Lodge when Judge Gossett stopped in for his daily visit. He made straight for this friend, but his usual smile and enthusiasm were absent, which told Major Smith that something was not quite right.

"It is good to see you, John," the judge said, shaking his hand. "I only wish the news about the Confederacy was as hopeful."

Major Smith nodded and told Gossett that he knew about the results of the two most recent battles.

"Our state has paid a higher price for our freedoms than anyone could have imagined," the judge said. "The reality of Lincoln's intent to free slaves and the certain reluctance of the European nations to rally to our cause makes the outlook bleak indeed."

Both men were quiet for a moment as the reality of what was sure to happen sank in. The likelihood of any peaceful resolution seemed to have vanished; more Southerners than ever seemed determined to continue the struggle. How things would turn out going forward remained to be seen. And Major Smith, with only one child left, was concerned about Berta's opportunities.

"I remember you mentioned an interest in Fairfield Women's College, and I have recently received more information about their activities which I'll share with you," Gossett said. "Doesn't your daughter possess excellent musical talent?"

As it turned out, one of the wounded Confederates from the battle of Shiloh was an adventurer from Europe, who came to aid the Confederate cause. He had recovered from his injuries sufficiently to take a position at the Fairfield College as instructor of musical arts. According to Gossett, this Rudolph von Godski claimed to be descended from a noble family in Poland. Whether or not that was the case, he was, in fact, reputed to be an accomplished pianist. Perhaps Berta would benefit from his instruction?

"This is interesting news, especially since we plan to visit there in the next month," Major Smith said. "The college has much to recommend it with its ties to Masonry and the Baptist church and the fine reputation of its president, Dr. Henry Graves. I hope that Berta will be amenable to attending."

When Major Smith returned to the hotel, he found Anna and Berta reflecting a much more somber mood that just a few hours earlier.

"What has caused my pretty girls to be so unhappy?" he asked. "Are the hotel rooms not to your liking, or did you find that mice had already occupied them?"

"We have heard about the terrible circumstances of our Crockett Southrons and their regiment in Maryland," Anna Jane said, shaking her head. "The news gives us no reason to smile."

"True, true, but I do have some good news to share," he said, taking a seat by the fireplace. "Our friend John Wootters has not only survived the ordeal, but he is now commander of their company. Lodwick Downes has asked me to bring this letter he had received, as it has a special message that is likely of interest to Berta."

With these words, Berta sat back in a large chair and began to weep, her shoulders shaking from the force of her sobs. Hannah, who was also crying, took the girl in her strong arms and held her tight. Their embrace provided palpable comfort.

"Now, this letter was written well before the army moved into Maryland, and while its optimism may not still be appropriate, it doesn't demand excessive tears," her father said. "I thought you will find it of interest as Wootters specifically asked his uncle to share it with you."

"Read the letter, child," a now-smiling Hannah said. "I want to know what the lieutenant has to say!"

Berta took the letter and opened it with a trembling hand. Dated September 1st, it was more than two months old. She briefly wondered if any of her letters had found their way to Mr. Wootters, especially since the troops seemed to move frequently. She cleared her throat and began to read:

> My Dear Uncle,
>
> I am writing this note more hurriedly than I would have wished as I have much to tell since my last letter. You have most surely learned about our brigade and its success earlier in the summer, even if you have not received the letters I wrote from Richmond. The complaint that we had journeyed all the way from Texas and had no one to fight was answered in May, when we were sent against the Federals at a port called Eltham's Landing on the York River. Although it was not a major battle, it gave us a chance to show General Johnston what Texans can do in a fight. At the end of June, after General Lee had taken the command, we had another chance at

a place known as Gaines Farm, where General Hood was called upon to save the day against a stubborn Union defensive line. Late in the afternoon our men charged over a quarter-mile of rough ground with loud rebel yells, despite their guns. This must have put the fear of God in them as their line broke and the federals fell back in defeat. The only thing that saved them was nightfall, but by the next morning their General Porter had removed his troops across the Chickominnie (sic) River burning the bridges in defeat.[39]

Berta's tears had subsided, but her voice softened to the point of a whisper as she continued her reading:

The Fourth and Fifth Regiments had the greatest losses, but our First paid its price as Colonel Rainey, our commander, was wounded. We are now led by Lt. Col. Philip Work. Our Crockett Southrons lost four men—Boykin, Morris, Manning and Montgomery, who will be greatly missed as they had each become my close friends. Our Lt. Sheridan was wounded, as was my good friend Lt. Wall, and will not be able to continue with the company. Willie will be returning home, but he has left one finger in Virginia as a result of his wound. He may have arrived in Crockett by the time you receive this, so please tell him that we wish him well and, if his finger regrows, he is welcome back here at any time.

[39] *Reference is to the Chickahominy River in Virginia.*

"How can they have such a cavalier feeling about such bloodshed and tragedy?" Berta turned to her parents. "What has happened to their minds?"

"It's only natural that men, when faced with the likelihood of death, remove that thought from their minds," he explained. "It is a way of confronting fear and keeping that feeling from preventing them from failing to act bravely."

Berta shook her head; she simply didn't understand. But she continued reading.

> *I suspect you already know of what I have written as I sent other letters from Richmond, where we spent a month trying to recover from our losses. During that time we became aware of the burden that has fallen on all of our Confederate brothers as the hospitals in our capital are filled with injured men, especially a very large one known as Chimborazo. The First Texas' numbers were far below last spring, and we gladly received a new company from Trinity County. They arrived in early August just as we were directed to march north from Richmond.*

During a pause, Oscar appeared quietly in the doorway to the parlor. The slave informed Major Smith that the team and carriage had been put away in the stable, and if all the tasks were done, he and his son, Edgar, would retire for the evening. Once again, Berta returned to the letter.

> *The next day we crossed the Rapahinik (sic) River to join Gen. Johnston's divisions, and the new Trinity troops were amused at their first combat action. General Lee has prohibited men from foraging*

at the expense of locals, but some troops were tempt-
ed by a field of ripening corn and set about to ob-
tain a meal. As they entered the field they met a
Union scouting party with similar intentions, and
the result was a fist fight suitable for any bar room
and roasting ears bombardments were hurled. The
Texans quickly took the field but our brigade quar-
termaster felt obliged to buy 100 acres from its own-
er. The Roasting Ears Fight was not a great benefit,
as we were ordered to continue toward the Bull Run
Mountains the next morning. The divisions succeed-
ed in clearing a gap known as Thoroughfare, and
over the next two days the federals took a great beat-
ing. Our brigade attacked a field called the Chinn
Ridge, where we met two regiments from New York
that were not prepared for the fight. These Zuvies
(sic) in their bright red and blue uniforms were near-
ly wiped out. Their fallen covered the field and have
been rightly described as appearing like the fields
covered with bluebonnets and paintbrush flowers in
Texas.[40]

"Is it possible that a human being's spirit can become so hardened that a scene of death and destruction can be so described?" Berta said. "I just don't know if I can continue to read of such horrors."

"Please finish the letter, Missy Berta, so we can know what he says to you," Hannah said. Instead, Berta handed the letter to her mother, who read on:

[40] *References are to the Rappahannock River in Virginia and to the regiment of New York Zoaves.*

I must close this as the postmaster is calling for any letters that are to be sent before we leave this place in the morning. Please tell my friend Miss Berta Smith, that I have received one of her letters and I am saddened about the loss of her brother Lucius. I am certain that he served bravely and that his actions would make any man proud. He must have stood valiantly with his comrades until God called him to real peace. Also tell her that I thank her for her words of encouragement and reassure her that I and my fellow soldiers are well aware that our faith is the only source of strength sufficient to sustain us as we complete our duty. Her letters are very welcome as others I have received are of such trivial content that I suspect the writer is unaware of what is happening in the war. We are indeed fighting not only because of our own pride and for our safety but to secure freedom for those of a gentle nature as she possesses. Please give my love to all of our family and ask them to write when they are able.

Your fond nephew, John Wootters.

As Anna Jane folded the letter, returning it to the frayed envelope, the room was silent. A few minutes later, Major Smith spoke.

"You have heard words from one who represents the best that our Southland can offer," he said. "We can only pray that he and his comrades remain safe and, if such is not to be, then that our Heavenly Father will receive each of them into eternal peace."

As each silently offered a prayer, Major Smith told his wife and daughter what Judge Gossett had shared with him: Fairfield Female College had engaged a new music instructor and the Smith family should visit there soon. They had discussed such a trip on several occasions, and now it seemed the time was right. They would go in December. Berta was looking forward to it.

On Sunday during church, Berta could not stop thinking about John Wootters and the letter he'd written. She didn't know him very well, but now she wondered if her initial impression of a gentle and thoughtful soul was wrong. The appalling loss of life that he seemed to readily accept was beyond her grasp. She had recurring thoughts about the role of divine intervention in the cataclysmic conflict, and she was certain that everyone in church and at such meetings across the north and south were offering similar prayers.

Having read the Book of Job in the Bible, Berta had concluded that many issues were simply beyond human understanding and that the only valid prayer request was that God grant each individual the ability to endure and to have faith. She could not, however, keep from asking God to spare the life of John Wootters and bring him safely home.

Once the service was over, she went looking for Lodwick Downes to return the letter. He suggested that Berta continue to reassure his nephew that there were many reasons for him to survive, that he was held in the highest regard and esteem, and his safe return was the subject of their daily prayers. Berta felt a brief urge to ask Downes about the effectiveness of prayer, but instead thanked him profusely and assured him that her prayers and letters would continue.

The return to the plantation saw the Smith family in an improved mood. They all were optimistic about their planned visit to Fairfield in the coming weeks.

January 1863 would always remain one of the most memorable of times in Berta Smith's life. It was the month she became a student at the Fairfield Female College. Their visit in December had allayed any concerns they had; Berta was especially excited about the piano instruction she would receive. The new music instructor's reputation had spread rapidly. He was, it seemed, an accomplished pianist from a Polish noble family, the House of Sobieski. The opportunity to study piano with him appealed to Berta, and she sensed, at the time of her visit, that the school would become like a second home to her.[41] Her initial impression of the college was boosted by the warm reception she received from the other students. The prospect of being with other girls with whom she had much in common was something she could look forward to.

Even before she matriculated, Berta, along with many other Texans, was in a mood of excitement over the remarkable triumph of the Confederates at the battle of Galveston on New Year's Day. The Valverde Battery, those guns captured by the heroic but fatal charge of Lucius Smith and other Texans in New Mexico one year earlier, had contributed to the victory.[42]

Most of Berta's new classmates had family members and friends serving the Confederate cause. Dr. Graves and his faculty members did their best to help the students focus on

[41] *Appendix I. Item 17. The Houston Chronicle, September 28, 1930.*
[42] *Appendix II. Item 13. Battle of Galveston.*

their studies and other activities, and the prevailing atmosphere of the college was one of optimism and enthusiasm. Even in her first weeks at the college, this clearly had a positive effect on Berta's attitude. She returned to the plantation for the last weekend of the month to pack up some additional clothes, sheet music and other items from her bedroom, and it was obvious to everyone in the Smith home that Berta's heart and spirit were lighter. They could tell just by the way she walked from room to room. They also knew she would step even more lively when she discovered the surprise that awaited her.

The carriage came to a stop at the front veranda of the Smith Plantation home. Hannah, who had made the trip to accompany Berta back home from the college in Fairfield, slowly exited the carriage. Oscar secured the horses first and then helped Hannah and Berta up to the front entrance, where they were greeted by a smiling Anna Jane.

"Welcome home! I hope you had a good trip and I can't wait to hear about your first weeks at college," she said. "Come in, come in, I have something for you."

"The college is a wonderful place in so many ways," Berta said, holding her mother in a warm but gentle embrace. "Dr. Graves and the faculty are interested in helping us learn and helpful when we need their attention. Our accommodations are just fine and the servants are very helpful with our laundry and keeping our rooms in good order."

Berta noticed that her mother seemed a little unsteady, but continued her description. The building and its surroundings were delightful, she said. Not only was it an elegant structure, it was also well heated, as there was a fireplace in her sitting room. The grounds, which were neatly kept, would be breathtaking with the spring flowers in full bloom. But the best part was the company of all the girls at the college.

There were only about thirty of them, and one named Martha Meriwether, who was a year ahead of Berta, lived close to Smith Landing plantation. There was a larger number of younger students in the lower school, which was known as the Academy, and they all lived in the Fairfield area. According to Berta, the girls in her classes, some of whom came from as far away and Louisiana and Mississippi, were very pleasant.

One thing she had noticed, she told her mother, was how strict Dr. Graves was with the girls' meal times and how insistent that they all follow their schedules with promptness and punctuality.

"If one of us is late for dinner, the door is locked and that person misses the meal," Berta said. "When that happens, some of the other girls will smuggle food out of the dining room and take it to the one being punished. But we are very careful to not be caught."

It seemed that Dr. Graves ran a tight ship. With so many girls in one place, her mother pointed out, it was likely necessary to have rules and to follow them.

"How is the music instructor I have heard so much about?" Anna Jane asked. "I gather his injury at Shiloh has not prevented him from teaching."

"Count von Godski, as he insists on being called, shows no signs of his disability other than a slight limp," Berta smiled. "He really is a very serious and excellent pianist, and I know he will greatly help me improve my playing."

Berta also thought the Count, who was very proud of his mustache, sometimes acted like a dandy. If she looked at him too closely, she found it hard to keep from laughing. As for his taste in music, he was partial to pieces by Frederic Chopin, perhaps because of the Polish roots he shared with that composer. Berta hadn't yet tried to play any of his music; she found the pieces very difficult to play, but beautiful. When Count von Godski played them, she could sit and listen for hours.

"Your Father and I have missed you, but it is reassuring to know that you are so happy and busy with your studies," said Anna Jane, whose fatigue was beginning to show. "The college certainly agrees with you, and I am sure that if you are careful to complete your studies and practice your piano pieces, you should not have very many occasions to have to forego your dinner. Now go unpack your bags because I have a surprise for you: a letter from John Wootters, delivered this week!"

Berta held her breath as she grasped the letter from John Wootters. She felt lightheaded, she felt dizzy, she felt a flushed sensation travel up her neck to the top of her head. Leaning on the bannister, she walked upstairs and directly to her room. Her first reaction was one of confidence: the company commander had responded to her notes with a personal letter. She recalled how strong and handsome he was, what an impressive figure he had presented the day he left with the Crockett Southrons. Quickly dismissing those girlish thoughts, Berta allowed insecurity to wash over her as she carefully opened the sealed envelope. Would he write descriptions of the terrible realities of war? What would the message reveal about him? She had not been able to forget the image from his earlier letter of the dead soldiers strewn across the fields like wildflowers. Many of those soldiers had been someone's brother or son, whether fighting for the North or the South. She took a deep breath and focused on the letter in her hand:

> My dear Miss Smith,
>
> I am writing you from our camp near the town of Fredericksburg, in what is said to have been the gentle countryside of Virginia. At this time, it is cold and barren except for the tents of our regiment and the trodden fields of what were farms. I want to express appreciation on behalf of the Crockett Southrons for the warm stockings and sweaters that you and the other ladies made for our dwindling number. We have even received a supply of shoes, which were badly needed as our only means of transportation is by our feet.

Berta's eyes were now free of tears as she tried to imagine the scene described for her. She had not considered how many of the 110 men that had marched from Crockett a year and a half ago were still alive, or still at their duties. It was certainly a smaller band than she remembered. She moved closer to the window to read by the fading light:

> It is likely that one could imagine that there are no acts of kindness to be found in an army's occupation, but I have just learned of such a case following the terrible battle at Fredericksburg.[43] The Federal general called for an attack that was doomed to failure and resulted in the loss of many of their troops.

[43] *Appendix II. Item 14. Battle of Fredericksburg.*

Our regiment and others in General Longstreet's command had been building a defensive position on high ground near the town. For reasons we could not imagine, their forces made a direct attack on the position with the results that we the defenders certainly expected. That night, a South Carolina sergeant, who must have been appalled by the suffering of the federals injured on the field, risked his life to take water to the men lying between the battle lines. The Union solders did not fire at him as he ministered to their wounded, when he would have been an easy target. My only regret is that I did not have such an opportunity or would likely not have been so brave as he was.

Berta could not continue after reading these words until her tearful sobs could subside. After an interval she resumed her reading:

I have written several letters but as you may not have received them I will write again that I thank you for the words you sent of your prayers for our safety and belief that only God's grace can give us the strength to perform our duties. We are aware that many on the opposing side of the battle share our faith. We can only do our duties with the desire to support our comrades and to defend the freedoms we hold so dear. One can only admire men who will sacrifice so much for this cause even though we hope for a very different outcome.

Please continue to offer prayers on our behalf We will also be praying that you will be able to face the

hardships in your path. Please give my love to your
family. I hope to be able to return to give all of you
my warmest regards.

Your friend far away,
Lt. John Wootters

Berta sat in wonder at what she had read. She had many
questions, more than before she'd read the letter. Sometime
later, she heard Hannah knocking on the bedroom door.

"Missy Berta, your supper is ready and your momma and
poppa are worrisome about you," she said. "They want you
to come downstairs when you are able."

"Oh, Hannah, I didn't realize how long I had been lost in
my own thoughts," Berta got up and opened the door. "Please
tell them that I am coming now."

———————

At the dinner table, Berta recounted her description of the
activities at the college for her father, who agreed that the
decision for her to attend was a good one. He was particularly interested in what had brought her piano instructor to the
Confederate army and seemed pleased that her studies were
both challenging and enjoyable.

Berta related much of what Wootters had told her about
the Crockett Southrons in Virginia. The conversation with
her parents left many of her questions unanswered, and she
realized that the mind and heart of a soldier facing such
dangers were not something she could fully understand. She
was glad to be returning the next morning to her college
and to activities that were far removed from the agony of
the battlefield.

XIII

LATE SUMMER 1863
HOUSTON COUNTY, TEXAS

THE SUMMER AFTER Berta's first session at the Fairfield Female College was hard for her; as much as she enjoyed being home with her parents, she also missed being with her school friends and in the classroom. During those moments of yearning to be back at school, she turned to her music, her parents' company and the wilderness around Smith Landing Plantation, all of which brought her great joy.

Although the property extended several miles from the river, it was the one-mile wooded area adjoining the river that she found particularly enchanting. The gentle Cedar Branch meandered through this section, carrying its clear water to the power-ful and often murky Trinity River; numerous trails coursed through the hardwood forests bordering the river. Thanks to her botanical studies at the college, Berta was much more aware of the plants and flowers that grew in the area. The forest floor contained numerous palmetto palm bushes as well as ancient-looking ferns and mosses; interspersed among the gigantic oak trees were magnolias with enor-mous white blooms and pecan trees heavy with nuts and possessive squirrels.

The variety of creatures living in the forest—raccoons, possums, deer, all manner of birds and creeping things, and the occasional black bear—seemed endless. Berta marveled at how these animals and plants were perfectly content with their place in the world. She couldn't help but wonder what it was about humans that made them constantly question their place in God's divine plan, and in idle moments, she would speculate about her own future, wondering what God intended for her and whether she was prepared for it.

She would often walk on the bluff and observe the river below. Once bustling with traffic, the Trinity was now large-ly quiet and empty. The packet boats that had made frequent visits to Houston County and occasionally to their dock be-fore the war were now absent, victims of a war that also seemed so far away. Down river in Galveston, the port re-mained blockaded by a federal naval force. Although the city had been free of the occupying Union troops since January, business activities remained moribund due to the blockade.[44]

On this afternoon, as Berta passed the front veranda she saw the garden and, in particular, the rose bush that her friend, Betty Graves, had given her in May. She was pleased

[44] *Appendix II. Item 13. The Battle of Galveston*

to see that it had a number of blossoms and a promising array of buds, and she reminded herself to take a supply of the flowers back to the college, for both Betty and her father, Dr. Graves. He would likely remember her confusion when he asked her about the plant at their final meeting of the spring session. At the time, she had been confused and uncertain about the idea of love and how she felt about it. Perhaps human nature resembled the river—languid during the dry season, a raging torrent after heavy rains—and the apparent chaos that was such a disruption to her world. Could a person be both gentle and violent? Was it possible for John Wootters to be a sensitive and kind person, but also someone who was capable of glorifying suffering and death? The answer would not come to her. She wondered if it ever would.

As she crossed the veranda and entered the house, she felt a sense of security and comfort surround her. The entrance hall offered a shady refuge from the afternoon heat and languid atmosphere. Occasional breezes swept up from the river, circulating cooler air through the house and dispersing the warm air through small openings near the tops of the large windows. The entrance hall had rooms that branched off from either side, rooms that were used for dining or visiting, a library and a music room that accommodated her piano. During the summer months, the kitchen area was kept cool from the lack of cooking, as those activities were confined to a structure separate from the main house.

Hannah supervised most of the domestic activities, including the meals, which were signaled by a large bell whose ringing could be heard across the property. The bell announced meals not only for the family but also for the more than ninety slaves who worked in the nearby fields and lived on the plantation. Because the Union blockade had halted all transport of the cotton crop to markets, the slaves had redirected their efforts to clearing the forest for firewood, lumber and future farmland and to the production of corn and other crops and livestock, such as hogs and chickens. They lived about one mile inland from the river, on high ground near the church that had been provided by Major Smith.

Berta entered the music room and noted that someone had placed a rose stem in a vase on the piano. The rose bush was flourishing, producing delicate pink blossoms that added color and cheer to the house as well as the garden. Hannah always made sure that one stem was in a vase on the piano and another in the nearby parlor where Anna Jane spent much of her time. Berta played the piano several hours every day and had dutifully worked on the Beethoven sonatas and Chopin pieces over the summer. Since beginning her studies with Count von Godski, her skills had improved significantly. Major Smith and Anna Jane were very pleased with her evident talent.

In addition to taking afternoon walks and practicing piano, Berta spent much of her time reading. She was fond of novels from Europe, especially books by the Brontë sisters, and she loved to pore over the large family Bible. Over the past year or so, she had become interested in the history of the ancient Hebrews and their subsequent Jewish generations as well as the more familiar New Testament scriptures. The community of Daly's had established a small Baptist church, which was more convenient for regular worship than the church in Crockett. Her parents were pleased that she was enthusiastic and curious about her faith.

Lieutenant John Wootters was never far from Berta's mind, and she spent hours writing letters to him. She had not received anything from him recently, but a letter from early in the summer sent to his family in Crockett had described the dissatisfaction that his company felt at their assignment to the southern Virginia and North Carolina border area. They had been sent there to get food and other supplies that the Army of Northern Virginia needed.[45] While they had succeeded in acquiring substantial supplies of pork and corn, local farmers weren't always eager to give up their crops or livestock. The diet of the Confederates was so meager, Wootters observed, that if the Union troops didn't kill them, starvation probably would. In an attempt at levity, he observed that the plump Union troops were much better targets than the gaunt Confederates. He had written that the greatest disappointment for him and his company was missing out on the battle at Chancellorsville, one of the greatest achievements of General Robert E. Lee and his Army.[46]

By the end of the summer, there had been no further messages from Wootters; Confederate supporters were aware of the disastrous events at Gettysburg, Pennsylvania, and the loss at Vicksburg, Mississippi, which gave control of the Mississippi River to the Federal forces. Further support of the Confederate armies east of the river would not be available from the states west of it, and future communications would be even less dependable. The telegraph carried some information that could only add to the gloom that pervaded Texas.

Hood's Brigade had suffered severe losses at Gettysburg; the First Regiment reported twenty-four men killed and fifty-four wounded. The town of Crockett was shocked by the

[45] Breiner, T.L. "Pork Belly Politics".
[46] Catton, B. "Never Call Retreat" p.144–156.

deaths of the Jones brothers and William House, who had been with John Wootters at the flag ceremony two years previously.[47] Berta was relieved by the news that Wootters had not only survived but had been promoted to first lieutenant and continued as their company commander. She vowed to continue praying for his safe return to Texas as well as for the preservation of his mind and spirit.

As the summer drew to a close, the Smith family remained anxious about the possibility of a Union invasion. Texas had been largely spared the destruction of warfare, but rumor had it that the presence of Union forces was eminent. Despite these great uncertainties, Berta seemed lighter in spirit and demeanor than she had in some time. Hannah, whose insights were most always accurate, was sure that John Wootters' continued safety and survival accounted for the spring in Berta's step.

Anna Jane and Major Smith also noticed their daughter's unusual radiance. They would be celebrating her sixteenth birthday on Friday, September 4, which coincided with her return to Fairfield for the next college session. Anna Jane, with Hannah's help, had made sure Berta would be appropriately clothed in the frilly and blousy skirts that were the fashion among the daughters of planters' families. Fancy cloth was scarce, but Anna Jane had been able to reuse and redesign older dresses to accommodate her daughter's wardrobe.

Major Smith and Oscar had recently returned from a visit to Crockett with a supply of new ribbon and a message that was both amusing and concerning. He told the family of a

[47] *Mainer, TN, Houston County in the Civil War. P 23-4.*

conversation overheard at the Masonic Lodge having to do with a certain local family and a gift of sweaters. Although it had taken nearly six months, the ne'er-do-well Jencks, who had previously accosted young Berta about teaching Oscar to read, had observed that his own children were wearing sweaters that he couldn't remember buying. When his youngest, who hadn't yet learned of the expediency of lying, identified the red-haired lady and the old slave as the source of the clothing, even Jencks was able to solve the mystery.

Jencks had confronted Oscar during one of his trips to Crockett and asked him who had given Berta permission to provide his children with such gifts. The somewhat abashed Oscar answered him in a way that Smith's friends at the lodge thought so amusing that they insisted he get a first-hand description of the event from Oscar. So, during their return trip, Major Smith asked him about his run-in with Jencks.

"I was just loading the wagon with parts for the plow that broke, when up comes that white man and he seemed in a rage about something," Oscar said, frowning. "I didn't even see him coming when he started yelling at me. He said, 'Hey, nigga, who done tole dat red-headed girl she could give dem clothes to my chilluns?' I didn't know what to say, so I just looked at him, and the longer I looked the madder he got. I couldn't think how to answer, so I said that the Lord told her to do it."

Smith couldn't help but laugh at this description of the conversation. "What did he say when you suggested that divine inspiration was behind it?"

"I don't think he knew what I said because he got even madder and said, 'Who is DiLaud and where in hell is dis Dilaud fellow?'" Oscar said. "I was so confused that I said I didn't know where the Lord is but I know he ain't in hell.

That just made his face turn even more red, and he still didn't know what I was saying because he said that he wanted to know who this DiLaud fellow is and that he and Missy Berta better stop meddling in his family's business."

That was exactly the story Major Smith had heard at the Lodge. What's more, it hadn't taken long for most of Crockett to find out and to have a good laugh at Jencks' expense. And that worried Major Smith, as it was unwise to have such an unpredictable and angry person as an enemy.

"I think it's best for you to avoid any dealings with Jencks, and the next time we have a reason for you to be in Crockett you should send Edgar," Major Smith said. "I doubt that Jencks will connect Edgar to our plantation, and there's no need to make more trouble."

Later that evening as the Smith family was having a celebratory supper in honor of Berta's birthday and the beginning of a new year at the college, her father related in a stern tone what he had heard in Crockett and from Oscar that afternoon.

"People like Jencks can pose significant dangers to you, Oscar and anyone else he associates with our family," he said, looking directly at Berta. "Please avoid any interaction or association with that man or his family, as even the most innocent gesture will just fuel his hatred. You or anyone else in our family should not leave our property without an escort. Although the sheriff has said that if Jencks causes any more trouble he will lock him up and throw away the key, you must assume responsibility for your own safety."

Berta nodded and looked down at her plate. She was sad to have caused problems for her family and even sadder for the children who had to live with the foul-tempered Jencks, but she would soon be leaving for Fairfield. From that safe distance, it would be no problem to avoid any unpleasant encounters.

DECEMBER 1863
FAIRFIELD, TEXAS

THE AUTUMN OF 1863 was a time of resolution for the Confederacy and for Berta who was now in the advanced class of the Fairfield Female College. More than a quarter of the young women expecting to return for the fall session had been unable to do so because of the economic hardships faced by the planters of Texas and throughout the South. Students whose families lived in Louisiana and Mississippi, where the war had become a constant threat, were facing very troubled times.

The faculty and other workers at the College did their best to create an air of stability for the students, but all felt the impending doom that was enveloping the Confederate states. Since the fall of Vicksburg, with the relative isolation of the western areas and the failure at Gettysburg of General Lee's planned invasion of the northern states, only the most optimistic Southerner expected the secession movement to succeed.

Although less widely recognized than the battles at Gettysburg and Vicksburg, the Union army's triumphant Tullahoma Campaign in Tennessee would have profound effects on the outcome of the war. The widely hailed victory of Texans at the Battle of Sabine Pass in September 1863 helped to restore some morale and enthusiasm across the state. The overall outlook for the Confederacy, however, was grim, as the Texas troops could not reach the battlefields in the east due to effective Union blockades.

On her return to college in September, Berta found that her friend and confidante, Betty, had been warmly received back home by her family after her elopement in May. Her husband, William, had been assigned to Walker's Greyhounds, a division made up of twelve regiments from Texas commanded by Major General John George Walker, and had gone immediately to northern Louisiana to try to support the Confederate efforts at Vicksburg.

Betty had resumed her duties at the academy, teaching young students who came daily from their homes in Freestone County; she also continued to nurture the rose garden. Both Betty and Dr. Graves were pleased that Berta brought them souvenir flowers from the plant Betty had given her and that Berta had aptly named The Rose of Love. In all her sixteen years, Berta had never heard anything quite so romantic as the love story of Betty and William. She marveled that something like it could happen outside of the pages of her treasured European novels.

Still, Berta struggled to understand Betty's distinction between loving with one's mind and with one's heart. She had sought an appropriate opportunity to question her older and wiser friend, and on a particular autumn afternoon when the crisp air represented a distinct change in the seasons, she got her chance. One of the reasons for her interest in visiting with Betty was the confusing feeling she had for John Wootters and the fact that a bond seemed to be developing between them. How could she have such feeling about someone she had not seen in more than two years? They had both experienced so many changes since then that they might not even recognize each other.

———

Certainly Berta was pleased that her child-like shape had developed into a more womanly figure; she felt confident in her growing attractiveness and maturity. The changes in her thoughts and feelings were a surprise to her as she was becoming aware of a growing desire within herself to nurture and care for others.

Her optimistic spirit had been tempered by the deaths of little Ossie and her dear brother, Lucius. The potential brevity of life and the reality of the separation resulting from death were thoughts that troubled her. Nearly everyone she knew, including her own family, had suffered hardship and upheaval, as lives were disrupted and torn apart by the war between states. It was enough to change her views, not only of the world but of herself.

As Berta approached the rose garden on that autumn afternoon, Betty offered her a smile and a greeting, but the younger woman did not respond with her usual cheer.

"I'm so glad to see you, but I fear that the number of roses in your garden is diminishing as quickly as our hopes for an independent South," Berta said. "I am afraid we are entering a winter that will last much longer than a single season."

"I must say that my cheerful confidante has taken on a cloak of gloom," Betty note. "It doesn't seem natural or fitting for you, Berta. Has something happened?"

"Only the letter received not long ago from my friend John Wootters, who is serving in Tennessee. Or perhaps he is back in Virginia with Hood's Texas Brigade," Berta answered. "He describes events that are so terrible I don't know how the human spirit can bear them. I am sure that his messages temper the reality of the situation. He likely does not want to review in his own mind or for me the actual horrors he has seen."

"Indeed, I understand and share your anxiety about the future," Betty said. "I pray daily that my dear William will return. Whatever you say about the terrible circumstance of the battlefield is certainly true. One cannot have seen those horrors without it having some long-lasting effect on one's mind and spirit. We can only ask God to bring them back and over time make them whole again."

Berta nodded, thinking again about the suffering John Wootters must have witnessed throughout the war and never told her. Sometimes, it was too much to bear. Betty distracted her with a question about Wootters, as she knew the pair had been writing for quite some time. The sun shone brightly as they walked through the garden and only the occasional chill of a breeze reminded them that the cold of winter was around the corner.

So Berta told her how she had met Wootters' family on arriving in Houston County from North Carolina, how his brother, James, had come to Texas to work with their uncle at his merchandise store in Crockett, and how their families had become friends. She recalled how her family attended the Baptist church in Crockett, and it was there she often saw Wootters and became aware of his knowledge of her faith.

"Although he was a grown man, my mother felt sympathy for him because his parents had both died when he was very young and he was raised and educated by relatives on the eastern shore of Maryland," Berta said. "Occasionally I would play piano for our church services, and Mr. Wootters seemed to appreciate it and encouraged my efforts."

Berta joined Betty in cutting dead branches from the bushes. As they continued working, Betty noted how interesting it was that he would notice her friend's musical talent. But Berta, who seemed lost in thought, continued talking. He was one of the first men from Crockett to join the Confederate army in the summer of '61, she pointed out, and he was also chosen to receive the company flag at a ceremony. His words that day had been thoughtful and brave; it would be impossible for Berta to forget them. She admitted to writing him letters that, at first, reflected her own naiveté about the war, and she worried that he may have thought them childish and frivolous.

"After Lucius died, I became very upset when I realized that I had never told him how much I loved him and how proud I was of him. And then he was gone forever," Berta said, choking up a little. "I resolved then never to make that mistake again. That's when the nature of my letters to Mr. Wootters began to change."

She wanted him to know how proud she was and how she respected the commitment he'd made to fight for his country; she wanted him to know that she prayed daily for his safe return. And while he wrote back that he appreciated her sincerity and concern, Berta continued to send him words of encouragement, interspersed with pleas that he not take any foolish risks, as his life was in enough danger already.

"I'm sure your messages have been very reassuring and important to him," Betty said.

"I really am very proud of him," Berta said. "He has been steadily promoted up the ranks and is now first lieutenant and commander of his company.[48] There is no question about his bravery and leadership, but I am concerned about the effects that so much death and destruction must have on his mind and spirit."

After a pause where the only sounds were the buzzing of insects in the garden, Betty smiled and took her friend's hands.

"My dear Berta," she said in a near whisper. "Have you ever considered that you may be in love with Lieutenant Wootters and that what you call friendship may have progressed to something more substantial?"

Berta looked at her friend with skeptical eyes. Of course that wasn't possible. How could she be in love with someone she hadn't seen in two years and then when she wasn't much more than a child? He could have changed so much that she might not even want to continue the friendship. Berta shook her head. No, that wasn't the answer. She was certain.

"I appreciate your opinion, Betty, since you are the person with whom I would be comfortable having a conversation about love," she said. "You had mentioned last spring before your

---

[48] *Appendix I. Item 6. Roster, Co. I, 1 Regiment Texas Volunteers, Texas Brigade, Field's Division, Longstreet's Corp, Army of Northern Virginia, July 15, 1863.*

marriage that you and William were very much in love. Ever since then, I have struggled to understand what you meant."

Betty's gaze drifted to the mounting clouds in the eastern sky and how they reflected the light of the setting sun. She paused briefly to catch her breath and blink away a small tear before continuing.

"William and I knew that we were in love, and we have publicly declared and vowed to honor that love forever," Betty said. "To describe how we knew it was love isn't easy to do. I will do my best to share some of my feelings and ideas. You can form your own conclusions."

Berta could not immediately respond to her friend's reaction, but she was reassured when Betty took her arm and walked with her to a nearby garden bench. In this shady spot, she continued. She spoke of the Biblical meanings of love, the love of God, sacrificial love and the unconditional love that Christ had for his followers and for all people. But an easier way, she noted, to describe love as a bond between a man and woman was the ability to love with mind and heart. Loving with the mind implied rational thought, while loving with the heart was a more emotional experience.

"I think that an enduring love has to involve an agreement between one's mind and one's heart," Betty said. "Without that agreement, it's difficult to imagine a substantial foundation for one's life."

Berta listened with rapt attention as understanding dawned on her. Her feelings for John Wootters, which were coming straight from the heart, had not been tempered by much thought. She realized that now, and she decided to pray for guidance.

"I will nevertheless continue to write him letters of encouragement," Berta announced. "Now, wise friend, we need to store these garden tools and put these few rose stems in some water as we will be expected at supper very soon."

Fairfield provided a secure home for Berta, where she could improve musical skills and general education. Count von Godski had departed the college for adventures in California, but Berta's playing continued to develop. She was now frequently the pianist at the Baptist church in Fairfield, where her own faith was nurtured. Her greatest pleasure at the college, however, came from the friendships she had with the other students. As there were no significant opportunities for social interactions outside the college, the young women amused themselves when not occupied by their studies. In the afternoon they would play games on the college grounds or stroll among the gardens and wooded areas of the property.

Dinner time remained a formal affair for the students. They were expected to arrive promptly at the designated time, dressed in their elegant dresses and white gloves. The workers at the college included seven slaves that Dr. Graves had assigned to help the young women with the housekeeping chores and their clothing, which was always kept cleaned and ironed and in appropriate condition. During the evening hours, the girls would occasionally amuse themselves by holding balls, during which they danced to their own music. Not having male dancing partners, some of the taller girls would dress the part and dramatize the roles of gallant escorts, even fashioning mustaches after the style of Count von Godski who, even in his absence, was a source of amusement.[49]

[49] *Burks, C. "Fairfield Female College."*

The evening entertainment would be interrupted by the bedtime ringing of the bell, after which one of the teachers would make rounds to assure that all were in bed. Occassional late-night visits would be cut short by the teacher on duty. For Berta, the coming of the Christmas season marked the end of the fall session at the college and the return to the Smith Landing Plantation, where she hoped a new letter from Lieutenant Wootters would be waiting for her.

1864
FAIRFIELD, TEXAS

T HE UNION VICTORY at Vicksburg in July 1863 had isolated the western Confederate states from the battlefields in Tennessee, Georgia and Virginia. The blockade of the Mississippi River and the Gulf of Mexico by the Union Navy helped to prevent any movement of troops from west to east. In Texas, the year had begun with the Confederate re-capture of Galveston and ended with the dramatic defeat of the Union invasion at Sabine Pass, but frustration was running high due to the state's inability to get past Union blockades and contribute to the Southland's effort.[50]

[50] *Appendix II. Item 17. The Battle of Sabine Pass.*

While messages from John Wootters continued to be sporadic, Berta learned of his promotion to captain of his company in March 1864.[51] He reported that the boredom of the brigade's long winter camp near Knoxville, Tennessee, and the uncertainty of future assignments had ended when the Texas Brigade, now under the command of Brigadier General John Gregg, received orders to return to Virginia at the end of March. General Lee was preparing for whatever the new commanding General of the Union Army, Ulysses S. Grant, might order.[52] The Texas Division and all of General Longstreet's Corps would rejoin the Army of Northern Virginia in an attempt to thwart General Grant's strategy to capture Richmond.

In early 1864, a large Union force was threatening the city of Shreveport, Louisiana; their success would open a direct route for an invasion of Texas. Following the defeat at Vicksburg the previous summer, the Walker Greyhounds and other Texas units had spent months marching in Arkansas and Louisiana without encountering significant combat. The mud, mosquitoes and hardships of the swamps and marshes had claimed the lives of many of the troops.[53] Morale was at a low point until February 1864 when they were placed under the command of Brigadier General T.N. Waul and assigned to the command of Major General Richard Taylor.[54] Their mission was to counter the invasion of the Federal army, which was now advancing up the Red River toward Shreveport.

---

[51] *Appendix I. Item 6. Roster of Commissioned Officers, Provisional Army Confederate States, Promoted Mar. 13, 1864.*

[52] *Appendix II. Item 22. Union Army Generals*

[53] *Appendix II. Item 18. Walker's Texas Division, the Red River Campaign and the Battle of Mansfield*

[54] *General Richard Taylor was the son of former U.S. President Zachary Taylor.*

The staff of the Fairfield Female College tried to remain cheerfully optimistic, and the young ladies in the now smaller college class continued their routine of studies. More than half of the students expected for the spring session had been unable to return.

Berta had assumed new duties, assisting her closest friend and confidant Betty Graves in teaching of the younger students at the academy. She followed her usual study program, which included piano exercises, and often provided music for the Fairfield Baptist Church. One morning in mid-May, Berta arrived in the classroom to help Betty and found she wasn't there. She instructed the students to continue reading their lessons from the previous session.

Half an hour passed and still there was no sign of her friend. Berta grew increasingly concerned; it wasn't like Betty to miss a class. Moments later, a faculty member appeared in the doorway, her face ashen. Berta felt a terrible knot of anxiety form in her stomach.

"Miss Smith, would you please come into the hallway for a moment?"

Once out of earshot of the students, the teacher spoke in a hushed voice.

"The most terrible circumstance has come upon us, and you must know that Miss Graves will not be attending your sessions this morning."

"Oh dear Lord, what has happened to Betty?" Berta felt tightness in her chest and throat.

"I don't know for certain, but there was a commotion at the front entrance just as everyone had left the dining room. A messenger from the Fairfield post office apparently delivered a letter to her, and I'm told that she collapsed and was being assisted to her bedroom by her parents."

Berta's mind flashed to the memory of the postmaster and minister arriving at Smith Landing. She knew immediately the contents of the letter—that dreaded message of regret from the Army. Covering her mouth with her hand, she could only utter, "Her dear William."

Later that day she learned what the message said. William had received a mortal wound in his service with the Waul's Brigade of the Texas Division in the battle at Mansfield, Louisiana. He had been taken to the nearby Keatchi Women's College, which had been converted to a hospital for the wounded Confederates. Despite their efforts, he died in the company of his fellow soldiers and was buried with full military honors with one hundred other members of Walker's Texas Division in a cemetery at the college.

Berta was initially overwhelmed, not only by her own grief and remembering the loss of her brother Lucius but also by her awareness of how much her dear friend Betty must be suffering. Betty had apparently collapsed before being assisted to her living quarters, where she remained sobbing uncontrollably.

Dr. Graves did his best to reassure Berta and her classmates that Betty was being attended by her mother and there was nothing else for them to do except to keep her in their prayers. Berta prayed that William would be received into the heavenly home promised to those who loved the Lord, and she prayed that Betty would somehow be able to find the peace that could heal her mind and her heart.

The next day, with the permission of Dr. and Mrs. Graves, Berta knocked on the door of Betty's room.

"Betty, my dear friend, it is Berta," she said. "With your permission, I would like to come in." After a few minutes with no response, Berta again spoke, this time more loudly. "Betty, if my presence does not add to your burden, it would help relieve my grieving heart to see you and hear your voice."

Berta heard movement from behind the door, and in another moment it opened slowly to reveal Betty, her eyes red and swollen.

"I am in no condition to be presented to any polite company," she said. "But if seeing me will relieve your mind, please come in."

On entering the bedroom, Berta offered her friend a rose from the special bush that, to her, represented William and Betty's love. The young women clung to each other. It was clear that Betty, whose hair and clothing were always arranged with the utmost care, had not changed her clothes since receiving the dreadful message.

"I have been so anxious about you as have all of your friends," Berta said. "Just to see you standing upright is a blessing to my saddened soul. Although your heart may be broken, the pain is shared by many who have been lifting you up in our prayers."

Betty, tear-streaked and disheveled, sat down on a divan, the rose resting on her lap. She gazed at the flower, twisting the simple gold band on the fourth finger of her left hand; the shadows under her eyes accentuated the pallor in her cheeks.

"I just don't know how I can go on," she said, her eyes filling again with tears. "The past day has been more than my mind can bear. I can't see any prospect for happiness."

"Few people can understand the grief that you feel," Berta said. "Many of us are sharing a small part of your pain, and we are praying for you to receive the peace that our Lord can provide."

"Indeed, Berta, you know that our Lord assures us that we will never be given a burden that we are unable to bear,"

Betty said in a quiet voice. "He promises that we will have the strength to overcome any grief we experience. Time will eventually heal my wounds. I know that William's pain is over and that he will have eternal peace. Someday I will join him in God's presence."

Betty's gaze wandered to the soft clouds drifting past her window, and Berta noted with some relief that her breathing was slowing down. She knew that her friend would never completely recover from this, that she would likely carry the scar on her spirit forever. But she hoped that Betty would recover enough to live a rich, fulfilling life.

"Please know your friends are outside praying for your mind and heart to heal," Berta said. "When you are able to join us, the grief will be much lifted from our hearts and from those of your family. We are here to love and support you in this desperate time."

Berta got up to excuse herself and saw that Betty was holding the rose close to her heart, a sad smile on her face.

"We all love you," Berta said.

The following day, college activities continued as usual, but a sense of gloom pervaded everything, from classroom sessions and study periods to recreational time. In place of the usual games and laughter, small groups of friends quietly discussed the disaster of war and the irreplaceable loss of loved ones. Many of the girls could identify with Betty as they had lost family members or friends in the war; some had lost their homes. Also absent was the irrepressible optimism about the future that girls their age typically embraced.

The evening meal was heralded by the usual ringing of the college bell. On this occasion every student was prompt in attendance as Dr. Graves blessed the food. Before the dishes had been placed on the table, the door at the back of the room opened and there stood a well-groomed Betty. Applause broke out across the room, as every girl stood up and clapped. Dr. Graves came forward to embrace his daughter and help her to her usual seat at the head table. As everyone sat back down, Betty rose from her chair and silence fell on the entire gathering. Even the servers stopped what they were doing as Betty spoke.

"My dear friends and family, I want you to know of my regret for any grief or anxiety that I have caused during the past days, and I want to express my heartfelt thanks for your prayers and friendship during this terrible time," she said. "Although I know William will not be returning to me, I have asked God to help me understand my feelings, and I am certain that he has sent me the love and affection of my friends and family to help calm my troubled mind. It gives me strength me to know that we will all lift each other up as we go forward to face an uncertain future. Again, I thank you for your friendship and for this Fairfield Academy and College, which reassures me that we will continue to have a place to serve and learn in this world."

As she took her seat, the meal was served and conversation resumed, albeit at a more subdued level. It was clear to everyone present that although life would go on, it would never be the same for Betty, for this group of young women or for the Southland.

The spring session at Fairfield College concluded in late May, and the girls prepared to return to home for the summer. Back at Smith Landing Plantation, Berta wondered what the future held for her and her family. Then, in mid-July a telegraph message arrived in Crockett informing them that Captain John Wootters had been wounded at Bermuda Hundred, Virginia en route to Petersburg and that he had been taken to Richmond for medical care.[55] His friends and family in Houston County did not know the extent of his injury, nor did they know how he was currently faring.

Not surprisingly, the news of Captain Wootters' injury and hospitalization caused Berta no end of distress. She was concerned that he might lose an arm or leg, as she was aware that amputation was often the expedient solution to badly injured limbs. Equally troubling was the fact that many soldiers and veterans who suffered those kinds of injuries often took to drinking to dull the constant pain. But what bothered her most was the relief she felt at hearing that John Wootters had been wounded. To her, the news wasn't necessarily bad; rather, it meant that he would no longer be able to serve in active combat. He was almost certain to survive the war, and would be returning to Houston County perhaps sooner than expected. It was, in some ways, the best news Berta could have wished for.

The news about her mother's health, however, wasn't quite as positive. Anna Jane had suffered a prolonged illness earlier in the summer and been so weakened by it that there had been some concern she wouldn't survive. But she had gradually regained her strength and was now able to join her family on the veranda for longer periods.

On one particular evening, they were sitting on the veranda overlooking the approach to the front of the house and the Trinity River. It was late in the season, and the flow

[55] *Appendix I. Item 6. Report of the 1st Regiment Texas Infantry. JH Wootters, June 17, 1864, Wounded right arm, severe. Register of General Hospital No. 9. Richmond, Virginia. Admitted June 17, To Howard Grove, June 19, 1864.*

of the current was slower than usual; the spring rains were a distant memory. It seemed unlikely that the packet boats from Galveston could manage the shallow water. Indeed, it had been so long since anyone in Houston County had seen them that the subject never came up. Back on the veranda, Berta asked her father about issues that were on her mind.

"It's nearly time for me to return to Fairfield College, and I want to thank you and Mother for sending me there," she said. "I miss my dear classmates and teachers and hope that the college will continue despite this terrible war."

"We would do anything to see that you continue," her father smiled and nodded. "The reports we have received from Dr. Graves indicate that you have benefited greatly from these experiences."

Her mother nodded in agreement. "You seem to have talents not only in your music but also in your academic studies," she said. "Dr. Graves says those talents should be nurtured beyond what he can offer at Fairfield. But the future is so uncertain we can only take one year at a time."

Major Smith frowned, his mouth a grim line. He and Anna Jane weren't optimistic about the future; in his heart, he knew it was only a matter of time before the Confederate troops were defeated and the Federal government declared all slaves to be free citizens. When that happened, he feared chaos would follow, which would benefit neither landowners nor slaves. Many of their slaves and their families before them had served the Smiths and the Pounceys for generations, and both Anna Jane and Major Smith felt obligated to help these dependents survive and succeed, whatever the future might hold. Smith Landing Plantation could not survive without the workers that tended the crops and livestock nor without those slaves, like Hannah, who tended to the family's personal needs. To that end, Major Smith would arrange for them to own land in their own right, as surely the laws in Texas would change to allow freed slaves to own property.

"I have discussed these matters with my friends in Crockett who have legal and judicial experience, and we will be preparing documents with provisions regarding the transfer of some property to each of the families who want to remain in this area," Major Smith said. "Those who are able will continue to plant and will share in the value we receive for our crops. And over time, they can pay for their land."

It seemed a logical approach to the situation. Things were uncertain and changing from day to day. It could be dangerous for their slaves to have no place to call their own, Major Smith noted, as a defeated Southland could also be a very hostile one, particularly in regards to freed slaves. Those who chose to leave could be subject to laws they did not understand. He already planned to meet with Oscar and Edgar to lay out his plan and discuss their reaction to potential changes that lay head. A number of slaves had disappeared from plantations near Crockett, and the militia had been on alert for the possibility of any major disturbances.

"Hannah and her family are very loyal to you and Mother, and many of them already consider the church and the cemetery that you provided for them to be their own domain," Berta said. "I am sure that once free, some will want to remain here, where they have the security of a home of their own."

Berta also had an idea brewing. Although her run-in with the cranky Jencks several years earlier had stayed with her, it had also inspired her to teach the slaves to read and write, if for no other reason than to prove that they could.

"Although I am certainly not as mad at him as I once was, I still don't like him at all," she told her parents. "But I must confess that it would give me pleasure to see his expression if Oscar was to read him one of Shakespeare's soliloquies from Hamlet."

"Now Berta, I am sure that some level of forgiveness may be available to you for harboring such thoughts, but the penitence would likely be long and arduous!" Major Smith said, attempting to smile. "I am confident that Oscar would have enough sense not to do such a thing, even if he were able to recite the part from memory. And I would urge you to temper your zeal for spreading knowledge, at least until we have a better idea about the future."

A few weeks later Berta returned to her beloved college for the fall session and immersed herself in her studies and the duties that marked her year as a member of the senior class. She had been at the school for only a few weeks before she was notified that Edgar, Hannah and Oscar's son, had arrived with a message for her.

Such visits made her anxious, as they were usually precipitated by bad news. On arriving, Edgar told her that Hannah and her parents had sent him with a copy of a letter sent to Captain John Wootters' family in Crockett. Edgar didn't know exactly what was in the letter, but that his mother told him that Miss Berta would want to know of it without delay. He had ridden his horse to the limit of its capacity to comply with her request.

Relief flooded Berta, as she had imagined the worst: that the emergency involved one of her parents. Opening the letter, she nearly fainted on reading the first lines. It was a copy of a terse telegraph message received in Marshall and carried to Crockett by a messenger as the wires between the towns were temporarily disrupted. It read: "Capt. John H. Wootters is on leave from the 1st Reg't. Tex and reassigned to the Trans-Mississippi Dept. for the purpose of recruiting duty in Texas. Will report directly to Gen. Edmund Kirby Smith on his arrival in the state. By Order of the Secy War, James A. Seddon."[56]

John Wootters, it seemed, was at long last coming home.

[56] Appendix I. Item 6. Inspection Report P, No. 51; enclosure 13.—Inspection Report of the Texas Brigade, Field's Division, 1st Army Corps, commanded by Col. F.S. Bass. Absent commissioned officers accounted for: By what authority—J.H. Wootters, Capt 1 Regt. Tex—Report dated: Exterior Line Richmond Defenses Chas City Road Jan 17, 1865—Recruiting in Texas—Secy War, August 1864.

XVI

WINTER 1864
SMITH LANDING PLANTATION

O N SEPTEMBER 2, 1864, the Confederacy's faint hopes of maintaining its independence vanished with the fall of Atlanta to the Union Army. That victory also virtually guaranteed President Lincoln's re-election, and two months later, the Radical Republicans gained a veto-proof majority in the U.S. House and Senate.[57] The Confederate forces had not been able to slow the progress of Union troops in either Tennessee or Georgia, and as the ranks of Union soldiers grew in number, the ultimate outcome appeared inevitable.[58]

---

[57] *Appendix II. Item 19. The U.S. Presidential Election of 1864 (from the Library of Congress)*
[58] *Catton, B. Never Call Retreat. pp. 383–395.*

As the Federal policy was to use emancipation as a military and political strategy, it was clear that social disruption across the South would proceed as rapidly as the invading Union forces. Major Smith had considered these matters, along with their inevitable outcome, and made plans to transfer ownership of some property to his slave families. Many of the slaves at the Smith Landing Plantation welcomed this solution. The Cedar Branch community had become an entity centered on its church; the stability of the plantation and security of its residents and their homes seemed assured.

With Hannah's devoted attention, Anna Jane managed to keep up her strength and stamina despite the cold winter weather. At the Fairfield Female College, Berta was nearing the close of the fall session, and everyone involved seemed pleased with her developing skills as a teacher of the academy's younger students. It was apparent to the faculty that Berta had considerable talent working with the children. Her piano studies continued to progress but at a slower rate, as her schedule did not allow her as much time to practice.

Among the things she most treasured were the friendships she had formed with her classmates. Only seven girls remained in her senior class, and although they had very different personalities, their unique camaraderie and sharing a love of the College gave them great comfort. With activities and friendships to fill her time, Berta was less anxious about the lack of communication from Captain Wootters, particularly since he was no longer on the battlefield. Moreover, she knew the journey from Richmond, Virginia to his new assignment in Texas would be arduous, so she did not expect to have any news from him for some time. She nevertheless continued to pray for his safety.

Back in Houston County, Major Smith was satisfied that life could move forward, for his family and his property despite the hopeless outlook for the Confederacy, and he remained fully engaged in the daily operations of the plantation. Although the economy of Texas and the entire Confederacy was in a disastrous condition, the plantation was nearly self-sufficient and able to provide for the needs of those who lived and worked on it. The Confederate currency was useless, merchandise goods were essentially unavailable for purchase at any price, and cotton production had come to a complete standstill as there was no market for the product. Warehouses throughout Texas and northern Louisiana were filled to overflowing with bales of cotton.

Across East Texas, information and news was slow to arrive. The telegraph was the only dependable source of communication, and even that was only occasionally so. There had been no further word concerning Captain John Wootters since August, when his family and friends were informed of his re-assignment to recruiting duty in Texas. The extent and effects of his injury were unknown.

At Smith Landing Plantation, Edgar had taken on more of the supervisory duties as his father, Oscar, showed signs of slowing down with age. Major Smith was pleased with Edgar's leadership and his ability to encourage productivity among the workers without treating them harshly, as was the case at neighboring plantations. Major Smith had always considered his slaves an asset of his property and believed that a valuable asset should be treated well.

Dusk arrived early on those December evenings, and the campfires in the slave community would glow brightly. On one particular night, Smith was standing in the roadway discussing the next day's plans with Edgar when a rider appeared at the distant end of the drive. Smith assumed that someone had lost his way while looking for the branch in the road that led to the Trinity River crossing. But as the figure slowly emerged from the shadows, they could see that he wore the military uniform of the Confederacy. It was then that Smith recognized the soldier.

"My God in Heaven, if it isn't Captain Wootters!"

Even as he spoke the words, Smith felt a twinge of uncertainty. The soldier's face was both familiar and unknown to him, and yet it must be Captain Wootters. What other Confederate captain would appear at his home on a chilly December night? The soldier's right hand and wrist were tucked inside his jacket, and he was holding the horse's reins with his left hand; he was lean to the point of appearing gaunt, and his face was covered by a well-trimmed beard, which contrasted sharply with his pallor.

"Truly, Major Smith," the mounted figure replied. "It is Captain Wootters, or what is left of him."

"Please come into my home as no one could be more welcome than yourself," Major Smith said. "I cannot tell you how pleased I am that you are back in Texas. Come inside and Edgar will take care of your horse." The slave took the reins from Captain Wootters as Major Smith gestured to him to come inside.

"Edgar, tell Hannah that we have a special guest for dinner," he said. "Anna Jane will be delighted that you are here this evening."

Wootters slowly dismounted and extended his left hand to Smith who clasped it in his two outstretched hands.

"Excuse my left hand, Major Smith, but the grip in my right hand is not sufficient to express the warmth of my greeting," Wootters said.

"That doesn't matter," Smith said. "What matters is that you are here. Please come inside our home where you can warm your arm and your spirits."

The two men entered the hallway from the veranda, but before they could advance beyond the front door, Hannah burst in from the rear entrance. She made straight for Captain Wootters, weeping openly, and encircled his gaunt body with her abundant arms.

"Oh, Dear Lord, thank you for answering our prayers!" she cried. "My goodness, Captain, you look like you could use a good meal and you have come to the right place for that. You can't know how hard we've been praying for your safe return."

"Hannah, it's been so long since I have been in Texas that I wouldn't recognize you if our friend Berta didn't tell me about you in her letters," Wootters said, at last smiling. "It is good to be back home, and I would much appreciate a warm supper."

They entered the parlor where Anna Jane usually sat in front of the fireplace and found her standing, a broad smile lighting up her face.

"Oh, Captain Wootters, it is so good to see you," she exclaimed. "I hope you are visiting long enough to tell us all about yourself and how your injury is progressing. Please come in and make yourself comfortable. I know Hannah will be setting a place for you at the table."

"Indeed, Mrs. Smith, a warm room and a good meal are just what my mind, body and soul have been longing for," Wootters replied. "I can't think of a more delightful place to enjoy them than in your gracious home."

Major Smith offered the young man a comfortable chair and asked Oscar, who was in eager attendance, to bring them a spot of bourbon, the special reserve that he kept in the library for honored guests. Turning back to Captain Wootters, he asked him to recount what had occurred over the past months and what he was planning to do now that his new assignment had sent him back to Texas.

In the brighter light of the parlor, the Smiths could more clearly see their visitor, and the changes in his appearance were stark. Other than his much leaner figure and right arm, which was supported by a sling, his face showed lines of worry and the sparkle in his normally bright eyes had dimmed. There was no evidence of the smiling face they had first encountered at the mercantile store three and a half years earlier. And when standing, he stood erect, as if expecting to review the troops and give them the orders of the day. John Wootters was indeed a changed man.

Oscar offered the visitor a portion of the special whiskey, and Wootters sipped it gratefully, staring at the fire before turning back to the Smiths.

"So much has changed in my life in the past half year that I can barely recognize myself or my homeland," he said. "There may not be enough pages in an entire library to describe all that has occurred, but of greatest interest to me is to know how the Smith family is faring and how Berta is getting along at Fairfield College."

Anna Jane nodded and went on to tell him that her daughter was well and making a good record at the school. The college was certainly the bright spot in her life, she noted, as it seemed to lessen the melancholy Berta felt when at home, which her mother was sure had to do with continuing sadness over the loss of Lucius and anxiety about Captain

Wootter's own welfare. Berta had grown into a very capable young lady.

"Her skills at the piano are improving nicely, and she often mentions the need to practice so she can play pieces for you," Anna Jane said. "She remembers your interest in her music and your encouragement."

As Wootters listened to the news about Berta, he thought that nothing would please him more than to hear her play again. He hoped the opportunity would present itself soon. Unfortunately, it would have to wait a little longer. His orders were to first report to General Edmund Kirby Smith in Marshall, which he had already done, and then proceed to Galveston to meet with Col. Ashbel Smith. After visiting briefly with his family in Crockett, Wootters would make his way to the port city.

He expressed concern to Major Smith about the state of the Confederate Army in Texas and General Kirby Smith's ability to inspire loyalty and make good, strategic decisions. General Smith had a long and distinguished military career, and had served the Confederacy well in the early years of the war at First Manassas and in Tennessee. As commander of the Trans-Mississippi Department, he had been instrumental in stopping the Union Army's Red River Campaign.[59] Since then, however, he had made unpopular—and unwise—decisions that had led to unrest among the Texas troops.

"The number of desertions from our Texas regiments is increasing daily, and those who stay are often disregarding the orders of their superior officers," Wootters told Major Smith. "There have been reports of soldiers stealing equipment and supplies from the storehouses to sell or barter for their own benefit, which demeans the sacrifices that have

[59] *Shehan–Dean, A. Struggle for a Vast Future: The American Civil War.*

been honorably made by so many. General Hood would never tolerate such behavior."

Smith could see the tension building in Wootters' face as his eyes narrowed and the lines across his forehead deepened. Hoping to diffuse the mounting tension, Anna Jane beckoned the men into the dining room in her most cheerful voice. Once they were seated at the table, the conversation turned to Wootters' physical well-being and the responsibilities of his new assignment in Galveston. He had been wounded on June 17, a day etched forever in his memory. The Crockett Southrons, along with what was left of the First Texas, were moving towards the city of Petersburg, after spending several days awaiting orders at the town of Bermuda Hundred, near where the James and Appomattox Rivers join in Virginia.

Biding one's time was a frequent activity for soldiers, he told them, and after the terrible battle of Cold Harbor, there was some uncertainty as to what Ulysses S. Grant and his army would do next.[60] When it became apparent that his objective was to capture Petersburg, General Fields' Texas Division was directed to go there and join the troops of General PGT Beauregard's command.

On that fateful day the sunlight was beginning to fade, as the Crockett Southrons were in camp for the night, when a Union sniper ended Wootters' service to that company.[61] His arm was flung into the air with an uncontrollable force that brought him to the ground and, in that instant, Wootters knew that he'd been hit. A searing pain coursed through his arm; soldiers around him fell to the ground, expecting further gunfire, but none came.

[60] *Appendix II. Item 20. The 1864 Overland Campaign–The Wilderness to Cold Harbor.*
[61] *Appendix I. Item 6. Report 1st (First) Texas: J.H. Wootters (sic) Capt., Co. I, 1Regiment Texas Infantry, Appears on a Report of casualties in the 1st Regiment Texas Infantry for A.D. 1864. June 17, 1864 Wounded right wrist–severe.*

"I felt a terrible pain in my arm and then nothing," Wootters told them. "It was just numb, and I couldn't move my hand. Unfortunately, those problems have largely persisted."

Lieutenant Aldrich, another soldier from Crockett, helped secure Wootters' damaged arm and took him to a more protected location. The next few hours were a blurred memory, but soon he found himself on horseback and heading toward Richmond about ten miles away.

Anna and John's attention was so focused on Wootters that they didn't realize Hannah had come into the room carrying a tray of additional servings. She placed the tray on the table and stood quietly as he continued talking.

"We were directed to the Receiving and Wayside Hospital, and by daybreak it seemed this would be my new abode,"[62] he said. "As the sun rose over Richmond that morning, I knew I had likely spent my last day with the comrades with whom I had shared breakfast every morning for three years."

The receiving hospital, he later learned, had been a municipal tobacco warehouse; in wartime, however, it was receiving up to three thousand patients every month.[63] Anna Jane shook her head, unable to imagine so many wounded young men lying in makeshift beds so far from home. From there, as he could not rejoin his unit, Wootters was transferred to Howard's Grove Hospital.[64] Once a picnic and recreation area, Howard's Grove had been converted to a hospital with more than sixty buildings and accommodations for up to eighteen hundred patients. It was nearly a city unto itself,

---

[62] *Appendix I. Item 6. Arch., Chap. 6, File No. 108, page 719. JH Wooters (sic) Appears on a Register of Receiving and Wayside Hospital, or General Hospital No. 9, Richmond, Virginia, Admitted June 17, 1864, Disposition Howard Grove, June 19, 1864.*

[63] *Information about General Hospital #9 in Richmond, VA during the Civil War. From Civil War Richmond.*

[64] *Information about Howard's Grove Hospital in Richmond VA during the Civil War. From Civil War Richmond*

with its own water supply, laundry, bakery, storehouses and other facilities.

Wootters continued his tale, as Major Smith and Anna Jane sat in grim silence, the remains of their dinner growing cold. Over the next few weeks, Wootters received attentive and excellent medical advice from the surgeon-in-charge, Dr. T.M. Palmer. He reported to Dr. William A. Carrington, medical director of Virginia Hospitals, who earlier in the war had served as the surgeon of the Seventh Virginia Regiment.[65] Even though the physicians and surgeons in attendance were highly skilled, they were limited in number; nor were there enough attendants to care for the patients.

The Richmond newspapers often published pleas for ladies to visit or to lend their servants to assist in the care of the men.[66] One of the services these ladies rendered was to assist the wounded in writing letters. Because of the injury to his right arm, Wootters could not hold a pen; however, a Richmond matron helped him write a letter to the family of E.M. Oliver, one of the privates who fought with him in Company I and had died in battle.

The painful duty of informing the Oliver family of their loved one's death was the last official function Wootters provided for Company I and the First Texas Infantry. Of the original 110 men who marched away from Crockett on that warm day in July three years ago, only nine remained alive and uninjured.[67] "The sadness and the knowledge of that fact will stay with me forever," Wootters said.

On the afternoon of his arrival at Howard's Grove Hospital, Dr. Palmer examined Wootters' wound; his arm and hand still had no sense of feeling. Following the examination,

---

[65] *T.M. Palmer CSR, M331, National Archives, Civil War Richmond.*
[66] *Richmond Examiner, 5/17/1864, Civil War Richmond.*
[67] *Mainer, T.N., Houston County in the Civil War, p. 31.*

Palmer told the young soldier that the future mobility of his arm remained in doubt, as the ulnar bone, while intact, was chipped and the radius had been crushed; the latter would likely not heal.

It was miraculous, in fact, that the shot had not severed any major arteries and that his nerves did not appear to be affected. This last was a point of optimism, as Palmer would not have to amputate the arm. He did, however, need to perform surgery to remove bone fragments and damaged tissue. Only time would tell how much function Wootters would eventually regain in his arm and hand, but surgery would certainly help things along.

———

At this point in Wootters' narrative, the Smiths had lost all interest in the meal. Their full attention was directed to their guest. Major Smith placed an additional log on the fire and motioned for Hannah to sit on a side chair so that she could continue listening.

"I told Dr. Palmer that the past six weeks had shown me that the outlook for our Confederacy was bleak," Wootters said. He stood and briefly paced around the dining room, rubbing his weakened right arm. "The battle at Cold Harbor resulted in a slaughter of their troops that would be appalling to anyone, regardless of what we have experienced in past years.[68] Any commander who regards the lives of his troops so cheaply as seen in these actions of the Union Army poses problems that the Southland will not be able to overcome."

When Wootters took his seat at the table, there was no trace of a smile on his handsome face. "Dr. Palmer later indicated that I was probably not familiar with the order of

[68] *Appendix II. Item 20. The Overland Campaign: From The Wilderness to Cold Harbor.*

President Lincoln for the conscription of 500,000 men by the Ides of March. Of course I knew nothing about such information," he said, looking directly at Major Smith.[69] "We agreed that it was best not to share that news with the men in the field as it could be very discouraging to our effort."

Major Smith understood and nodded in agreement. He expressed his family's thanks that Wootters had seen some progress in his health and urged the younger man to eat his fill, as he had lost much weight in the past three years. It would also not do to disappoint Hannah, who liked nothing better than to see young men enjoying her cooking. "When we received a copy of the wire indicating that you were returning to Texas for recruiting purposes, we couldn't help but wonder where you could possibly find enough men to form a single regiment," Major Smith said to Wootters. "The eastern states must be equally or even more depleted of men than Texas."

His assumption was correct. As Wootters went on to tell them, his arm had improved noticeably by early August, but had not progressed beyond that. While he was determined to rejoin his company, Dr. Palmer advised him against it and within twenty-four hours, Wootters had received a summons to report to the General Headquarters of the Army of Northern Virginia. It seemed that Dr. Palmer had practiced medicine in Richmond for years before the war and was highly regarded among that city's elite. Wootters suspected the good doctor was behind his new orders.

Fortunately, the hospital staff were able to procure a proper uniform for him; he was, in fact, still wearing it. He was to meet with a senior general, and he was, under no circumstances, to complain or question anything that was said or

---

[69] *"The Draft for Half A Million of Men", New York Times, February 1, 1864, The New York Times Complete Civil War. p. 300.*

prolong the conversation in any way. This last order brought a smile to Major Smith's face. Hannah, who had been serving berry cobbler, stopped abruptly to listen.

"I was ushered into a room at the headquarters, where a number of staff officers were meeting, and was stunned to see General Lee sitting at the table," Wootters continued. "I saluted him, which required that I use my left hand to prop up my right wrist, and General Lee introduced me to the group as a member of Hood's Texas Brigade who tried to give him orders."

General Lee continued by saying that Wootters' unit had ordered him to take a position at the back of the brigade when he was attempting to lead us in an attack on the Union line at the Wilderness.

"What did you say when the General took you to task in front of the other officers?" Anna Jane asked. "What did you do?"

"I was stunned and could only remain at attention, feeling my pulse beating at a mighty pace," Wootters said. "I did manage to say that it was the best order I had ever given, and I had no regrets about it."

It was then that General Lee admitted the intelligence of the Texan's plan, while also indicating that he would be the one to give any new orders. For now, he told the younger man, Wootters would not return to his company at Petersburg and would instead be reassigned to recruiting duty in Texas. Furthermore, Wootters was to deliver two messages: one to General Edmund Kirby Smith announcing his presence and assignment, and another to Col. Ashbel Smith with the Second Texas Infantry in Galveston concerning the injury to his own right arm. After issuing those orders, General

Lee told Wootters he was dismissed, and wished him a safe passage and a successful journey.

Col. Ashbel Smith was a highly respected physician who had served with General Lee in the war with Mexico and whose medical advice was highly valued. It seemed that Col. Smith had also suffered an arm injury—his in the battle of Shiloh—and might have some personal experience to share. The group sat silently as all were stunned by what they had heard.

"I must say, Captain Wootters, when General Robert E. Lee issues an order and it is signed by the Secretary of War, it would be unlikely that anyone would question the directive," Major Smith said.

"I agree, sir, but I must confess that leaving my troops is much more difficult for my mind to accept than anticipating a direct assault on any enemy position," Wootters said. "I must, however, agree with you that an order from General Lee would be willingly accepted by any soldier who has served with him. If he were to order us to walk on water, I suspect all of his troops would try to do just that."

As Hannah finished serving the cobbler, Oscar stoked the fire, which began to burn more brightly. With his story told and the whisky warming him from the inside out, Wootters finally reached a degree of contentment.

"I don't recall ever having such a fine meal, certainly not since being in the army or even before leaving Crockett," he said to his hosts. "You are more than kind to provide such a feast."

"Captain Wootters, we are so thankful that you are back in Texas, and we hope that you never have to face such horrors again," Anna Jane said, going slightly pale. "I will pray that this violence has not left scars on your mind and spirit and, if so, that the Lord helps to heal them. While you and Major Smith finish your conversation, I will excuse myself as I am very tired."

With Hannah's help, she left the men to their own deliberations. After a second helping of berry cobbler, Major Smith showed the young captain to his bedroom and facilities for the night, with the invitation that he was welcome back any time and for as long as he wished.

———————

After Major Smith retired, Wootters went back to the dining area where Hannah was clearing the last of the dinner dishes and requested a few minutes to visit with her. After offering her guest a third helping of cobbler, which he accepted, Hannah sat down and waited for Wootters to speak.

Throughout the evening, she noticed that he seemed alert, not relaxed. But he captured the last berry in a spoon, the tension in his face softened as he exclaimed, "Hannah, that was the best meal I have ever had!"

"Captain Wootters, I didn't know you had such a sweet tooth!" Hannah said, returning the smile. "I'd give you more but that is the last of the cobbler. I'll make more if you are staying over for a few days."

"Unfortunately, I will be leaving tomorrow," Wootters said. "After seeing my family in Crocket, I have to continue on to Galveston."

"Captain Wootters, how long have you been back in Texas?" Hannah asked. "And what have you seen before coming here tonight that is so worrisome?"

Wootters arose from his chair, the tension in his body immediately evident.

"I have been in Marshall meeting with the commander of the Texas troops in Texas," he answered. "What I heard has been as hard for my mind as the sniper's minie-ball was for my arm."

Virtually nobody in Texas was aware of what was happening in this war, he told her. From the commanding general who imagines continuing the war after the Confederates in the east are annihilated to the privates who were deserting their posts and plundering the supplies, they all seemed to lack any awareness. And that lack of awareness failed to honor those who had served and died for the Confederate cause.

Hannah was surprised by these angry words; John Wootters had always presented himself as a mild-mannered and calm sort. Seeing the look on her face, he apologized for his outburst.

"You don't need to apologize for your feelings, Captain," she said. "Sometimes it's best to let them out where you can see them."

Wootters sat down again and looked directly at Hannah.

"What I really wanted to ask you was about my young friend Berta," he said. "As you see, what I have experienced in this war has hardened my heart and spirit so that being around me may be something that her gentle nature can't accept."

Ever observant, Hannah noted that his eyes appeared to moisten and his voice wavered slightly at the mention of Berta's name. She nodded and kept her tongue.

"Berta is very special to me, as she was the only person who wrote to me and seemed to understand what I was experiencing," he said. "Her words gave me hope that there would be something, or someone, surviving this war who had the strength to carry on to the future. I don't want her to be frightened of me."

Hannah smiled broadly, her teeth shining in the dim light of the dining room.

"Although Miss Berta is still young to me, she is very much a grown woman and has changed greatly in the past three years," she said. "About the only things that are the same are her red hair and her sweet disposition. She has a very smart mind and thinks about everything more than anyone I ever met. Of all the people she knows, I think she has more concern about you than anyone, and I know that she prays for your safe return every day of her life. Now I don't know everything that is in her mind but I am not sure she is as delicate as she seems."

"No person should ever have to know what we have endured in this war," he said in a low voice.

Hannah, who had taken a seat in front of him, looked directly into his eyes told him exactly what she thought. He needed to take some time to heal, physically and spiritually, before he could plan what to do with the rest of his life. It would be good, she thought, for him to stay close to his fellow soldiers, who had seen and done what he had seen and done. She suggested that this might lead him to some peace of mind.

"White people can't really understand what it's like to be a slave, but other slaves do understand," she said. "One of the ways our people keeps up their spirits is by visiting with each other about the hardships and bad things they've seen. Soldiers have shared the same bad times, just like slaves have. You are going to be all right, Captain Wootters, but it's going to take time."

And with that, Hannah announced that she would see him in the morning at breakfast and he should bring a hefty appetite to the table.

Captain John Wootters went to sleep that night in a most comfortable bed. While the turmoil and concern that often kept him awake still lurked in the corners of his mind, he thought for the first time in ages that there might be a path that could lead him out of the darkness.[70]

---

[70] *Appendix II. Item 22. Union Army Generals*

MAY 1865
FAIRFIELD, TEXAS

A S THE FATEFUL YEAR OF 1865 began to unfold across the South, spring did not bring with it the usual air of hope, rebirth and anticipation. It was apparent that the dwindling numbers of men in the Confederate ranks could not hold back the advancing Union forces. In Texas, frustrations were running especially high, as the state's 60,000 troops were unable to help their comrades east of the Mississippi due to the blockades by the U.S. Navy. Morale was low, desertions were on the rise and the economic impact on the civilian population was reaching crisis proportion.

Anxiety was rampant throughout the Confederacy. Most people were aware that the South's military and economic capabilities were exhausted. Then on April 9th, nearly every city, town and village received the dreaded, but expected, news that General Lee had surrendered the Army of Northern Virginia to General Grant at Appomattox Court House, Virginia. As it had become clear in recent weeks that General Lee could no longer defend against the siege of Petersburg, his army evacuated the Petersburg and Richmond defenses and moved westward on the second day of April. Their attempt to escape across the Roanoke River was thwarted, and the 28,000 poorly fed and under-equipped Confederates were no match for the 100,000 well-supplied Union soldiers.

With the agreement of his senior generals—Ewell, Gordon, Longstreet and others—General Lee agreed to meet with General Grant on the morning of April 9th. General Grant, showing his great respect for the Confederate leader and his troops, allowed General Lee to select the place of his surrender, and he chose the home of Wilmer McLean in the town of Appomattox Court House. That afternoon, the two leaders met and the surrender terms previously declared by General Grant were accepted. The terms were as generous as could be anticipated: "the officers and men will be allowed to return to their homes, not to be disturbed by United States authority so long as they observe their paroles and the laws in force where they reside." The officers were permitted to retain their side-arms and personal equipment. Grant also allowed the defeated Confederates to take their horses and mules, and provided Lee with food rations his starving army so desperately needed.[71]

[71] Foote, S. The Civil War. Volume Three, pp. 907–956.

At the formal ceremony on April 12, the Confederates were permitted to surrender with honor and respect as the 28,000 soldiers stacked their arms. Although the war in Virginia was over, it was uncertain how troops in other parts of the Southland might react, however, leaders of other principal commands began surrendering their troops soon thereafter, due, in part, to their respect for General Lee and the lack of appetite for continued bloodshed. Two weeks later, General Joseph E. Johnston surrendered his troops in the southeastern Confederate states at Durham, North Carolina, and on May 8, General Richard Taylor, commander of the Department of Alabama and Mississippi and the Army of Tennessee, surrendered at Citronelle, Alabama. The only significant Confederate force still active at the time of the Fairfield graduation ceremony in mid-May, was the army of the Trans-Mississippi Department, commanded by General Edmund Kirby Smith.

The Southland's uncertain future cast a pall of gloom as Fairfield Female College prepared for its closing ceremonies. The spirit of gaiety that would usually accompany a graduation was nowhere to be found in Freestone County, and as the spring session drew to a close, the seven members of the senior class were a pensive and somber group. They remained bonded by the experiences that they shared, and the responsibility for writing and delivering an essay for the graduation ceremony fell to Berta Smith, who had been named class valedictorian.

It was a task that weighed heavily on her; she wanted to express her love and appreciation for the many individuals associated with the college as well as for her classmates. The seven senior girls had dubbed themselves The Mystic Seven, reflecting their close friendships. All were aware of the great uncertainty they would face on returning to their homes and families after graduation. The one comfort sustaining them was the friendship they shared; as the time of separation drew nearer, they seemed to cling to each other in a bid for reassurance.

Major John Smith and Anna Jane would attend the graduation ceremony, accompanied by Hannah, Oscar and their son, Edgar. The Smiths had arrived in Freestone County the afternoon before the graduation and stayed at an inn for visiting Masons. The evening before the ceremony, Hannah went to Berta's college home to help her pack for the return to the Smith Plantation the following day.

On arriving, Hannah was directed to Berta's room on the second floor. She reached the top of the circular stairway and entered the parlor connecting to the bedroom. There was Berta, sitting at a desk with tears in her eyes.

"Missy Berta!" Hannah cried out. "Why are you so sad? Are you feeling all right?"

"Oh, Hannah! I am so glad to see you," Berta said, rushing into her confidante's comforting embrace. "I have been so worried about reading this message tomorrow at the ceremony, and I'm sad to think about my college days coming to an end. I will miss my friends and teachers so much."

"Of course it's natural to grieve when you leave something you love," Hannah said, smoothing back Berta's hair. "One thing you can't do is keep time from passing. We get older every day, whether we want to or not."

"You always know how to make me see things clearly, no matter how frightened or sad I may be," Berta sniffed and wiped her face. "I hope my mother is feeling well and that the trip wasn't too hard for her."

GALLERY

1. Holy Bible of the Smith Family
2. Berta Smith's Upright Grand Piano
3. Coin Silver Flatware of the Smith Family
4. Present Cedar Branch Church,
   Houston County, Texas
5. Val Verde Cannon, Fairfield, Texas
6. Smith Landing Ferry Site, Trinity River,
   Houston County, Texas
7. Major Dick Dowling and Sabine Pass Battle Monument,
   Houston, Texas
8. Valedictory Essay, Fairfield Female College, May 1865
9. Graves of Anna Jane Pouncey Smith and Major John Smith
10. Fairfield College Marker, Freestone County, Texas
11. Pennepack Baptist Church, Philadelphia, Pennsylvania
12. Welsh Tract Baptist Church, New Castle County, Delaware
13. Restored Flag of the 1st Texas Regiment
14. Bermuda Hundred Historical Marker, Virginia

15-18. Desserette – The Smith Plantation in Bladen County,
   North Carolina (Restored)

19. Berta Smith & Capt. John H. Wootters at the
    Time of Their Wedding
20. Berta Smith Wootters & Capt. John H. Wootters Later in Life

Holy Bible of the Smith Family
FIGURE 1A

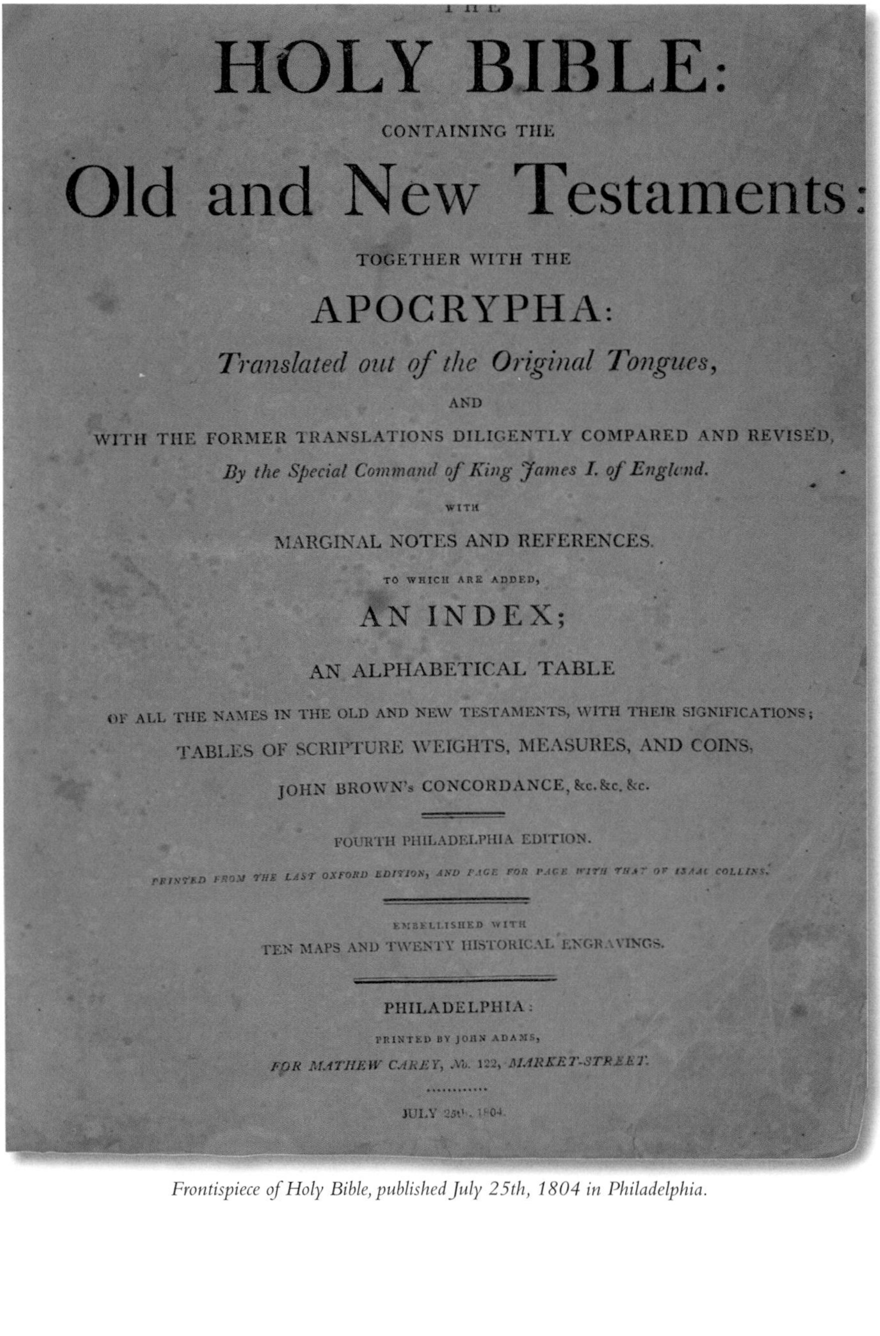

THE

HOLY BIBLE:

CONTAINING THE

Old and New Testaments:

TOGETHER WITH THE

APOCRYPHA:

Translated out of the Original Tongues,

AND

WITH THE FORMER TRANSLATIONS DILIGENTLY COMPARED AND REVISED,

By the Special Command of King James I. of England.

WITH

MARGINAL NOTES AND REFERENCES.

TO WHICH ARE ADDED,

AN INDEX;

AN ALPHABETICAL TABLE

OF ALL THE NAMES IN THE OLD AND NEW TESTAMENTS, WITH THEIR SIGNIFICATIONS;

TABLES OF SCRIPTURE WEIGHTS, MEASURES, AND COINS,

JOHN BROWN's CONCORDANCE, &c. &c. &c.

FOURTH PHILADELPHIA EDITION.

PRINTED FROM THE LAST OXFORD EDITION, AND PAGE FOR PAGE WITH THAT OF ISAAC COLLINS.

EMBELLISHED WITH

TEN MAPS AND TWENTY HISTORICAL ENGRAVINGS.

PHILADELPHIA:

PRINTED BY JOHN ADAMS,

FOR MATHEW CAREY, No. 122, MARKET-STREET.

JULY 25th, 1804.

Frontispiece of Holy Bible, published July 25th, 1804 in Philadelphia.

FIGURE 1B

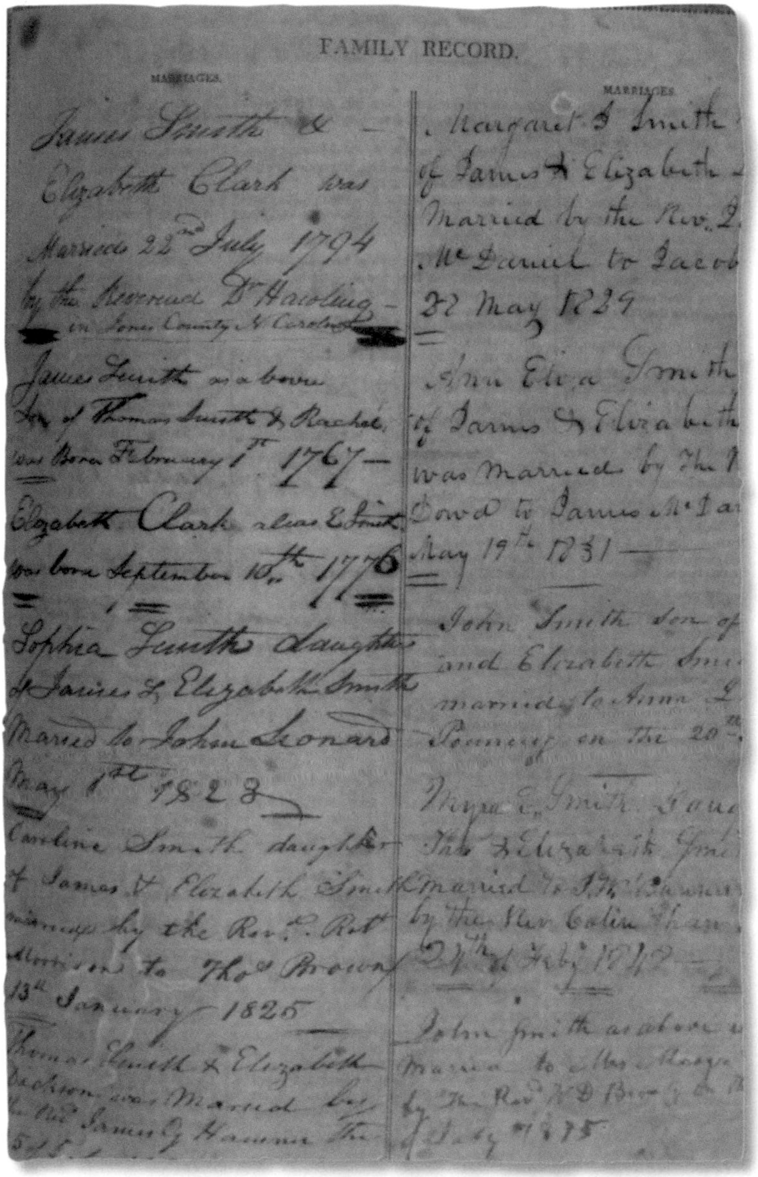

FAMILY RECORD.

MARRIAGES. | MARRIAGES.

James Smith & Elizabeth Clark was Married 22nd July 1794 by the Reverend Dr Hawling – in Jones County N Carolina

James Smith as above Son of Thomas Smith & Rachel was Born February 1st 1767 —

Elizabeth Clark alias E Smith was born September 10th 1776

Sophia Smith daughter of James & Elizabeth Smith Married to John Leonard May 1st 1828

Caroline Smith daughter of James & Elizabeth Smith married by the Revd Robt Morrison to Thos Brown 13th January 1825

Thomas Smith & Elizabeth Jackson was Married by the Rev James G Hanna the 5th ...

Margaret J Smith of James & Elizabeth Married by the Rev. D. McDaniel to Jacob 22 May 1829

Ann Eliza Smith of James & Elizabeth was married by the ... Dowd to James McD... May 19th 1831 —

John Smith son of and Elizabeth Smith married to Anna J Pouncey on the 20th ...

Handwritten page listing marriages including: James Smith and Elizabeth Clark, married July 22, 1794 by Reverend Dr. Hawling in Jones County, North Carolina, John Smith married Anna Jane Pouncey on February 20, 1834 and John Smith married Mrs. Marge Dailey by the Reverend W.D. Bromly on July 1, 1875.

Upright Grand Piano
FIGURE 2

*Piano purchased by Major John Smith for his daughter, Berta Smith,
in 1856 for the price of 18 bales of cotton.*

Coin Silver Flatware of the Smith Family
FIGURE 3A

Flatware of John and Anna Jane Smith with their monogram – JAJS

FIGURE 3B

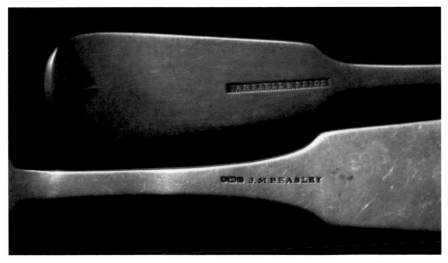

Lettering on reverse of spoons. Campbell & Prior was a silver merchant in Fayetteville, NC from 1834-36, firm bought by John M. Beasley, a silversmith and Baptist minister, in 1845 (John and Anna Jane married 2/20/1834).

Present Cedar Branch Church, Houston County, Texas
FIGURE 4A

FIGURE 4B

Text from historical plaque reads: Cedar Branch began as a settlement of freedmen. John Smith (1809-1890) and Anna Jane Pouncey Smith (1811-1874) deeded a parcel of their cotton plantation to each of their former slaves. The freedmen organized a church in 1862 and built a sanctuary in 1864. Lev Leonard chose the name Cedar Branch for the chapel and community. He and Alonzo Campbell selected a cemetery site. By 1888 a school was established and classes were held in the church building. In 1952 it became part of the Grapeland School District. The church continues to serve as the focus of this community. (1998)

Val Verde Cannon Fairfield, Texas
FIGURE 5

Text from Historical Plaque in front of Freestone County, Texas Courthouse

State Historical Survey Committee
Val Verde Battery
C.S.A.
Six brass field guns taken by Lt. Joseph C. Sayers company in Civil War Battle of Val Verde N. Mex., 1862, and brought back to Texas with incredible difficulty, armed a new unit of hand-picked men. Sound of the Val Verde guns in action set pace for other outfits, helped secure such victories as the recapture of Galveston 1863. At Mansfield, LA, April 1864, captured new longer range guns. Unwilling to lose their guns when the war ended, the men buried four. The last commander T.D. Nettles, brought this one home to Freestone County. (1960)

Smith Landing Ferry Site, Trinity River, Houston County, Texas
FIGURE 6

The site of the ferry across the Trinity River at the Smith Landing Plantation is shown by Edgar Pouncey, grandson of Addie Pouncey, to Drs. Carlos Hamilton Jr., John H. Wootters and Carlos Hamilton Sr. (left to right).

Major Dick Dowling and Sabine Pass Battle Monument
FIGURE 7

Monument in Hermann Park, Houston, Texas in honor of Dick Dowling, members of the First Texas Heavy Artillery unit and their victory at the Battle of the Sabine Pass, September 8, 1863 (Text is from the Texas Historical Commission plaque.)

Major Richard William (Dick) Dowling, C.S.A. January 14, 1837 – September 23, 1867

For complete text of historical plaque, see Appendix II, Item 17.

Valedictory Essay, Fairfield Female College, May 1865

FIGURE 8A

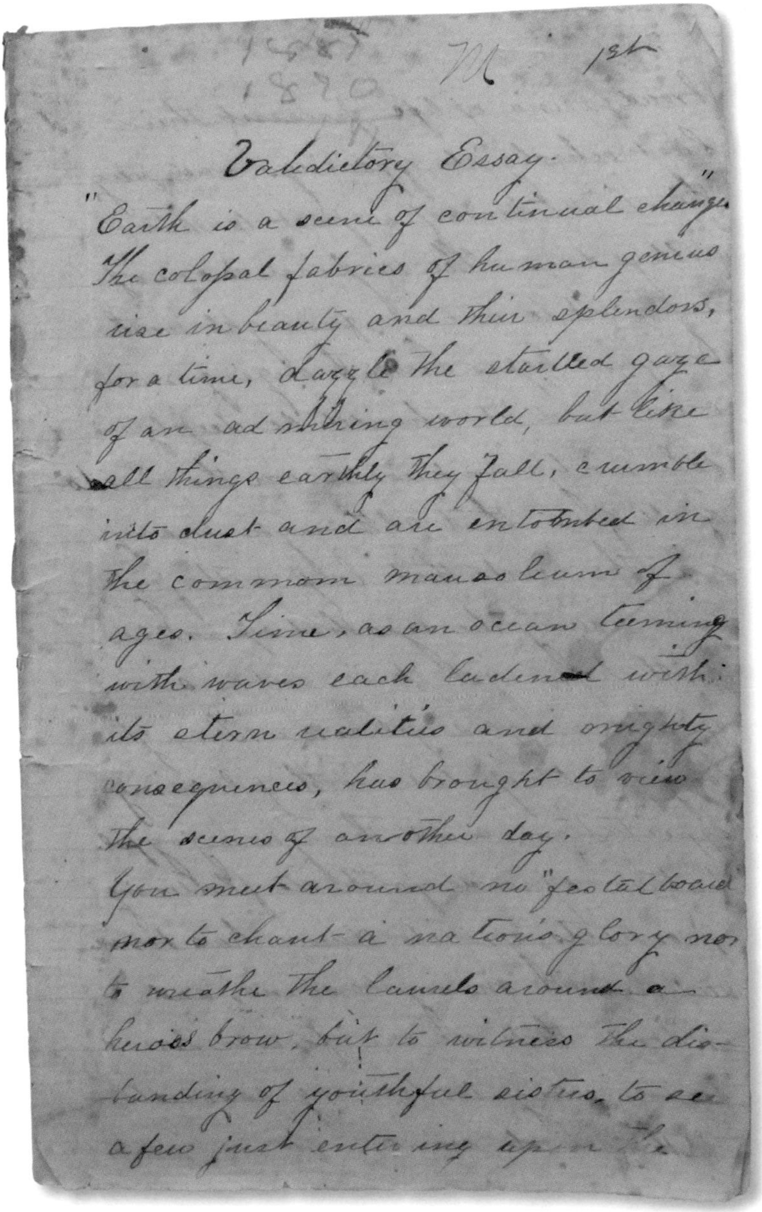

M 1st

Valedictory Essay.

"Earth is a scene of continual change"
The colossal fabrics of human genius rise in beauty and their splendors, for a time, dazzle the startled gaze of an admiring world, but like all things earthly they fall, crumble into dust and are entombed in the common mausoleum of ages. Time, as an ocean teeming with waves each ladened with its stern realities and mighty consequences, has brought to view the scenes of another day.
You meet around no "festal board" nor to chant a nation's glory nor to wreathe the laurels around a heroe's brow, but to witness the disbanding of youthful sisters, to see a few just entering upon the

Handwritten text of the Valedictory Essay presented by Miss Berta Smith at the graduation ceremony of the Fairfield Female College May, 1865, page one of essay.

Valedictory Essay, Fairfield Female College, May 1865
FIGURE 8B

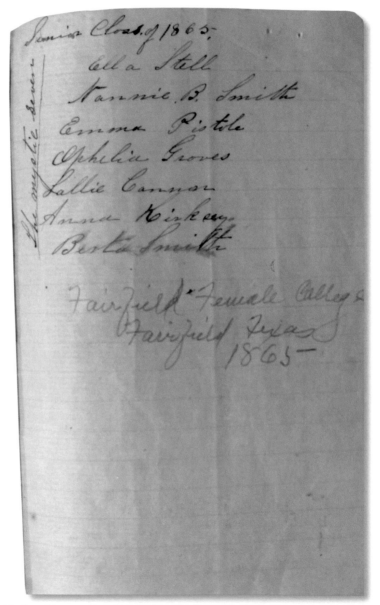

Members of the senior class of 1865: Ella Stell, Fannie B. Smith, Emma Pistole, Ophelia Graves, Sallie Cannon, Anna Kirksey and Berta Smith – The Mystic Seven.

Graves of Anna Jane Pouncey Smith
and Major John Smith
FIGURE 9

*Grave sites on the Smith Landing Plantation being shown to Dr. John H. Wootters and
Mrs. Berta Denman Hamilton, grandchildren of John and Berta Smith Wootters, and Dr. Carlos Hamilton
Jr., their great-grandson, by Mr. Edgar Pouncey, the grandson of Addie Pouncey and great-grandson
of Hannah and Oscar Pouncey (left to right).*

*The grave markers read: In Memory of Mrs. A. J. Smith, born Oct. 23, 1811, Died Aug. 5, 1874.
and Maj. John Smith, Born Dec. 21, 1809, Died July 29, 1890.*

Fairfield College Marker, Freestone County, Texas
FIGURE 10

*Marker placed in 1936 by the Texas Historical Commission at the site
of the Fairfield Female College in Freestone County, Texas.*

Pennepack Baptist Church, Philadelphia, Pennsylvania
FIGURE 11

Pennepack Baptist Church, In the latter half of the seventeenth century Baptists from England and Wales settled in the County of Philadelphia. Their gathering as baptized believers led to the formation of the Pennepack Baptist Church (text from the marble marker in front of the church). See Appendix II, Item 9, for complete text.

Welsh Tract Baptist Church, New Castle County, Delaware
FIGURE 12

The Welsh Baptists, that arrived in Pennsylvania in 1701 and worshipped at the Pennepack Baptist Church, purchased a 30,000 acre tract from William Penn and relocated there in 1703. They built a church known as the Meeting House at Iron-hill in New Castle, Delaware. The original log building was replaced by the present structure (above) built in 1746. The James family and others had already emigrated to the Old Cheraw area of South Carolina in 1735. The James' lived across the Welsh Tract Road from this church where they owned a tavern which was said to have later sheltered Generals Washington, Greene and LaFayette when they had been atop Iron Hill spying on the British in the nearby Chesapeake Bay. At one time the Welsh Tract Road passed behind this church building and continued up and over Iron Hill. Traces of this abandoned road can still be seen southeast of the church. The oldest tombstone in the walled cemetery is inscribed in Welsh and dated 1707.

Restored Flag of the 1st Texas Infantry Regiment
FIGURE 13

Flag carried by the 1st Texas during the Peninsula Campaign, at Second Manassas and Antietam.

This flag was reported to have been made by the wife and daughter of the regiment's first colonel, Louis T. Wigfall and at least the star was said to have been made from material of Mrs. Wigfall's wedding dress. In the summer of 1862 the four battles named on the flag were added. At Antietam on September 17, 1862 the 1st Texas Regiment lost 186 of its 226 men including nine standard bearers of this flag. It was captured by a Federal soldier who was awarded the Congressional Medal of Honor for the deed. The flag was returned to Texas in 1905 and is in the Texas State Library and Archives.

Bermuda Hundred Historical Marker, Virginia
FIGURE 14

Desserette – The Smith Plantation in Bladen County, North Carolina Restored
FIGURE 15

Desserette main house entrance.

FIGURE 16

Brick piling foundation of Desserette home.

FIGURE 17

Original kitchen of Desserette of lopped cypress siding.

FIGURE 18

Original cypress weatherboard smoke house.

Berta Smith & Capt. John H. Wootters
At the Time of Their Wedding
FIGURE 19

*Captains John H. Wootters and William B. Wall
at the time of the wedding of John Wootters
and Miss Berta Smith. (This photo shows
evidence of their Civil War injuries—
Wootters right wrist injury and Wall injury
to right hand with missing thumb)*

*Berta Smith at the time of her wedding—
January 17, 1867*

Later in Life
FIGURE 20

Hannah nodded and reassured her that Anna Jane was just fine. Both of her parents were so proud of their daughter that nothing could spoil this day for them, not even economic and political turmoil. And Berta, too, should let nothing distract her from the joy of her graduation ceremony. But the younger woman, it seemed, had something else on her mind.

"I am so happy that Captain Wootters has returned to Texas," Berta said casually. "Have you seen him since he visited just before Christmas?"

"No, child, he is very busy with his duties in Galveston," Hannah said as she began the job of packing Berta's trunks. "He has only passed through our neck of the woods without visiting."

"He wrote me a short letter last month saying that his arm was improving and that he was so thankful for Col. Ashbel Smith," Berta said.[72] "He said he was hoping to come for our graduation but he wasn't sure about his assignment. I do not expect him to be able to attend, as it sounded as if he has been very occupied."

"He will come if he can," Hannah said. "Now you don't need to keep reading your paper, but you do need to help me pack your trunk so we can leave tomorrow."

Berta, now smiling, agreed that she was finished re-reading her essay and turned her attention to the packing job at hand.

Warm sunshine greeted them on the morning of the graduation. The sky was clear, and all signs pointed to a pleasant day for this ceremony. The morning activities included tours of the college for the families of the younger students and a

[72] *Appendix II. Item 23. Col. Ashbel Smith, M.D.*

music recital, which the senior girls would perform for those in attendance. The instructors had selected Berta to give the final performance, and she had decided to play two piano compositions by Beethoven. The first was "Bagatelle in A Minor," better known as *"Für Elise,"* one of her favorites; the other work was the second movement of a sonata often referred to as the Pathetique, which reflected in many ways her own sadness about the state of the Southland.

The audience was awed by the sensitivity and skill she showed in her presentation of these pieces. The applause was loud and appreciative, so much so that Berta responded to calls for an encore performance.

On returning to the piano, she played variations on a tune that, when played in a slow metric, was not immediately recognizable. But after the first stanza of the work, she broke into a lively traditional rendition of "I Wish I Was in Dixie's Land," which elicited a rousing cheer and singing from the audience. The response to her music lifted her spirits, and Berta thought for the first time that morning that she would be able to complete the day's activities, including the reading of her essay, with a smile on her face.

The graduation ceremonies were held early in the afternoon at the front entrance of the college before an audience that was smaller than in previous years. Parents, family members, friends and guests were in attendance. Dr. Graves and other faculty, as well as the college overseers, sat on the veranda, which was decorated with patriotic bunting and flags. As usual, the students were seated at the front of the audience, grouped by seniority in chairs on the lawn facing the building's entrance. After the requisite prayers, welcomes and salutations, Berta was introduced and came to the podium with a sense of trepidation.

Berta began her essay with a quotation and paraphrase from Charlotte Brontë's Jane Eyre at the point when the main character's spiteful aunt is dying and reveals the letter written three years earlier to Jane from her uncle, John Eyre, promising her a better future.[73]

"Earth is a scene of continued change," Berta said. "The fabrics of human genius rise in beauty and dazzle the admiring world, but like all things earthly they fall, crumble into dust."

"This occasion is one of moment to many," she continued. "To our friends of this vicinity, we gladly thank you for the favors we have enjoyed at your hands. The time has come when we must return to our cherished homes and, we ask a place in your memories and with you, leave our blessings and ardent wishes for your happiness."

She went on to thank the college and its founders, and to express gratitude on behalf of the senior class for the privilege of having received such a thorough and important education.

The clouds that had partially blocked the sunshine had drifted to the south, and the bright rays brought a glow of perspiration across her brow. As she dabbed her face with her handkerchief, some thought she was drying tears, as many in the audience were also feeling the emotion of the moment. She concluded her presentation by addressing her fellow seniors, the Mystic Seven.

"Beloved classmates, begging your kind hearts to bear with us, we must bid a last farewell. Though our bodies be far removed, our spirits shall linger, the time for parting comes, and it is with deep and heartfelt emotion that I think of it."

[73] *Brontë, Charlotte. Jane Eyre, Chapter XXI.*

Not to ignore the crisis of their beloved Confederacy that was foremost in her audience's minds, she added: "God only knows when shadows gather thickly around and disappointments hide from your anxious view the long wished-for headland toward which you press. We know that the bright sunshine succeeds the storm, and the future is before us radiant with the light of hope. Now run, my bursting heart— say farewell to your companions of my college days. Dear friends, instructors and classmates, we extend to you all a heartfelt good bye."[74]

Berta left the podium to thunderous applause interspersed with the occasional sigh. Those in attendance knew they were witnessing the end of an era in the history of their country and their own lives. As she walked to her seat, her gaze was directed to the periphery of the audience where, standing in the shade of an oak tree, was a group of men wearing the Confederate Army uniform. Looking at them more closely, she realized that the man at the edge of their group was her friend, Captain John Wootters, but his appearance seemed so changed that she couldn't be sure. She looked again, with greater effort, and saw that it was, indeed, John Wootters. Had she not been about to sit down at that moment, she might have fainted from her surprise.

Light-headed, her heart racing, Berta remain seated a bit longer when the students were called to receive their certificates of graduation. By the time the ceremony had ended, she was feeling more herself. She went to greet family and friends, and acknowledge their congratulations before focusing her attention on the person who had been central to her thoughts, yet seemed like a stranger to her mind.

[74] *For complete text of essay, see Appendix I, Item 7.*

Berta made her way to the edge of the crowd as she saw John Wootters moving in her direction. She was suddenly seized by a sense of panic. He was unsmiling and sporting a beard, and he seemed taller than she remembered. He had an air of authority and strength in his stride, but as their eyes met, a radiant smile lit up his face. At that moment, Berta experienced an unfamiliar feeling, one that she would later compare to her feelings after the church service in Crockett four years earlier. Wootters approached her with outstretched arms and pulled her toward him. Berta stood motionless for a long moment.

"Oh, John, it is so very good to see you," she finally said.

At those words, she felt a tightness in her throat. Her arms encircled his neck and, after a gentle hug, they looked into each other's eyes. Neither said anything for what seemed like several minutes. Then they both began to laugh, softly, as Berta found herself able to speak again.

"Oh, Mr. Wootters, it is fortunate that I was unaware of your presence before making my presentation," she whispered. "I might have been speechless at an inopportune time. I am very glad you could be here today."

She stepped back and took a visual measure of him. "I have been very concerned about your well-being, and seeing you looking so fit and handsome is truly a blessing and answer to my prayers."

"I cannot tell you how thankful I am to be here today," he said, noting that it had been nearly four years since he'd left Crockett. "I not only was able to hear your words which were the most beautiful and gentle messages that I have ever heard, but your piano pieces earlier this day were exquisite and encouraging. Certainly the music of heaven couldn't be more pleasing to my ears."

This lavish compliment made Berta's cheeks flush bright pink. She appreciated his kindness, she told him, but he was much too generous with his praise. Of greater concern was his health and recovery from his injury. And while he was handsome and elegant as she had imagined he would be, he was also considerably leaner. The war years had taken their toll on his body as well as his spirit.

"Please walk with me to the flower garden and tell me what you have experienced since your visit with my parents last winter," Berta said, taking his good arm. "I have, of course, heard what you told them as they were amazed by the events following your injury. We are all so thankful and relieved with your return that words can scarcely describe my happiness."

She led them in the direction of the rose garden, where there was privacy as well as shade. She attempted to tuck her hair back into place—a few strands had come undone as she returned Wootters' embrace—but gave up after repeated attempts. They passed her special rose bush, and she broke off a stem with a large pink blossom, placing it in the lace handkerchief her mother had given her as a birthday gift. It was a treasure she carried with her on special occasions.

"When I had stopped for that pleasant visit with your parents, I was en route to Galveston," he said. "My visits to troops in Tyler, Huntsville and Hempstead made it clear that recruitment to the chaotic condition of our troops was not possible."

"Your surprise visit was certainly the high point of the season for my parents," Berta said. "They could hardly speak of anything but how honored they were that you paid them a call. Nor could Hannah."

That visit had also been a high point for Wootters. As he noted, the meetings with the troops and officers across the state were disappointing. Even as he continued to emphasize the importance of maintaining the honor and integrity of the forces, he could see the lack of discipline was pervading the ranks. After being in Galveston a short time, news came of General Lee's surrender and that other Confederate generals had followed suit. Only Col. Ashbel Smith's leadership was able to prevent outright mutiny among the remnants of the Second Texas Infantry in that city.

That Berta and Captain Wootters appeared to be renewing their acquaintance did not escape Hannah's sharp eyes. She wisely suggested to Major Smith and Anna Jane that they all retire to the rooms Berta occupied during the school year and make certain that everything was in order for the return trip home. As the crowd attending the graduation ceremony gradually dispersed, Berta and Captain Wootters continued their stroll through the rose garden.

"You have had such experiences in the years since you and the Crockett Southrons marched away from town on that July day four years ago that it would likely take a lifetime to relate them all, and I suspect there are many you would rather not discuss," she said. "You mentioned that the past few months have been distressing to you. What have you seen that caused you to say that?"

"You are quite correct in saying that much that has happened is difficult to revisit, but many of those experiences are so tightly secured in my memory that they are not likely to ever fade," he responded. "What has grieved me in the past few months are the actions of many so-called soldiers who seem determined to shun all order and discipline and to only take whatever they can for themselves. Rioting and plundering do nothing to honor the memory of the brave soldiers I have known."

Somewhere in the garden, an agitated mocking bird cried loudly to discourage a squirrel from coming too close to its nest. Here, there was peace, and Berta wanted very much to envision a more hopeful future than what the present world seemed to offer.

"I have no right to burden you with my own anxieties, and I apologize for having done so," Wootters said, suddenly aware of having bared so much of himself to the young woman. "This has been a beautiful occasion, and I share with your family a great sense of pride in your accomplishments."

"Hearing about your experiences, both good and bad, would never be burdensome to me," Berta said. "I look forward to hearing as much about them as you are willing to share. I am just thankful that you have returned and seem so well physically. Nothing could detract from my happiness at this time."

They talked about Wootters' plans after that day. He was, he told her, on his way back to Houston at the direction of General Kirby Smith, who was en route to hold a court of inquiry to investigate the causes of the disorder and lawlessness that had become so prevalent. Once that was finished, he would accompany Col. Ashbel Smith and William Ballinger, a Galveston attorney, to New Orleans to arrange for peace terms for Texas. The group would then return to Galveston, where they hoped General Kirby Smith would sign the terms and officially end the war in the state. Beyond that, Wootters planned to arrange business activities he could pursue after the war was over.

His hope was to start a cotton brokerage business; he had already met with several individuals who were interested in joining him in such a venture. They would manage an office in Galveston, and Wootters would meet with planters in East Texas to encourage them to market their products through his firm. He was confident that demand for cotton would continue to grow. During his absence, his older brother, James, also known as J.C., had continued to manage the mercantile business. Following the unexpected death of their Uncle Lodwick's partner, Col. Long, the elder Wootters had married Long's widow, Emily, and they now had two children of their own. During the war, J.C. had served for a short time with the Thirteenth Texas Cavalry, after which he had returned to his work in Houston County and served one term in the Texas Legislature. Wootters' sister, Sarah, who was six years his senior, lived in Crockett with her husband, W.H. Moore, and their children.

As the afternoon wore on, the sun moved behind a stand of tall pines and the shadows seemed to dance about the garden. The temperature cooled a bit as clouds began moving in. Captain Wootters and Berta sat down on a bench. Berta laid the rose wrapped in her lace handkerchief on her lap.

"It is very sad that your parents died so young and did not have the opportunity to see their children become such valued citizens," she said. "You and your brother and sister were very fortunate to have such caring relatives."

"Truly, we were blessed in many ways," Wootters nodded. "But I have always regretted losing them and having to rely on the kindness of others. Now it seems that I will be dependent on my comrades-in-arms and others close to my heart to be able to move ahead with my life. You have helped me to know that our ultimate purpose in life is to understand and live the plan that God intends for each of us. Tell me what you anticipate doing, now that you have finished your courses here."

Berta told him that she would be returning to Houston County. She wanted to be of help to her parents, especially to Anna Jane whose health continued to be quite fragile. Her father, she said, had already taken steps to provide land that could be owned by the family-owned slaves who had, over the years, contributed so much to making the Smiths' lives comfortable. Berta had no doubt that once they were free to leave, some certainly would. But a number of them had already indicated they would remain close by to raise their own families in the area. And then she told Wootters her biggest secret.

"This summer I plan to begin teaching some of the slave children to read just as I have been teaching the younger students at the Fairfield Academy," she revealed. "It seems unfair to expect people to be able to function as freedmen when they lack many of the skills needed to succeed in any capacity."

Wootters was surprised by these plans, but decided not to pursue that conversation. He did, however, promise not to reveal her plans to anyone.

"I don't think anyone would fault you for your feelings," he said. "You are the child of gentle people, and despite these harsh times, you have all persevered."

As they walked towards the college building, Berta took the rose and the handkerchief in which it was nestled, and placed them in his hand. "Please take this bloom as it comes from a particular bush that is very special to me," she said.

Nearing the driveway, they saw the Smith family standing near the loaded carriage, with Edgar ready to guide the horses back home. After greeting Major Smith, Anna Jane and Hannah and her family, Wootters said his goodbyes to Berta, but with the expectation that it would not be for long.

He waved until he could no longer see the carriage and then took the lace handkerchief, inhaling the faint rose fragrance. Smiling to himself, he carefully placed the handkerchief in his coat pocket. It had, indeed, been a very pleasant day.

LATE SUMMER 1865
ON TEXAS ROADWAYS

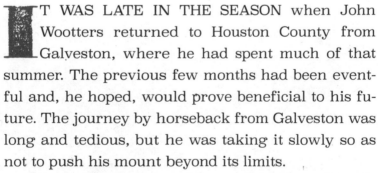

IT WAS LATE IN THE SEASON when John Wootters returned to Houston County from Galveston, where he had spent much of that summer. The previous few months had been eventful and, he hoped, would prove beneficial to his future. The journey by horseback from Galveston was long and tedious, but he was taking it slowly so as not to push his mount beyond its limits.

The months after his return to Texas had affected him perhaps as much as the previous three years of combat duty with Hood's Brigade. Some of his embittered fellow soldiers would conclude that the only thing he had gained from those experiences was this aging horse and three uniforms. One of the uniforms was as worn out as the horse, but he had received a new suit for his trip to New Orleans with Col. Ashbel Smith. As he made his way through the towns of Houston, Huntsville and Trinity toward his destination in Crockett, he had ample time to reflect on the events of the past several years. He could only smile to himself and be grateful that the prospects for the future, as far as he could tell, seemed reasonably bright.

He would never be able to erase the memory of so many comrades who had served in the First Texas Regiment with him, especially those in the Crockett Southrons. How naïve they had been when they so proudly marched out of town on that July afternoon in 1861. He marveled at their enthusiasm while training on the field at Howard's Grove in Richmond and their disappointment and boredom on the Potomac defense lines later that winter. Their first real action at Gaines' Farm the next spring showed them the death and injury that would be their ever present companions.

Little did they know what lay ahead at Sharpsburg when it became apparent, to those that survived, that there would be nothing glorious about this war. This idea was further reinforced at Gettysburg, Chickamauga and the Wilderness. That the soldiers serving on both sides were brave was clear in those battles; for the Union Army, that courage shone through further at Fredericksburg, Spotsylvania Courthouse and Cold Harbor. Following those debacles, it became obvious that no amount of Confederate zeal could overcome the vast resources of the Federal government. With the Union willing to sacrifice its men in mass charges despite extraordinary losses, eventually the southern defenders would not be able to persevere. Their bravery, persistence and devotion to their comrades, however, would never be forgotten.

As the summer months had been warm and largely dry, John Wootters took every opportunity to provide water for his horse and enjoy shady respites on this journey. The most hopeful event of recent months had been his visit with Berta at her graduation in May. Although he had passed through Houston County several times since then, his visits had been brief due to the urgency of his duties. He had promised himself and Berta that, whenever possible, he would not continue to be such a stranger.

Indeed, his visit to Fairfield had been a revelation. Not only had the young girl become a beautiful woman, but she was also certainly a lady of substantial intelligence and insight. He had learned of her significant faith from her letters, but he had not been aware of the extent of her musical talents and the depths of her mind.

After taking his leave from the Smith family in May, he had proceeded to Crockett for a visit with relatives and then on to Houston, to assist General Kirby Smith with his inquiry into the rioting and mayhem that had occurred there.[75] He had been dismayed by the desertions and looting going on in that town, but before General Kirby Smith arrived, Wootters had received a message directing him to report to Col. Ashbel Smith in Galveston. He was to be an aide for a special mission to New Orleans.[76]

---

[75] Cutrer, T. W. "Smith, Edmund Kirby," Handbook of Texas Online.
[76] Silverthorne, E. "Smith, Ashbel," Handbook of Texas Online.

Wootters was aware that both General Kirby Smith and the governor of Texas, Pendleton Murrah, shared the idea that Texas might be able to continue down the secessionist pathway despite the collapse of the rest of the Confederacy.[77] Murrah had asked Col. Ashbel Smith and William P. Ballinger, a highly regarded attorney in Galveston, to journey to New Orleans to determine what terms of peace could be expected for Texas.[78] Col. Smith had specifically requested that Wootters accompany them as an aide.

The Texas delegation expected that the Union commander in New Orleans would only discuss terms of surrender and then only with his Confederate military counterpart. On their arrival they learned that the expectation was accurate. The Federal commander, General Edward R. S. Canby,[79] had indeed refused to meet with their delegation. However, he did offer General Kirby Smith's chief of staff the same terms as had been extended to Generals Lee, Johnston and Taylor. On June 2nd, when their boat returned from New Orleans, General Kirby Smith formally signed the documents of surrender. The most destructive era in American history was officially over in Texas.

---

[77] Wooster, R.A. "Murrah, Pendleton," Handbook of Texas Online.

[78] King, C.R. "Ballinger, William Pitt," Handbook of Texas Online.

[79] General Edward R.S. Canby led the Federal troops of the Department of New Mexico and after forcing the retreat of General Sibley's Brigade following the Battle of Glorietta Pass, he was reassigned to the east. By 1864, he commanded the Union troops in the Battle of Mobile, Alabama and its capture in April 1865. He had accepted the surrender of General Richard Taylor in May 1865 at Citronelle, Alabama.

On June 19, General Gordon Granger and two thousand Union troops arrived in Galveston to establish Federal control in Texas. On that day from the balcony of Ashton Villa, General Granger read aloud the General Order No. 3, which officially freed all slaves in the state.[80] No one in Wootters' family had ever owned slaves, but he had expected to become an owner once he started his life as a planter. He had learned from Major Smith and Anna Jane that slavery was not necessary for a viable agricultural economy. Wootters suspected that the economy might be more effective without the oppressive presence of that institution.

Major Smith had agreed to help him establish a plantation of his own and, while in Galveston, Wootters had been able to obtain property near Daly's in Houston County where he planned to begin his farming activities. He had also made arrangements to start a cotton brokerage operation. He and a new acquaintance, Mr. Duble, who had experience in the warehouse and brokerage business, had agreed to form a partnership. Wootters was convinced that they could successfully compete for the business of planters in the Trinity River area.

While in New Orleans, Wootters consulted with physicians about his injury, and they had told him to expect continued improvement in the function of the nerves in his hand and arm, even as some of the medical professionals expressed concern about possible persistent inflammation in his arm bone. Injuries such as this one could affect one's heart and kidneys, and it would be difficult to know whether or not

[80] *"General Order #3: The People of Texas are informed that, in accordance with a proclamation from the Executive of the United States, all slaves are free. This involves an absolute equality of personal rights of property between former masters and slaves, and the connection heretofore existing between them becomes that between employer and hired labor. The freedmen are advised to remain quietly at their present homes and work for wages. They are informed that they will not be allowed to collect at military posts and that they will not be supported in idleness either there or elsewhere."*

this inflammation was present as he had little sensation of pain in the injured arm. Since amputation was the only suggested alternative treatment, Wootters was willing to wait for signs of further improvement.

The late afternoon sun offered little relief from the heat. With drops of sweat falling into his eyes, Wootters instinctively raised his right hand to wipe his face and realized that there was some feeling in the thumb, which although hardly more than a tingle, was at least an encouraging sign. Perhaps he would soon be able to write a letter to Berta with his preferred hand.

Indeed, his thoughts kept returning to Berta, with her lovely face and fiery red hair. She was constantly in his mind. After hearing her speak at the graduation, he understood that she was also living through a difficult time of transition. Although his experiences had been of the harshest sort imaginable, hers had caused her great anxiety. She had lost her brother, young Ossie and Betty's husband, William. Berta seemed to have responded to these experiences by gaining strength from her faith. Although she was still affected by them, her faith seemed to have grown, and she clearly was able to move forward with her life. Wootters thought he had much to learn from the Smith family, and he considered that Berta's parents could have been like the parents that he had never really known. He appreciated Major Smith's interest in helping him learn the skills he would need to successfully manage an agricultural enterprise.

As he neared the town of Trinity, he came upon a boy who was trying to persuade a young heifer to follow him through a gate to a path leading away from the road. Wootters stopped to observe the predicament of the youth and to allow his horse to have some water from a nearby tank. When he asked the boy if he needed some help the response was that he sure did and that he couldn't understand why the animal so disliked that particular path. Wootters suggested that the heifer probably didn't know what was at the end of the path and whatever was there would not be an improvement over where she had already been. As he and his horse approached the heifer, she promptly went through the gate; the youth said that he was much obliged for the help. Wootters smiled as he thought that he really had not done anything to help. In fact, the heifer had concluded that being in close proximity to a horse was less desirable than whatever was down the path. It made Wootters recall Berta's interest in teaching slaves to read, but he had significant misgivings about how such an effort would be perceived by much of the white population.

Noting the significant number of freedmen walking along the roadways, Wootters realized that the freedom to determine their own destination was a new experience for them. Although he had dealt with many slaves during his years at the mercantile store, none had paid him as much attention as Hannah. She had, in fact, given him sage advice during his visit in December, and he had often thought back to her words. Truly, Hannah had exceptional abilities and insights; with educational opportunities, she would have been able to have significantly improved her life.

Wootters expected the coming generation to see a vastly different world than his own, and he was thankful to be present for its unfolding. Sharing that world with Berta seemed like a goal he must pursue.

As he entered the town of Crockett, he was eager to visit with his brother and sister and their families and with his aging uncle. He hoped to find lodging, depending on his now worthless Confederate money or the generosity of the owners of the inn or at the Masonic lodge. Once ensconced, he would post a letter to Berta announcing his return and hopefully would be invited to pay a call at Smith Landing plantation.

Although the almanac indicated that summer would soon be ending, the heat in the Trinity River bottom-land showed no sign of easing. The corn fields, brown and barren as their crops had been long ago harvested, were awaiting rainfall. Once the soil was more pliable, the fields would be plowed and prepared for future use. As planters throughout the area knew, the end of the summer farming season heralded the beginning of autumn with the promise of cooler tempera-tures to come.

There was also another beginning on the horizon: the new school that Berta would provide for children in the Daly's area. She had anticipated and planned for this ven-ture since returning home from college in May. At Fairfield, she had learned much about teaching young students, and she looked forward to helping children discover the pleasure of reading and learning. As to where she would conduct the lessons, she was fortunate that Reverend Joseph Pritchard had volunteered the use of the church building for that pur-pose. Berta felt very blessed, indeed.

On this particular afternoon, she had been at the church preparing a room for the dozen students she expected to at-tend her class the following week. Oscar was driving the carriage back to the Smith plantation as he had been in-structed to do by her father. As the carriage ride was prov-ing too bumpy for her to concentrate on a book, she took the opportunity to revisit in her mind the events of the summer.

Graduation and the reality of not returning to Fairfield Female College had been more challenging than she had expected. Although she would miss her friends and especially her mentor, Betty Graves, her days had been filled with activities. She had spent time knitting and sewing with her mother over the past months, and was pleased to note some improvement in Anna Jane's strength and stamina.

She recalled Reverend Pritchard's visit to their home not long ago. As pastor at the Baptist Church in Crockett and a part-time pastor of the mission church at Daly's, the Reverend Pritchard held services at Daly's on late Sunday afternoons twice a month; the congregation was too small to have a full-time minister. However, more people were building homes in the area, and the numbers at his afternoon services were increasing. Berta suspected that one of Reverend Pritchard's reasons for visiting their area was her parents' frequent invitation to dine at their home before his return to Crockett. Hannah always prepared his favorite meal—fried chicken, greens, cornbread and gravy—and he never seemed to lack an appetite.

A man much admired by all who knew him, Pritchard had served the church in Crockett for as long as Berta could remember. He was a jolly, avuncular minister whose message of forgiveness and kindness was more appreciated than the harsher version of Christianity found occasionally at other churches. His large size indicated that he had missed few meals in his lifetime; he was easy with a smile and knew the names of every member of the congregation and their children.

Over dinner at her parents' home one evening early in the summer, Berta was telling the Reverend Pritchard about her interest in teaching young children to read and how she longed to open a school for local youngsters. That conversation led to another regarding the need for education for children in the Daly's area as none was presently available. It was then that the Reverend Pritchard suggested that the church building would be an appropriate location for such a school, as the facility went unused several days of the week.

On another of his visits, the conversation had included comments about the handiwork that she and Anna Jane undertook to amuse themselves and to provide attractive items for their household use. Much to Berta's chagrin, the Reverend Pritchard brought up the episode between Oscar and Jencks, which he found entertaining, and wondered if Berta had made any more clothing for those children. In deference to her father's warning, she had not. Nor was she planning to in the future. Major Smith had used that occasion to once again emphasize to Berta the importance of never leaving home alone; hence, Oscar's main duty had become driving her to Daly's and to other destinations when needed. This wasn't something she regretted; riding in the carriage would allow her to wear better clothes to school in place of riding attire.

Now, with summer nearly gone, Berta eagerly anticipated the start of school in one week. First, she wondered what to wear the first day of classes and decided that since the students at Fairfield College were expected to dress nicely for class, she would continue that tradition at her own school. Presenting herself neatly would establish a level of decorum for the classroom that she would expect to be reflected in the efforts of the students. She wondered briefly if the Jencks children would attend her school but was not surprised when their names did not appear on her roll.

Berta was aroused from her reverie as the carriage came to a stop at the front veranda. Hannah was there to greet them, and her broad smile indicated that she must have something special on her mind.

"Missy Berta, there was someone here to see you this afternoon," she said. "You must have passed him on the road."

"Who might be paying a visit on such a warm afternoon?" Berta asked, stepping out of the carriage.

The clerk from the store at Daly's had just departed after delivering a letter addressed to her. Glancing at the letter, Berta saw that it was from Captain John Wootters, and she felt a sudden knot of anticipation in her chest. She opened it and read:

My dear Miss Smith, your friend and obedient admirer has returned to Houston County from his duties and would beseech you to grant him the privilege of visiting with you at your convenience. Please reply to the undersigned by return post to the Masonic Lodge at Crockett where he will be anxiously awaiting and hoping for a favorable response. Your humble and expectant friend, Cap't. J. Wootters.

As Hannah suspected the origin of the letter, she was standing by with evident curiosity, waiting to hear the contents of the letter. Once Berta finished reading it, Hannah smiled broadly and instructed the younger woman to respond right away.

"You write him back, and I'll have Oscar take it to the post office at Daly's right this minute," she said. "Tell him that I am making the biggest batch of berry cobbler he's ever seen, so he better show up hungry."

Unable to refuse such a directive, Berta wrote back, inviting Wootters to call at the plantation the following Saturday.

If his schedule permitted, she wrote, he would be welcome to stay for supper and that the entire Smith family would look forward to his visit.

SPRING 1866
HOUSTON COUNTY, TEXAS

THE EARLY SPRING MORNINGS were still cool, but soon after the sun rose above the treetops, the air turned sultry. Oscar knew this meant that catfish would rise to the surface from the depths of the lake at Elkhart Creek. With some fat pork belly for bait tucked into his basket, he was eager to hook a giant fish that was likely to be found near his favorite fishing spot. He had already driven Miss Berta to the school at the church in Daly's and was now on his way to the lake. For a brief moment, he considered driving to the nearby town of Augusta, which he had never visited. But as Augusta was regarded among freedmen as a place best avoided, the desire to go fishing won out.

After leaving the church, he turned down a road along the creek that led to the lake. Oscar smiled to himself as the carriage rumbled toward the water. One who had never been a slave could not appreciate the excitement of being able to decide on their own what they wanted to do on a particular day. His only responsibility was to drive Miss Berta and her mother whenever they needed to be away from the plantation. In return for this service, Major Smith had deeded him the homesite at Cedar Branch, where he and Hannah lived. While Berta was teaching her class, he was able to do whatever pleased him, and nothing interested him more than trying to catch that big fish. He had seen its back and fins rising above the waterline and thought it must be as long as a man is tall.

Oscar often marveled that slavery had really, finally ended; it was something he and his forbearers had been born into and from which they had all prayed for deliverance. That he could move about at will and that his descendants would choose the direction of their own lives filled him with a wondrous new sense of happiness. While some of the younger men in the Cedar Branch community had left for parts unknown, he was thankful that their son, Edgar, had decided to stay close to home and work in the fields that Major Smith had sold to him.

Major Smith had even agreed to help Edgar acquire an education in the future, if and when such an opportunity became available. Edgar had expressed an interest in preaching the gospel and realized that his effectiveness would be greater with the appropriate training. In the meantime, under Berta's tutelage and with Hannah's help, he was learning to read. Oscar was proud that his son had such lofty aspirations and the will to work for them.

Oscar and Hannah's desire to remain close to home surprised nobody, as Hannah had occasionally said that she wanted to be laid to rest near their son, Ossie. That desire was further encouraged by rumors that bands of hostile Ku Klux Klansmen had been seen throughout the area. These white men had been known to kill unsuspecting freedmen under the cover of night, and their white-hooded garments, used as disguises, made them even more terrifying. Oscar did not want to do anything that would attract their attention; appearing in an unfamiliar place like Augusta might do just that.

As he continued towards the lake, Oscar noted that the creek was somewhat higher than expected as they had received more rain this spring than usual. Although it would be much lower later in the summer, the creek always had some flowing water. Several miles below Daly's, the creek formed a lake before continuing on to the Trinity River about half the distance to Crockett.

The lakeshore was partially obscured by dense grapevines that grew in profusion near the water. There were trails made by deer and other animals leading to the lake so that one could easily reach its banks. This was widely known as an excellent fishing spot, and local people could often be found there trying to lure the resident catfish to the water's surface. In April and May, the bushes that protected the shoreline provided large quantities of a reddish fruit that women from the area would turn into mayhaw jelly. As he neared the lake, he noted that the crop had not been completely harvested. If the fish weren't biting, he would instead gather fruit for the jelly and berries for future cobblers.

Oscar was very content to spend the remainder of his days with Hannah in their home. He realized that without an education, one's prospects were very limited unless he had skill in a craft or the ability to learn one. The demand for able-bodied workers was said to be great, and a number of the younger freedmen had already left for larger towns. While he remained concerned about what the future held in store for that younger generation, he knew that at least it could be the potential for a better life. He also knew that it might hold the prospect of trouble for which many were unprepared.

As the sun passed the noon hour, Oscar walked the short distance back to the carriage. He had left it not far from the lake, where the road ended and became a narrow trail. The large catfish had not appeared, but he was pleased nonetheless with the number of fish he had caught. These and a basket of berries represented a good day's effort, and he whistled merrily to the horses as they made their way back to Daly's.

Once there, he found a shady spot beside the general store near the church building. It was here that he usually stopped the carriage to wait for Berta to finish her work in the school room. As he sat there recalling his successful day, who did he see walking in his direction but Jencks, with a scowl on his face sour enough to curdle milk. Oscar sat still and quiet as Jencks walked by, grateful that the man had not stopped to torment or provoke him. Minutes later, Berta emerged from the church, and he urged his team forward. After helping her into the carriage, he proudly showed off the abundance of mayhaw berries and the good catch of fish; Berta would later recall Oscar saying that he thought he had enough berries for Hannah to make as much cobbler as Captain Wootters might want.

The return trip to the plantation was most pleasant, as a cool breeze tempered the heat of the afternoon sun. As she considered the abundance of fish and berries, Berta wondered if John Wootters enjoyed visiting with her as much as he enjoyed Hannah's cobbler. The thought of his occasional visits made her smile, as it had been apparent from their conversations that his agricultural and business ventures were proving both satisfying and successful; and the idea of some future visit from him awakened in her a sense of excitement. She also reasoned that if the prospects of berry cobbler would tempt him to come more often, she would ask Hannah to show her how to make the dessert on her own.

———————

Late that afternoon, Anna Jane and Berta were sitting on the front veranda discussing the day's activities, and knitting socks and sweaters for the new Dorcas Aid Society to distribute to families in need of winter clothing. This effort had been particularly pleasing to Reverend Pritchard, as there were many children who would need warm clothing. The women of the church in both Crockett and in Daly's had responded enthusiastically to his request for help with the knitting. Berta cherished this time as it gave her the opportunity to visit with her mother for long periods, which had been less frequent when she was at college.

As they spoke of Berta's teaching and other news, Anna Jane expressed concern that her daughter's piano skills were suffering from a lack of practice. Berta spent more time preparing for class and visiting with her mother, and her music was being neglected as a result.

"It's true that I haven't been playing the piano as much as in the past, but unless I am learning new pieces, I don't need to spend as much time playing as I did at college," Berta admitted. "The time I spend with you is very important to me, and I wouldn't want to exchange it for any other pastime."

"Have you considered what you want to do in the future with your music?" Anna Jane asked. "Your father and I had always imagined that you would want to study at one of the conservatories or colleges in the East when the war was over. You really do have skills that all of us, especially your instructors, feel should be nurtured."

Berta blushed at the compliment. She wanted to correct her mother's statement by adding that she wouldn't attribute her musical efforts to inherent skills; it was only after hours of practice that these so-called skills were evident.

"I am thankful that I can create music from my excellent instrument, and doing so is one of my greatest pleasures," Berta said carefully. "I have asked God to guide my thoughts about these matters, and I feel in my heart that He has opened other opportunities that make it difficult to know what is the correct path to pursue. I feel that He wants me to also use what skills I have to teach people who wish to learn."

Anna Jane smiled at her daughter and marveled at how her last child seemed to have suddenly grown into a thoughtful young woman. As she had so often expressed, she could only hope that she would live long enough to see the story of Berta's life continue to unfold.

"In the past year, I have also learned that my heart has great concern for my friend Captain Wootters," Berta continued. "He is in the process of establishing future directions for his life, and I want to be available to help him if I'm able."

At that, both women stopped their knitting and looked at each other, as though seeking some unspoken meaning in Berta's words. She cleared her throat and told her mother that, happily, she did not think leaving home and her family was part of God's plan for now. It did not seem, she said, the best path to follow.

"Berta, my dear child, you are truly a thoughtful and spirit-filled young lady, and your father and I respect your ideas and plans greatly," Anna Jane said. "Of course, I am delighted that you want to remain near us, but I do not want my own selfish desires to stand in the way of your dreams. Tell me, are Hannah's suspicions correct? Has your interest in Mr. Wootters progressed beyond friendship to love?"

At those words, Berta's tendency to blush betrayed her.

"Mr. Wootters has been away for so long that I am not certain we really know each other," Berta said, choosing her words carefully. "It makes me very happy to see him back in Texas and showing evidence of recovering from his injury. But although my heart holds him in a very special place, my mind has yet to understand the course his life will take. I am confident that he will find the correct path for his future; it is possible that such a future may include the two of us, but right now I just don't know."

"You have been such a blessing to all of us," Anna Jane said, hugging her daughter. "I will also pray for both you and Mr. Wootters in your understanding of these matters."

The sun had sunk below the tree line, and evening shadows had overtaken the veranda. As it was too dark to continue sewing, Berta and her mother moved indoors to the music room to look for the sheet music of a scherzo that Berta had not played in some time. Anna Jane seemed more energetic than usual and was helping sort through the pages of music with great enthusiasm. There was a knock on the door, and Hannah entered, announcing that a visitor had arrived.

"Hannah, you know Major Smith won't return from Crockett until this time tomorrow," Anna Jane said. "Who is it that is surprising us with the visit?"

"It's that young deputy sheriff who we see sometimes down at the store at Daly's," Hannah answered. "You'll know who I mean. He's the one who looks too young to actually be a deputy."

"Please show him in, and I will explain that he must wait until tomorrow to see Major Smith, unless he goes to Crockett before then."

In a moment Hannah returned, followed by the deputy. He had forgotten to remove his hat and was fidgeting nervously. When he entered the parlor, Anna Jane stood up and extended her hand; that seemed to put the young man somewhat at ease. He jerked his hand back abruptly and took off his hat, as if suddenly remembering his manners.

"Hannah tells me that you are here to see Major Smith," Anna Jane said. "I am sorry that he isn't here this evening, but if you are going to Crockett you may see him. He is there on business. but he should return tomorrow if you want to wait and see him then."

The deputy stammered as he tried to answer Anna Jane, who was smiling somewhat impatiently. "I-I-I would rather speak to y-y-you in confidence i-i-if that is possible," he said.

"Of course," she said, turning to Hannah. "Why don't you finish setting the table, and we will be through here very soon, I am sure. Deputy, do you mind if my daughter hears what you have to say as she may remember more clearly than I?" The deputy nodded in agreement and shuffled his feet as Hannah closed the door behind her.

"Now, what brings you to our home on such an unexpected visit? I hope nothing is amiss."

"I am here because of a most disturbing situation, Mrs. Smith, and we need your help in resolving it," he said. "A man named Jencks from the Daly's area has filed a complaint. He is well known to law enforcement, as he has often been the cause of controversy and an occasional resident in the county jail in Crockett. He has just this afternoon made an accusation against the freedman named Oscar who lives on this plantation."

"What on earth could cause that devil Jencks to complain about anything except his own rudeness?" Berta gasped, forgetting herself.

Taken aback by the young woman's direct manner, the deputy told them that Jencks claimed the new calf from his black and white cow was with the herd yesterday but today had disappeared. He believed that Oscar had taken it because he had seen Oscar riding down the road to the Elkhart Creek lake that day. The road to the lake ran by his property line, and he hadn't seen anyone else in the area. Moreover, he planned to file a complaint stating exactly that in Crockett; Oscar would be required to come to town to answer the charge.

"If you know anything about this situation, you may be able to help resolve it," the deputy said.

"How could Oscar possibly have taken a calf from that horrible Jencks?" Berta said, her face flush with anger. "After he left me at the Daly's church for my school class, he went to the lake to fish and gather berries, and before returning to our plantation he waited at the church building to bring me back home. If he had a dead calf in the carriage I certainly would have seen it and even more so if it had been alive!

I don't think Judge Gossett or any other reasonable person will think Oscar is the culprit."

The deputy continued to fidget with his hat, as if embarrassed. He hadn't wanted to bring this news to Smith Landing plantation, but there were procedures, and they had to be followed. He agreed with Berta the accusation was likely groundless, and urged both women to provide any information they could to help resolve the matter quickly.

"I will be in Crockett tomorrow, and hopefully the situation can be dismissed quickly," he said.

With raised eyebrows, Anna Jane thanked him for his visit and his advice, and asked him to relay the message to Major Smith if he happened to run into him in Crockett that evening.

"I might add that Oscar and Hannah, as well as this family, will be having catfish for supper," she said. "I assure you there is no likelihood that we will be having veal."

After the deputy made his exit, Berta and Anna Jane agreed that under no circumstances should Oscar leave the security of the plantation and that legal measures would have to be forthcoming from the County Court before the deputy would be re-admitted to the property. Moreover, Oscar and Hannah did not need to be told of the visit until Major Smith could advise them. Berta resolved to have Edgar drive Hannah and her to Crockett the next day so she could inform her father of the situation and hopefully meet with Judge Gossett about the matter.

———————

After a restless night, Berta arose early and informed Hannah and Edgar of her wishes. They left for Crockett shortly after breakfast. Berta had some additional plans, which she decided to not share with her mother, and as the three travelers crossed the creek at Daly's, she asked Edgar to stop at the general store. Berta asked the proprietor if he could recall any people traveling towards the lake on the previous day, any strangers he did not recognize. Regrettably, the answer was no.

She thanked him and asked Edgar to then proceed in the direction of the lake. When asked why they were taking this detour, she said that she wanted to see the spot where Oscar thought a certain monstrous catfish was hiding out.

Hannah and Edgar silently thought that this was a most unusual request but proceeded as Berta directed. It was easy to identify the homestead property inhabited by the Jencks family. Beyond it was wooded land unclaimed and uninhabited by any settlers in the area. A considerable amount of Houston County was unclaimed land; from the road the area did not look very amenable to agriculture in Berta's eyes.

Berta had heard about this area from her brother, Lucius, who had enjoyed many hours of exploring the sand canyon. About a mile past the boundary stream, Berta was startled by the raucous cries of a flock of ravens. An upward glance revealed a similar number of buzzards circling. Noting the number of birds, she asked Edgar to stop the carriage and wait while she and Hannah made a short foray into the wooded area. Hannah protested mildly that she was too old to venture into the woods, but decided that she had better accompany her younger charge, just to keep her out of trouble.

A short distance later, the two women came upon a clearing and saw the beginning of a washed out sand formation. Within one hundred yards was a small canyon, and on coming to the canyon rim, Berta saw something that truly offended her sensibilities.

There in the bottom of the canyon about thirty feet down were the remains of a black and white calf, with at least twenty turkey vultures, also known as buzzards, feasting on the remains. An equal number of ravens perched further back were adding their cries of disdain.

"Oh Hannah, I have never seen such a horrible sight," Berta cried out. "That poor calf must have gotten too close to the edge and fallen to its death. Let's go now as I have an unusual request to make of Edgar."

Hannah, of course, had no idea why this discovery startled her young friend, whose face was now nearly the same shade of red as her hair. On returning to the carriage, Berta made a request of Edgar that gave Hannah pause. What she wanted was for Edgar to follow the trail to the calf's carcass, cut off its tail and bring it back to the carriage.

Hannah was too stunned to speak, much less to inquire as to the purpose of this bizarre request. She sat silently in the carriage and prayed that Berta hadn't completely lost her mind and that if she had, the loss was only temporary. After Edgar returned, tail in hand, the trio proceeded to Crocket.

On arriving in town, Berta found her father at the office of Judge Gossett, where they were discussing matters related to the Masonic lodge.

"What a surprise to see you here at the Court House when I didn't even expect you to be in Crockett today!" Major Smith said. "What is the occasion of your visit?"

Berta told him about the unexpected visit from one of the sheriff's deputies, the missing calf and Jencks' accusation, which was preposterous because Oscar was the last person on Earth who would steal anything, especially a calf. She had come to Crockett to counsel with her father and Judge Gossett, and felt fortunate to have found them together in the same place. She planned to give the sheriff a thorough explanation of what she thought had actually happened. Major Smith agreed that Oscar was most certainly not guilty, but that the accusation alone could make his life more difficult.

Gossett, who had been sitting quietly, listening to the conversation and thoughtfully stroking his ample chin, nodded.

"This could be a problem for Oscar, especially if there was a jury trial involved. Fair trials for freedmen like Oscar may be difficult to obtain in our present circumstance," he said. "The best alternative for Oscar would be to avoid any legal proceedings at all by discussing this with the sheriff."

Major Smith looked over at his daughter to find her smiling. "Berta, you seem happier than I would expect, considering the gravity of this situation."

"That's because there is more to the story than I have told you," she said, her dimples deepening. "I decided to investigate with Hannah, and we found the calf."

Berta then proceeded to tell her father and Judge Gossett about how she and Hannah had seen the birds, followed them and eventually found what remained of the calf.

"There wasn't much left of the poor beast, but I did ask Edgar to fetch me the tail so I could show it to you and the sheriff when I told him my story," she said. "The evidence is still in the carriage as I didn't think it appropriate to bring it into such a proper building as this."

"Young lady, you have very likely saved your man Oscar's hide," Judge Gossett exclaimed. "It would appear that neither Jencks nor the deputy spent much time looking for the calf, when blaming Oscar was such an easy remedy." He urged her to go with her father to the sheriff's office and explain what had happened. And when they were finished, they were to report back to Judge Gossett.

"Your bravery is remarkable for one so gentle-appearing," the judge said "But celebrating your accomplishment would be unwise."

Berta and her father thanked him for his advice and set off to find the sheriff's office.

——————————

It took some time, but Berta relayed the true story of the "stolen" calf, much to the surprise and consternation of the sheriff and the deputies present in his office. By the time she finished, she was reassured that no charges would be filed against Oscar. The sheriff also supported concerns expressed by Judge Gossett for Berta's safety in this matter, while Major Smith pointed out that he had expressed such warnings in the past.

As they were returning to Smith Landing Plantation, Hannah and Edgar were very curious about the tail of the deceased calf. Major Smith explained what had happened, warning them that any interaction with Jencks or others like him was best avoided. Thanks to Berta's bravery and initiative, a situation potentially dangerous for Oscar had been avoided.

——————————

Two weeks later, John Wootters attended a Masonic lodge function where he encountered Judge Gossett. The older man asked about Berta, as he was aware of their friendship, and Wootters told him of her various educational activities and charitable efforts as well as her devotion to her family. The judge, in turn, revealed the story of the calf's tail and cautioned Wootters that this information was not for public consumption for fear of some retaliation from Jencks.

For the first time, it dawned on Wootters that residing alongside Berta's gentle mind and spirit were an iron will and formidable sense of duty; she was indeed a match for any imaginable hardship or circumstance. In that moment of realization, he understood that the opportunity to spend the rest of his life with her might be the greatest single blessing God could ever bestow on him. He would pray that his own mind and spirit would continue healing so that he could be worthy of such a companion.

AUTUMN 1866
SMITH LANDING PLANTATION

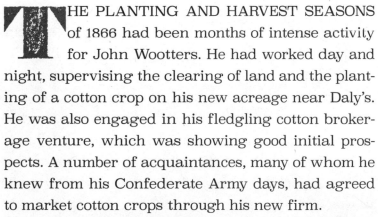

THE PLANTING AND HARVEST SEASONS of 1866 had been months of intense activity for John Wootters. He had worked day and night, supervising the clearing of land and the planting of a cotton crop on his new acreage near Daly's. He was also engaged in his fledgling cotton brokerage venture, which was showing good initial prospects. A number of acquaintances, many of whom he knew from his Confederate Army days, had agreed to market cotton crops through his new firm.

Houston County was home to many survivors of the war who, as former comrades-in-arms, were a close-knit group. Some had served in Hood's Brigade, including three of his best friends: Willie Wall and the Aldrich brothers, Gus and Colin. Lieutenant Wall had been one of the original officers of the Crockett Southrons and one of its first casualties. A severe hand wound at Gaines' Mill in 1862 had resulted in the loss of a thumb. That had ended his active military career, but his health and enthusiasm for life had apparently made a full recovery. Wootters had recently learned that Will and Miss Nettie Cooper were to marry on December 6th.[81] On learning that he would be asked to participate in the ceremony, Wootters promised himself that he would purchase a dress suit as soon as he was able.

As for the Aldrich brothers, Gus had been wounded in the battles of Gettysburg and Chickamauga but had recovered enough to remain active in their company. He served as commander of the dwindling Crockett Southrons after John was unable to continue, and was present at Appomattox when General Lee surrendered. Gus' younger brother Colin, who had served as mess sergeant for the Crockett Southrons, was one of the few men of their company to not be injured throughout the war. He quickly readjusted to civilian life and had recently married Miss Betty Kyle, whose family lived in Augusta.[82]

Gus and John Wootters had recently attended a social event at the home of Dr. Francis Lewis Meriwether and his wife, Ethalinda. They were a well-regarded couple, and they seemed to enjoy hosting parties at their plantation, especially for the younger, unmarried people of the area. These socials were characterized by piano music, often provided by Dr. Meriwether and Ethalinda, with enthusiastic singing and dancing. Their daughters, Martha and Frances, were

[81] *History of Houston County, p. 609.*
[82] *Ibid. p. 226.*

friends of Berta and had also attended the Fairfield Female College.[83]

When Wootters attended these events, he would notice that Berta was a vivacious and beautiful part of the celebrations. He would feel a twinge of irritation to see her surrounded by friends, as he knew that people were drawn by her radiant smile and inclusive nature. He even suspected that he was slightly jealous when those friends included overly attentive young men. Wootters made a special effort to be present at these gatherings.

Even so, agricultural activities and business ventures occupied much of his time and efforts, the latter requiring him to travel to plantations and communities in the area where there were prospects for his brokerage firm.[84] The management of his property near Daly's had benefitted from Major Smith's frequent and insightful advice and from the opportunity to employ freedmen living in the Cedar Branch community.

During the summer and early autumn, he visited the Smith plantation as often as possible to consult with Major Smith and to visit Berta. He never turned down an invitation to stay for supper. The meals provided by Hannah and Addie, a daughter of Hannah's who had grown old enough to help with the cooking, were delicious, and certainly much better than what he could provide for himself. Although Wootters had erected a small cottage on his property, it was far from commodious. The expansion of these living quarters to a more developed home would be a project for the winter months. He did not want to delay this activity. If he

[83] *Ibid. p. 472–73.*
[84] *Appendix I. Item 8. Letter from Berta Smith to John Wootters.*

were ever able to persuade Berta to marry him, he needed to offer her better accommodations.

In late October, after the final harvest welcomed the first chill of the season, Berta received a letter from John Wootters that made her smile. Unlike the usual brief notes she was used to receiving, this carefully written missive formally requested an afternoon visit to her home and indicated that he would be anxiously hoping for a welcoming reply. She informed Hannah and Anna Jane of the request.

"This is an unusual note from Captain Wootters," she said, her face lighting up with a smile. "Now that he has completed his successful harvest, he must want to adopt the airs of a gentleman planter with such a formal request!"

"You know he has something more on his mind than an extra helping of berry cobbler," Hannah shook her finger at the younger woman. "I sure hope you plan to make him welcome!"

"Truly, Berta, your father and I want him to feel very much at home here, and I am sure that you will write him to accept his visit," Anna Jane was also smiling. "I know that he and your father have had much to discuss in recent months, and I suspect that he may have something to ask about other than the preparation of cotton seedlings."

In truth, Anna Jane knew that her husband had already had a conversation with Wootters about a marriage proposal and had advised him that such a marriage would certainly have their blessing. He had also told the young suitor that his daughter had very definite ideas and a mind of her own, and that her parents' influence might not carry much weight.

Berta discussed the anticipated visit with Hannah and Oscar as she wanted to welcome her guest with more gentility than usual. Hannah would provide his favorite items for dinner, but dessert would be a berry cobbler prepared by Berta. It was one of the many skills she'd acquired during the summer months.

Although both Hannah and her mother had suggested that Captain Wootters was likely planning to propose marriage, Berta wasn't convinced about the purpose of his visit; she was even less certain about her response. After all, she had spent only brief intervals with him in recent months, and those had usually been on his visits to discuss his cotton farming with her father or at the occasional social event.

She had noted, however, that his demeanor had changed over the past year. Wootters had become more like the cheerful, optimistic person she remembered from previous years, and their friends all seemed to hold him in high regard. He was clearly a leader among the young people in their circle of acquaintances. Berta had also heard about his concern for the well-being of his former comrades and the efforts he devoted to helping them recover, both physically and spiritually, from the war.

Although she had long been aware of the love that she had for him in her heart, she was reassured by the gradual reconciliation of her mind to this idea that he was, indeed, the one whom God had provided to be her mate. Even so, it did occur to her that he may have a very different purpose for this visit. What if he merely wanted to celebrate the successful completion of his first year as a planter? What if he had other plans for his life other than staying in their community? She decided that trying to predict a life for the two of them was beyond her and that she could only rely on the Lord to answer her questions and provide directions for their lives.

As the day of Captain Wootters' visit neared, Berta made certain that the event would be a memorable one, whatever its purpose. The front parlor, which doubled as her music room, was suitably arranged and decorated with the last blooms of the year from Berta's special rose bush. She herself would be wearing an elegant dress and playing her favorite piano music. The hallway, dining room and parlor would be cheerfully illuminated by an extra supply of candles to be lighted at the appropriate time. She would welcome her guest and have time to visit with him before her parents joined them at the dinner hour.

As she was reviewing the evening's arrangements in her mind, Berta sat at the piano playing the gentle notes of *"Für Elise."* The late afternoon sun shone through the pine trees and into the windows, illuminating the sheet music on her piano stand. It reminded her that the piano and her attempts to produce music had been one of her greatest pleasures in life.

A slight breeze fluttered the curtains, and she heard a faint sound, a distant honking that could only be a flock of geese making its way from the distant north to their winter home in Texas. She felt her throat tighten with emotion as she was reminded that the God who directed those creatures and their companions on vast migrations also directed her own life's journey. At that very moment, she was certain that John Wootters was the person with whom she was meant to spend her life.

A soft knock on the door brought her back to the present. It was Oscar.

"Miss Berta, you have a guest," he said. "I believe you are expecting him."

Berta stood up quickly, perhaps too quickly because she felt a rush of faintness and had to hold onto the piano. John Wootters walked into the room behind Oscar.

"Miss Smith, I hope we didn't disturb you as I may be a bit earlier than you had been expecting."

"No, I was just daydreaming, and the sound of wild geese passing by aroused a bit of unexpected melancholy," Berta shook her head. "I am so pleased that you are here. I hope everyone has made you feel welcome."

"Indeed they have," he smiled. "Edgar has taken my horse to the stable where he will be glad to have some much needed rest. We have had a busy week, and he has covered more miles than he would prefer."

As she sat back on her piano bench, Berta found herself looking up into the most gentle and caring expression she could have imagined.

"Please, Captain Wootters, won't you sit down?" she motioned to a chair in the sitting area. "Would you like some tea? Oscar will be happy to bring some. Yes? Then please tell me what you have been doing and how you are feeling now that the harvest is completed." Berta covered her agitation with conversation. She stood up and followed her guest to a pair of chairs across the room.

With an elegant bow, Wootters offered her a bouquet of autumn flowers.

"I have brought you some wildflowers, but I fear that they are too rustic to adorn such an elegant room as this," he said. "They could not add to the roses that you have arranged."

"You are very kind to say such things," Berta said. "But I am sure that these will be the last rose blossoms of the season and what you have brought will be a very nice addition to the décor."

Berta looked more closely at her guest. He wore a gray army uniform, although it seemed much newer than his usual attire, and his beard was neatly trimmed. She thought he exuded maturity and confidence, which could have been intimidating except that his eyes and smile radiated the enthusiasm of youth.

Oscar entered the room with the tea service, which he placed on the low table beside the chairs, and she asked him to place the flowers from Wootters in a suitable vase on the dining table.

"I hope you are planning to dine with us this evening, Captain Wootters," she said. "My parents and I will be very disappointed if you have other plans."

"Hannah will insist that Captain Wootters stay, as she has already set a place for him," Oscar said. Berta noted that he looked elegant in his suit; she was very pleased with his genteel presentation of the tea set.

"I will be honored to stay for dinner," Wootters said. "I can think of no greater pleasure than sharing a meal with you and your parents in your lovely home."

He noticed that Berta was wearing a white, frilly skirt, enhanced by petticoats, with a blue bodice and a white lace collar. Her red hair was adorned by a blue ribbon. She was, in his mind, the picture of beauty.

"Miss Smith, you have never looked lovelier," he said. "That blue ribbon, is it the same one I helped you select some years ago when we first met at my uncle's store?"

"Thank you for your compliments," Berta said, turning several shades of pink. "But we have obtained new ribbons in the past five years. I certainly remember our first meeting, however, as you made an encouraging remark about my piano playing. Your kind words then may have been responsible for my continuing efforts to improve my technique."

"You were very skilled then, but the level of your expertise at the graduation recital last year was truly remarkable," he said. "I have heard your parents mention the possibility of you seeking further training at prestigious institutions in the east. Does that interest you?"

Berta noticed that with that question, Wootters' eyes reflected a certain tension that she did not understand. Perhaps he did not think she was old enough to be away from home. Not wanting to encourage that impression, Berta sat up straight as she looked directly at him.

"I have thought that travel to the great cities and conservatories of the east, or even in Europe, would be a wonderful adventure and could certainly help me achieve the full use of whatever talents I may have," she said. "At the time of my graduation I was seriously considering such a plan."

"And what have you decided?" Wootters said, leaning forward.

"Over the past year, I have become aware of different opportunities I think I must consider," she said. Wootters could see the enthusiasm in her eyes and in her face as she described for him, in some detail, her efforts at teaching reading and writing skills to the local children and to others at the Cedar Branch community. Moreover, he was not aware of the her mother's frail state and the satisfaction that Berta got from being there to help and comfort her.

The late afternoon passed quickly as she showed him some of the knitted and embroidered items that she and Anna Jane had made on behalf of the Dorcas Aid Society. She described for him her pleasure at the success of her rose gardening efforts, and he was amused at the pride she had in her ability to make a cobbler.

Their conversation was interrupted by Hannah, who came in to light the candles. It was then that Berta realized their visit had extended into the early evening hours, and she had not given her guest the opportunity to do much of the talking.

"I am sorry to have been so talkative," Berta said, feeling flustered. "I haven't given you a chance to tell me about your activities and plans for the future."

Wootters laughed. He enjoyed hearing about her activities; he was, in fact, more than pleased that she was finding life in Houston County to be so interesting and productive. His life, on the other hand, had been rather ordinary, but he was hoping that his efforts would have reasonable prospects. His land had enjoyed a much better harvest than expected, and the cotton brokerage company was growing, although it required more travel than he would have liked. It would take time for that venture to produce results, but the first year of work had seemed favorable thus far.

The sun had sunk below the horizon and the golden puffs of clouds reflected its departing rays. Candles illuminated the room with their flickering light. As she looked at her guest, Berta's eyes fell on the rose sitting behind him; it was on her piano in a slender vase at the end of the keyboard where candles would usually sit to illuminate her music. She felt somewhat overcome by the moment.

"I am very pleased to see you feeling so well and appearing as happy as one could ever hope for," she said. "Tell me about the plans for your future as this year's planting efforts have met with such success."

He wanted to further expand his farming acreage and cotton brokerage business. Over the next year, he and his partner would have their finances in order to begin accepting consignment of cotton crops. There were plans, he said, to build a railroad line to Crockett from Galveston through Houston, but it would still be several years before that could be completed. The track, which was supposed to extend to Palestine, would greatly improve the delivery of crops to the markets.

There was even talk of a new town where that line would cross the roadway between Augusta and the Trinity River. Wootters was anticipating these developments and had already bought land in the area, land that would be suitable for a house, as it was close enough to both his famlands and to the major roadways and eventually the railroad.

"It sounds as if you have made excellent plans," she said. "I am very happy for you, and from the enthusiasm in your smile, I can see that these activities have brought you much satisfaction. I have no doubt you will succeed."

"There is one matter that I have not been able to resolve," Wootters said casually. "That is my wish to share the future with the one person in the world that means more to me than any other. That person is you, Miss Berta Smith, whom I love with all my heart and mind."

Suddenly the world stopped. Berta felt as if she couldn't breathe; then everything around her seemed to spin. She could feel a sensation of heat spreading up her neck. Was she blushing, or was she simply overcome by joy? At last, she was able to catch her breath and speak.

"That particular Miss Smith has been prayerfully considering her own future," she said with a smile in her voice. "There is no name by which she would prefer to be known than Mrs. John Wootters. She has loved you with her heart for a number of years, and now her mind has reached the same happy conclusion. I could never, however, agree without the blessing of my dear parents."

Wootters, who had reached out to prevent her collapsing when she turned red, held her closely as she fell into his arms. The relief that he felt from having avoided a dreaded rejection of his proposal made him laugh aloud as he suppressed a brief urge to release a rebel yell.

"Berta, I have had such a conversation with your father and received his tentative blessing depending on your willingness. He has informed me that you have a mind of your own, and he would only agree to whatever you have already decided."

"Indeed, if I have such a mind, then it is fully made up and is very pleased to say 'yes' to your proposal," she said, as they shared gentle kisses. "I really do love you, John Wootters, and you have made me a very happy person."

Soon thereafter Hannah knocked on the parlor door and announced that Major and Mrs. Smith were seated at the dining room table and would be very pleased if Berta and Captain Wootters would join them."

When the couple entered the dining room, Major Smith arose and extended his hand in greeting to Wootters, who greeted them with a lilt in his voice.

"It is a great pleasure to be here and to have you be the first to know what is, for me, the best news imaginable," Wootters said. "Berta has accepted my proposal of marriage and made me the happiest man in the state of Texas. We would ask for your blessings on this happy circumstance."

Major Smith embraced the young man and Anna Jane clasped her arms around Berta, as both women's tears of happiness began to flow.

"I am so happy for you!" Anna Jane said. "I thank the Lord that I have lived to see this day."

Major Smith, who was overcome with emotion, wiped his eyes with a handkerchief.

"This is the happiest of days. Not only do I have a daughter, but I will also now have a son. The Lord took Lucius from me, but has given me John," he said, grasping the younger man's hand. "In honor of this occasion, I want you to have a certain horse. He is the son of Magnus, the horse that Lucius would be riding today if he were alive. I know he would want you to have him."

"I am honored by your gift," Wootters said, humbled by his future father-in-law's gesture. "As I ride him, I will always be reminded of Lucius' service and devotion to his country."

In anticipation of this announcement, the servants had gathered just around the corner and heard all that happened. Berta asked her mother to ring the bell so they could share the good news with them. On the first tinkle of the small bell, they burst into the dining room, faces beaming, and added their embraces to the celebration.

"Just as the Bible's Abigail found her King David, my own Abigail has her Captain Wootters!" Hannah exclaimed. "Praise the Lord!"

After an extended round of congratulations, Hannah's daughter Addie entered the room carrying a large platter of fried chicken and warned them cheerfully to not be too slow in beginning their meal as the dinner wouldn't stay warm for much longer. The four members of the soon-to-be-extended family sat at the dinner table where, after saying grace, they enjoyed an abundant and delicious meal.

Anna Jane seemed more vigorous than usual and eagerly engaged Berta in a discussion of the upcoming nuptials. It was determined that the wedding would be held at their plantation home and that Berta would have as her attendants

Fannie and Martha Meriwether, her friend Betty Graves and as many of The Mystic Seven as would be able to attend. John would ask his brother, Major James Wootters, and his comrades from the Crockett Southrons, especially Captain Wall and Lieutenant Aldrich, to be with him for the ceremony. His sister and her family and James Wootters' wife and children would also be part of the celebration.

Although Captain Wootters wanted to marry in the next few weeks, it was agreed that they would wait until after Christmas. That time would also give him the opportunity to further the construction of his new home, where the couple would eventually live. They would ask the minister from Crockett, Reverend Pritchard, to perform the ceremony.

Once the meal was over and Berta had been complimented on the berry cobbler, Anna Jane excused herself and went to bed. The excitement of the evening had taken its toll on her stamina. Major Smith agreed that it had been one of the most eventful days he could remember and assisted her upstairs.

As Hannah and Addie cleared the table, Berta and Captain Wootters retired to the front veranda, where the cooling breeze welcomed them. They sat holding hands on the porch swing. Berta was reminded of the many times she had enjoyed similar peaceful moments. Things would be different from now on; peaceful still, but on a different course. She realized that her life had taken a fork in the road that would be the most important decision she had ever made.

Would she regret not pursuing musical opportunities and expanding her experiences with distant travel? What would be the future of her homeland as it faced the uncertainty of becoming a new society? She silently thanked God for having answered so many of her prayers, and she knew she had made the right decision.

Berta excused herself as she got up from the porch swing and went into the music room. Taking the rose from the vase on her piano, she returned to the veranda and after a gentle kiss she offered it to her future husband.

"Take this, John, it's for you," she said. "It is my rose of love, and it has finally bloomed."

EPILOGUE

THE WEDDING ON JANUARY 17, 1867, concluded my story. However, this event began the life journey of Berta Smith Wootters and Captain John Henry Wootters and their family. The Wootters had seven children; their first child, John Smith Wootters, was born on October 3, 1870, at Smith Landing Plantation, and was followed by two girls, both of whom died in infancy. In 1877, the family moved to Crockett, which would be their home for the rest of their lives and where their subsequent children were born. These included daughters Ethel (1877), Lucia (1879), Frances (1883) and a son, Leon Blum Wootters (1886). It has been suggested that the need for better educational opportunities for their children was a factor in their move to the county seat.

John Smith Wootters, their first born, attended the University of Texas and received his M.D. degree from Tulane University in 1891. He also studied at the Jefferson Medical College in Philadelphia and received another degree in 1892. Dr. Wootters practiced medicine in Crockett for fifty-eight years until shortly before his death on October 23, 1950 at the age of eighty.

The oldest surviving daughter, Ethel, studied piano and voice during her college education at North Texas Female College and Conservatory of Music in Sherman, Texas.[85] This institution was preeminent in fine arts and musical education, and attracted many distinguished teachers from Europe. Ethel gained recognition for her performance at the World's Fair—the Columbian Exposition in Chicago—in 1893. Two years later, she received two certificates of proficiency from the president of the college, Lucy Kidd-Key.

In 1909, Ethel married Willis Higginbotham and moved to Stephenville, Texas, which was his family's home. There, she taught piano at Tarleton College, now known as Tarleton State University, which has been part of the Texas A&M University System since 1917. The school continues to offer educational opportunities in piano and other musical performance. After the death of Mr. Higginbotham, she returned to Crockett where she taught music until a few years before her death in 1973 at the age of ninety-six.

The second daughter, Lucia, attended the University of Texas and married James H. Painter, an attorney who practiced law in Galveston, Crockett and Houston. The youngest daughter, Frances, attended Hollins College in Virginia

[85] Wolz, L. "Kidd-Key College," Handbook of Texas Online.

and, on graduating, became the first student from west of the Mississippi River to receive the medal for piano performance. She moved to Lufkin, Texas, at the urging of her Hollins classmate, Lillian Denman, and obtained a certification to teach in Texas public schools. While teaching music in Lufkin, she met her future husband, Dr. Peyton R. Denman, her former classmate's older brother. Once married, Dr. and Mrs. Denman moved to Houston, where they lived for the remainder of their lives.

The youngest child of Berta and John Wootters, Leon Blum Wootters, graduated from Baylor University in 1909 and became a banker in Santa Fe, New Mexico, and in Houston.

Although the availability of educational opportunities for their children was certainly a factor in the family's move to Crockett, it is likely that business factors were also a consideration. In the first few years after the Civil War, due to the great demand for cotton and the fortunate relationships with the population of freedmen in the area, both Captain Wootters and Major Smith prospered in their agricultural activities, and Wootters' brokerage business seemed to have a bright future.

The agricultural economy in Texas prospered; in 1870, the price of cotton and the value of the crop were the highest that would be recorded for the next 140 years. The arrival of the Houston and Great Northern Railroad in 1872 proved to be an economic boost for Houston County. This railroad offered passenger and freight transport between Houston and Crockett via the town of New Waverly. In 1873, the line was extended through Grapeland to Palestine, Texas, which was a center for more widespread rail service. The availability of dependable transportation was a boon to cotton production in the area and contributed greatly to its prosperity.[86] The town of Grapeland, Texas, located between Crockett and Palestine where the road crossed from Augusta to the Trinity River, was developed with the arrival of the railroad in Houston County; and Wootters was an early property owner in the town. Grapeland was so named due to the profusion of wild grapevines in the area. That fruit, and the mayhaw jelly into which it was made, was a great favorite of the local residents.[87]

This economic activity and prosperity did not reach the public sector for a number of years after the Civil War, as the tax base for public services had been decimated. It would be several years before local communities recovered enough to provide both effective law enforcement and educational opportunities. Although the idea of public education had been discussed since the establishment of the Republic of Texas, such institutions didn't yet exist at the end of the war.

The economy of rural Texas, as throughout the South, was moribund, and education for the children was not at the top of the priority list. With the elimination of slavery, a major component of the tax base for both the state and counties was also eliminated. Slaves had constituted more than half of the taxable property and accounted for 36 percent of the total tax assessment. Farm values in Houston County would fall from over $1.1 million in 1860 to $57,000 in 1870.[88] Road improvements that had, in the past, been undertaken by slave labor (which the plantation owners were required to provide as an in-kind assessment) became an unaffordable luxury.

In March 1865, the Federal Congress established the Bureau of Refugees, Freedmen, and Abandoned Lands, known as the

[86] Young, N.B. "Houston and Great Northern Railroad," Handbook of Texas Online.
[87] Bishop, E. "Houston County," Handbook of Texas Online.
[88] Campbell, R.B. "An Empire for Slavery: the peculiar institution in Texas, 1821–1865."

Freedmen's Bureau. It was led by a national commissioner, Union Army General Oliver Otis Howard, who appointed assistants to head the program in states that had a large population of former slaves. The Bureau in Texas was led initially by Edgar M. Gregory; his position was considered to be the "post of greatest peril," as the program faced considerable hostility from some of the state's white citizens.

Those who supported the program believed that long-term protection of the freedmen depended on the establishment of a free agricultural labor system and of schools to help prepare them to function in a literate society.[89] This program, which began in January 1866 with sixteen schools, ten teachers, and 1,041 students, had within six months expanded to ninety schools, forty-three teachers and 4,590 students, both children and adults.

The other major function of the Bureau was the supervision of labor contracts; that function soon evolved into a military court system handling legal issues. However, the Bureau's most widely recognized achievements were in the field of education: by the end of 1865, more than 90,000 former slaves were enrolled in schools across the Southland.[90]

Although the 1870s began on a positive note for the agricultural economy in Houston County, 1873 marked the beginning of the worst economic depression to date in the U. S. and around the world, although the Great Depression of 1929 would surpass it. There were a number of factors leading to this circumstance, referred to as the "Panic of 1873" and the subsequent "Long Depression," which in some European markets persisted until 1896.[91]

[89] Harper, C. "Freedman's Bureau," Handbook of Texas Online.
[90] McPherson, J.M. "The Abolitionist Legacy: From Reconstruction to the NAACP." (1975)
[91] Moseley, F. "Depression of 1873-1879." In Glasner and Cooley, eds. Business Cycles and Depressions: An Encyclopedia.

This particular economic disaster can be traced to the collapse of the Vienna Stock Exchange on Black Friday, May 9, 1873. Inflationary factors related to the large war debt incurred by France for reparations resulting from the Franco-Prussian War caused a speculative boom in central European financial markets.

The Panic began in the U.S. on September 18, 1873 with the failure of Jay Cooke and Company, which had incurred large amounts of debt for the Northern Pacific Railway expansion. The overbuilding of railroad facilities in the U.S. through the use of excessive debt led to the collapse of major national banks. The German Empire discontinued the use of silver to back its currency. Similar measures by the U.S., in an attempt to return to the gold standard after the Civil War, contributed to a depression in silver mining activities in the West. Ensuing high interest rates and a slowdown in the domestic money supply had a negative impact on agricultural interests, which depended greatly on the credit markets.

The value of cotton fell drastically, as the crop in 1880 was twice as large as in 1860 but had only 25 percent the value. In addition, the opening of the Suez Canal gave cotton production in Egypt and India greater access to European markets; British shipping interests took a thumping, and tariffs increased as a result. Between 1873 and 1875 in the U.S., a total of 18,000 businesses folded, while unemployment reached a staggering 14 percent.

One of the businesses that failed was the cotton brokerage firm of Duble and Wootters. With the downturn of his personal agricultural venture, it is likely that John Henry Wootters faced challenges as difficult as those he and his unit encountered with Hood's Texas Brigade ten years earlier. I do not have definite evidence of the role played by Mr.

Duble, but the obituary of Captain Wootters suggested that Wootters personally accepted the responsibility for the firm's debts and eventually satisfied his creditors without the assistance of his former partner.[92]

In later years, Wootters was actively involved with his brother in the mercantile business known as the J.C. Wootters firm. Their letterhead stated that they were a Dealer in Staple and Fancy Dry Goods, Groceries, Ready Made Clothing [including] Hardware, Saddlery, Plantation Implements and Machinery at Factory Prices. Wootters was also one of the founders of the First National Bank in Crockett, and he continued his agricultural ventures with the advice and counsel of his father-in-law, Major John Smith.

Berta Smith Wootters devoted much of her efforts towards the care and nurture of her family, including her parents. Her mother, Anna Jane Pouncey Smith, died on June 9, 1874, from complications due to her progressive disability; she was buried in a family cemetery on the Smith Landing Plantation property.[93] According to his family Bible, Major John Smith was remarried to Mrs. Margie Dailey on July 1, 1875, and they lived in the plantation home until her death in 1883 from tuberculosis. Soon thereafter, Major Smith moved to Crockett, and lived with John and Berta Wootters and their children until his death in 1890.

His obituary stated that "Major John Smith had owned one of the finest plantations in East Texas and was regarded as one of the county's most successful planters. For several years he has done nothing other than exercise supervision over some farming interests of his son-in-law, Capt. John H. Wootters. Major Smith was a gentleman after the old school

[92] *Appendix I. Item 14. Obituary of Capt. John H. Wootters.*
[93] *Appendix I. Item 11. Obituary of Anna Jane Pouncey, June 1874.*

type—highly educated, intelligent, courteous, and patriotic."[94] He was buried next to Anna Jane in their family cemetery at Smith Landing Plantation.

Berta Smith Wootters was an active member of the First Baptist Church in Crockett, and provided inspiration and leadership to the Dorcas Aid Society throughout her life. She had her oversized piano moved from Smith Landing Plantation to their home in Crockett, where she continued to both teach and perform. Captain John Wootters was also an active member of the First Baptist Church, where he served as a deacon and leader of the Sunday school. He was active in the Masonic lodge and the Hood's Brigade Association, whose yearly reunions he regularly attended throughout his lifetime.

Captain Wootters died on January 21, 1892, at the age of fifty-two after a short illness that may have been congestive heart failure. Berta Smith Wootters died unexpectedly on February 5, 1915, at sixty-seven, following an apparent myocardial infarction. She was attended in her final illness by her son, Dr. John Smith Wootters.[95] Berta and John Wootters' five surviving children all had the benefit of university educations, despite their father's untimely death when the youngest child was five years old. Their Christian faith and dependence on the direction of God's will for their lives were guiding principles for their family.

Betty Williams Graves, friend and mentor of Berta Smith, was born in 1840 and continued to live and teach in Fairfield, Texas after the end of the war. In 1870, she married Theodoric G. Jones, a distinguished lawyer and judge who had completed his education in Tennessee and practiced law in Mississippi before moving to Texas. They had one son and

[94] *Obituaries, Houston Co., TX, Ancestry.com*
[95] *Appendix I. Item 14 and Item 16. Obituaries of Captain John Wootters and Mrs. Berta Smith Wootters.*

lived in Palestine, Texas, until Judge Jones died in 1898 at the age of seventy-five.[96] Betty Graves Jones subsequently moved to Dallas where she lived until her death in 1935 at the age of ninety-five.[97]

The comrades of Captain John Wootters who returned to Houston County included his close friend Captain William B. Wall, who recovered after his injury at the battle of Gaines' Mill in 1862. He married Miss Nettie Cooper on December 6, 1866, and they had long and productive lives in Crockett. Wall was elected county judge in 1878, serving for eight years, and was elected state representative for Houston County in 1896.[98] Albert Augustus (Gus) Aldrich married Miss Josephine Coleman, but they had no surviving children. Gus was the commander of Company I of the 1st Texas Regiment following the injury to Captain John Wootters. His younger brother, Colin Aldrich, was the mess sergeant for their company and later married Miss Bettie Kyle of Augusta. Bettie died after the birth of their first child and Colin married Bettie's sister Julia. They lived in Crockett and had a large family.[99]

Hannah and Oscar Pouncey lived at the Cedar Branch community their entire lives. A daughter, Addie Pouncey, continued to work in the home of Captain and Mrs. John Wootters for many years. Her grandson, also named Edgar Pouncey, was a well-educated man and served on the Board of Trustees of the Grapeland School District with which the Cedar Branch school had affiliated in earlier years.[100] Those who maintained their ownership of the land from Smith Landing Plantation likely benefited from the discovery of oil in the Navarro oil field in that area in the 1930s.[101]

[96] Obituary, Theodoric G. Jones, Ancestry.com.
[97] Obituary, Betty Graves Jones, Ancestry.com.
[98] History of Houston County, Texas 1687–1979, p. 609.
[99] Ibid. p. 226.
[100] Ibid. p. 573.
[101] Ibid. p. 26.

To complete this story, a brief word about the piano is in order. After its move to Crockett, the piano gradually lost its ability to sustain proper tune and was replaced by more modern instruments. Because of its size, beauty and historical significance it remained at the home in Crockett until their youngest daughter, Frances Wootters Denman, brought it to Houston following her marriage to Dr. Peyton R. Denman. Despite their best efforts, the piano could never be restored to a functional musical instrument status. It was left to me, Frances' grandson, in her will when she died in 1975 because I had apparently expressed appreciation for the piano as a child while living with my grandparents during World War II. I continue to provide it a home. Thanks to the benefit of modern electronics, the piano now produces acceptable quality sounds. I enjoy hearing such works as *"Für Elise"* and *Pathetique* sonatas, although they are probably not rendered with the same sensitivity demonstrated by a young, red-haired girl one hundred and fifty years ago.

APPENDIX I

LETTERS, MILITARY RECORDS AND NEWSPAPER ITEMS IN CHRONOLOGICAL ORDER

Item 6 Confederate War Records, John H. Wootters

Item 7 Transcription of Valedictory Address Fairfield Female College, 1865

Item 8 Letter from Berta Smith to John Wootters, December 1866

Item 9 Letter from John Wootters to Berta Smith, December 1866

Item 10 Letter from Berta Smith to John Wootters, January 1867

Item 11 Obituary of Anna Jane Pouncey, June 1874

Figure 9

Item 12 Letter from John Smith to daughter, Mrs. Berta Wootters

Item 13 Obituaries of Major John Smith, Rev. J P Pritchard, Judge A. E. Gossett

Item 14 Obituary of Capt. John H. Wootters, January 1892

Item 15 Letter from Mrs. Samuel Landrum to Miss Ethel Wootters, 1905

Item 16 Obituary of Mrs. Berta Smith Wootters, February 1915

Item 17 Transcription of Houston Chronicle "Ante-bellum Women Cherish Texas College Memory," September 1930.

Figure 10

Figure C

Item 1
AMERICAN REVOLUTIONARY MILITARY
RECORD OF THOMAS SMITH

American Revolutionary Military Records of Thomas Smith of North Carolina in the First
North Carolina Regiment 1776-1780 and 1781-1782

Roll dated Sept 8, 1778,
Inlisted(sic) July 25, 1776

Date of enlistment 15 May, 1781
Term 12 Mo.
Left service 21 May 82

1 | 1 | N. C.

Thomas Smith

Appears with the rank of .... on a

Roll

of Colonel Thomas Clark's Company—First N°
Carolina Battalion Commanded by Colonel
Thomas Clark

(**Revolutionary War.**)

Roll dated ....
.... *Sept 8* , 17*75*.
Inlist⁴, ... *July 25*, 17*76*.
War, ...
Yⁿ, *3*
Remarks : ....

(555)

2 | | N. C.

.... *Thomas Smith*

.... Q........ ... Co.,

.... N. Carolina Regiment.

(**Revolutionary War,**)

Appears in a book *

Copied from Rolls

of the organization named above.

Date of enlistment }
or appointment } .... , 17*81*.

Term ....

Casualties ....

Remarks ....

*This book appears to have been copied (from original rolls in the
Office of Army Accounts under the Paymaster General, U. S. A.,
who was authorized by Congress, July 4, 1783, to settle and finally
adjust all accounts whatsoever between the United States and the
officers and soldiers of the American army. (Journal American
Congress, Vol. 4, page 237.)—K. & P. 433,786.

Vol........ page ....

(575)

Item 2
TRANSCRIPTION FROM THE FAMILY
BIBLE OF JAMES SMITH

(1 Feb 1767-17 Oct. 1838)

The Holy Bible
containing the
Old and New Testaments
together with the
Apocrypha:
Translated out of the Original Tongues,
and
with the former translations diligently compared and revised
By the Special Command of King James I of England,
with
marginal notes and references
to which are added
An Index;
An Alphabetical Table
of all the names in the old and new testaments with their
significations;
Tables of Scripture Weights, Measures, and Coins,
John Brown's Concordance, &tc, &tc, &tc.

Fourth Philadelphia Edition
printed from the last Oxford Edition, and page for page with that
of Isaac Collins,

Embellished with
Ten Maps and Twenty Historical Engravings Philadelphia
printed by John Adams,
For Matthew Carey, No. 122, Market Street July 25th , 1804

[677]

FAMILY RECORD †
(SEE IMAGE IN GALLERY)

Marriages

James Smith & Elizabeth Clark was Married 22nd July 1794 by the Reverend Dr. Hawling in Jones County N Carolina

James Smith was born Son of Thomas Smith & Rachel Was Born February 1st 1767

Elizabeth Clark alias E. Smith was born September 10th 1776

Sophia Smith daughter of James & Elizabeth Smith married to John Leonard May 1st 1828

Caroline Smith daughter of James & Elizabeth Smith married by the Rev Robt Morrison to Thom Brown 13th January 1825

Thomas Smith & Elizabeth Dickson was married by the Rev James G. Hammer (?) The 25 of July 1827

Marriages

Margaret J. Smith daughter of James & Elizabeth Smith was Married by the Rev. James McDaniel to Jacob Leonard 28th May 1829

Ann Eliza Smith Daughter of James & Elizabeth Smith was Married by the Rev Patrick Dowd to James McDaniel May 19th 1831

John Smith son of James and Elizabeth Smith was married to Anna Jane Pouncey on the 20th Feb 1834

Myra E. Smith, Daughter of Thomas & Elizabeth Smith was married to J.W. Bannerman by the Rev Colin Shaw on the 24th of Feby 1848

John Smith as above was married to Mrs. Margie Dailey by the Rev W D Bromly on the 1st of July 1875

---

† Unreproducible records and letters are transcribed as written.

[678]

FAMILY RECORD

Births

Maria Smith Daughter of James Smith & Elizabeth Smith was born 12 July 1795

Caroline Smith Daughter of James Smith & Elizabeth his wife was born 11th June 1799

Sophia Smith Daughter of James Smith & Elizabeth his wife was born 20th March 1803

Thomas Smith son of James Smith & Elizabeth his wife was born the 1st day of November 1805

Margaret Smith Daughter of James Smith & Elizabeth, his wife was born the 5th March 1808

John Smith Son of James Smith & Elizabeth his wife was born the 21st day of December 1809

Births

Anna Smith, daughter of James Smith & Elizabeth Smith was born 28 April 1813

William Sidney Smith son of James Smith and Elizabeth his wife was Born December 24th 1816

James Austin Smith Son of James Smith and Elizabeth Smith was born December the 28th 1821~

Edward Smith Leonard son of John & Sophia Leonard born on the 23rd February 1824

Thomas Fredrick son of John & Sophia Leonard born 3rd Septr 1825

Theodore Brown Son of Thomas & Caroline Brown, Born 31st October 1825

[679]

Births

James Smith Brown son of
Thomas & Caroline Brown
born 7th of April 1827

Mary Elizabeth Leonard Daughter
of John & Sophia Leonard born
4th January 1828. John D. Smith
son of Thomas & Elizabeth Smith
born 21st April 1828

Sophia Caroline Brown Daughter
of Thomas & Caroline Brown
born 27th March 1829

Elmira Smith Daughter of Thomas
& Elizabeth Smith was born
6th Octr 1829

Jarmy(?) Smith Leonard son of
John & Sophia Leonard was born
22nd July 1830

William Probart Smith son of
Thomas & Elizabeth Smith was
born 5th December 1830

George Clark Leonard son of
Jacob & Margaret Leonard was
born 22nd February 1831

Rebecca Ann Leonard Daughter of
Jacob & M Leonard was born
30th January 1833

Deaths

Maria Smith Daughter of James
& Elizabeth Smith died September
25, 1795

William Sidney Smith son of
James & Elizabeth Smith died
March the 22nd 1822

James Austin Smith, son of James
& Elizabeth Smith departed this
life on the thirty first day of
August 1825

Theodore Brown died 25th
October 1826

John Dickson Smith son of
Thomas & Elizabeth Smith departed this life 27th Decbr 1828

James Smith Brown Son of
Thomas & Caroline Brown died
April 39th 1833

Caroline Brown departed this life
6th July 1835

[680]

Births

Elizabeth Margaret Brown was born the 31st March 1831

Benjamin T. Leonard Son of John & Sophia Leonard was born 26th January 1833

John Owen Brown son of Thos & Caroline Brown was born 10 June 1835, Died 31st July '35

Deaths

Died August 1st 1832 ???

Margaret Leonard Departed this life 6th August 1836

James Smith Proprietor of this book Departed this life 17th October 1838 in the 72nd year of his age

James S. Leonard son of John & Sophia Leonard died 3rd September 1841

Sophia C Brown daughter of Thom & Caroline Brown died 11th Octr 1841

Elizabeth C. Smith consort of James Smith Departed this life on the 22nd day of March 1850 in the 74th year of her age

Thomas Smith oldest son of James & Elizabeth Smith Died in ??? County Texas on the ?? 11th ?? 1865

Item 3
LETTER FROM REBECCA CROSLAND
TO MRS. JOHN SMITH

Address: Mrs. John Smith
           Prospect Hall
           Bladen County, N.C.

Bennettsville Oct 7th 1841

My Dear Uncle and Aunt
It is with feelings of the deepest sympathy and regret that I write
you this morning. Yesterday's mail brought your letter announcing
the dear of your dear little boys. We had heard a few days since,
through Mr. Floyd, the Methodist minister, that your family was
sick, but did not hear what was the matter. I hope the Lord will
enable you both to bear your affliction with Christian fortitude
and enable you to say as one of old did, the Lord giveth and the
Lord taketh away, and, blessed be his name.

Mother has been at grand Fathers ever since Sunday morning,
though the family is not more unwell than usual. We heard on
Sunday and aunt Mary was a little complaining. Grand Mothers
health is as good as it has been for some time. We are looking for
Mother this morning. I hope she will come before the mail closes
so you can hear particularly from them. ? Par says he would go
immediately out to see you but the situation of grand Father's
family will prevent, but some of us will go next week, either sister
and Par or uncle will if nothing prevents.

My dear aunt we will expect you to return with us if possible for
I think you would feel better after your fatigue and distress to be
away from home a while.

Par received a letter from Uncle Cochran this week, their family
is well but it is very sickly near him. Uncle Corgill's family have
all been sick with fever and all better except the old gentleman
who is still sick.

It is two weeks this morning since cousin John Corgill left us for Alabama. He was very anxious to visit you before he left but hearing of the ill health of his Father's family he hurried home.

Our family is quite well at present though brother William and Margaret Du Pre ? have had an attack of fever. Sister ? affectionately in love to you both and if nothing prevents he will be with you by the middle of next week.

May the Lord protect, guide and comfort you is the prayer of your affectionate niece.

Rebecca Crosland

Note: Rebecca Crosland was a daughter of Sara Pouncey and Mr. D.M. Crosland and a niece of Anna Jane Pouncey Smith. Sara was an older sister of Anna Jane Pouncey and hence Berta Smith's aunt.

Item 4
NOTE FROM ANNA JANE SMITH TO LUCIUS SMITH

April the 20 1856

My dear Son Lucius

Today is your birthday. I hope you may have a pleasant & a happy life. You will accept from your Ma a small present which you will find on your cake, remember your creator in the days of your youth. Happy you must be with your Brother & Sister.
I am your fond Ma

Anna Jane Smith
Written on outside of folded paper:
Master Lucius W. Smith
From Anna at home

Item 5
TRANSCRIPTION OF CROCKETT ARGUS "FLAG PRESENTATION"

July 1861

Transcription of a copy of the original print prepared by Mrs. Sarah J. Monroe Holmes in New York, February 27, 1913 when she was sixty-five years old and preserved by Mrs. Frances Wootters Denman, daughter of Captain John Wootters.

Flag Presentation in Crockett, July 17th, 1861 to Dr. Currie's Company copied from the original print, from the "Crockett Argus" by Mrs. Sarah Monroe Holmes, at the request of Mrs. D. A. Nunn. The "Crockett Argus" was edited and published by Col. John Hay and John C. Hepperla for several years before the War and during a part of the first year of the War, and was a very excellent paper. This Company was named the "Crockett Southerns."

"The Flag Presentation"
A flag, the handiwork of the patriotic ladies of Houston County, Texas, was presented to Capt. Currie's Company on Wednesday last, in front of Mrs. Hall's Hotel by Miss Sarah Jane Monroe, in behalf of the donors.

The speech of Miss Monroe was neat and appropriate, and the reply of Mr. John Wootters, who received the Banner, was in excellent taste.

The circumstances, the parting of friends perchance to meet no more, the stern necessity that had called so many of the hope and pride of our Country to a distant land, cast a gloom on the least sensitive heart, while the trickling tear from eyes unused to weep, evinced that however stern might be the hearts that beat in those manly breasts, the fountains of affection for home and kindred still flowed.

Go match the foremost ranks
In danger's dark career
And be sure the hand most daring there
Has wiped away a tear.

Miss Monroe, on presenting the Banner said, "Sir: The pleasing task has been assigned to me, of presenting to you this Flag made by some of our Country-women, which they beg you to accept as the Banner of your Company.

In presenting to you this glorious symbol of Southern Independence, we feel that we intrust it to brave hearts and strong hands who will never permit it to trail dishonored in the dust.

When the toils and deeds of the day are over and you repose at night on your soldier couch our prayers will mingle with yours and ascend to the "God of our Fathers", imploring your preservation, and the success of your arms in defense of this flag, as the emblem of Confederate Liberty. When victory shall have perched upon your standard and peace and independence shall have crowned your efforts, how gladly will we hail your return to your homes, and our homes, which you are determined to defend, or "in death be laid low, With your backs to the field and your feet to the foe". Take soldiers, this flag, which has been consecrated to Freedom, with our prayers. Should it be moistened with the blood of the Sons, remember that it has been bedewed with the tears of the Daughters of your land, thus bathing its bright folds in the two purest libations to liberty. With hearts full of grateful emotion, we now bid you all a sad but proud farewell."

Mr. John H. Wootters reply:

"Miss Monroe, I've been honored with the pleasing and grateful duty of receiving this beautiful flag at your hands, and of expressing, on behalf of the Company, of which I am an humble member, their heartfelt thanks to the fair and patriotic donors, and to you Miss Sarah for the happy and flattering terms in which the presentation has been made.

There is no greater incentive for the soldier, after his love of Country, than the smiles and approving words of the mothers and daughters of his Country. In the camp, when the toils of the day are over and midnight stillness reigns around him, his thoughts will revert to loved ones he has left behind him and the consciousness that he has their sympathy and prayers nerves his heart for the toils, or, it may be, the deadly conflict of tomorrow.

When this beautiful token of encouragement presented by you, fair lady, on behalf of your Country-women, shall be unfurled upon the battlefield, we promise you that so long as a heart pulsates and an arm is nerved it shall be protected from the foul pollution of an enemy's hand, and so long as one of us shall survive to bear it in triumph from the battlefield we will preserve this beautiful Banner, not only as a memento of the gallant patriotism of Texas' noble daughters, but also to remind us that it should never be sullied or dishonored by any act of ours unworthy the soldier or gentleman.

We are going far from home, we are called upon to sever many fond attachments, but our Country calls for our services and we will respond. We must not allow the fond endearments of home to overcome our love of liberty. We go forth putting our trust in God and the justness of our cause and hope, under this beautiful Banner, to accomplish an honorable peace or, if this is denied us, to fight and, if necessary, die in defense of our country's rights and the liberty and homes of the Daughters of the Sunny South; and if Providence, in his wise dispensation, shall permit us to return to our homes, we desire no prouder or higher commendation that woman's approbation, and though it may be in the evening of declining years, yet may the remembrance of this occasion be a vivid to our minds as now.

Again permit me to return to you our sincere thanks for this precious gift, and on behalf of myself, and those I have the honor of representing, bid you all a fond farewell."

Item 6
JOHN H. WOOTTERS' CIVIL WAR RECORDS

Item 7
VALEDICTORY ADDRESS – BERTA SMITH
FAIRFIELD COLLEGE – MAY, 1865

On the occasion of the graduation of the Senior class of 1865 a
Valedictory Essay was written and read by Berta Smith at the
time of their graduation from the Fairfield Female College. She
read as follows:

"Earth is a scene of continual changes. The colossal fabrics of
human genius rise in beauty and their splendors, for a time,
dazzle the startled gaze of an admiring world, but like all
things earthly they fall, crumble into dust and are entombed in
the common mausoleum of ages. Time, as an ocean churning
with waves each ladened with its stern realities and mighty
consequences, has brought to view the scenes of another day. You
meet around no 'festal board' not to chant a nation's glory nor
to wreath the laurels around a hero's brow, but to witness the
disbanding of youthful sisters to see a few just entering upon the
proud arena of life present their last school girl offerings and pay
their last tokens of respect to their college days.

"The occasion is one of moment to many, fraught with buoyant
hopes and thronging memories and it should be deeply and
solemnly impressed on the minds of all of us that although many
are the hearts that leap with joy and many the eyes that sparkle
with hope yet it is not a scene of unmingled pleasure. Though
long anticipated with pleasing expectations and though a joyful
future spreads forth its flattering prospects, yet its dawn has basic
sadness to many bosoms and indeed that we are forever severed
from every endearing association of the school room.

"Many countenances seem already to have grown sad at the
approaching of the word farewell. Ere it be spoken we will
attempt to give utterance to those emotions which crown
themselves upon our overflowing hearts.

"To our friends of this vicinity we gladly improve the opportunity
of returning our ever most thanks for the favors we have

enjoyed at your hands. Though our stay has been short and our acquaintance limited yet many have been our moments of pleasantness, many the incidents in memory store, to which we will delight to revert as we think of things that have vanished dear and cherished. They will be bright flowery isles in the wide sea of Eternity. In solitude's lonely hour as we muse over youthful scenes, perchance, when evening casts her mantle over us, at dusky brown of night, when the azure face of heaven is jeweled over with glittering gems, such reminiscences will come as welcome messages of departed days.

"They will tell of girlhoods mirth—of youthful associations—and friends that were. They will tell us hopes that dawned upon youth's merry morn, hopes that were bright and fragrant as the lili's opening bloom; often will their influcnce cheer and bless us as we advance on the great drama of life and lend cheering rays though gathering storms would daunt us. Kind friends the time has come when we must again return to our cherished homes, with you we can no longer stay. In our separation we ask a place in your memories and with you leave our blessings and ardent wishes for your temporal happiness and eternal glory beyond the grave.

"Stranger—whoever you are where ever be your home; whether amid the balmy breezes and fragrant blossoms of the Sunny South; among the snow capped mountains of the North, or far away in the wild prairie West you too hope though your life may have been but a series of disappointments yet your presence presupposed that you had some expectations in coming hither. May we ask what that hope was? Was it merely to criticize our failings—to find some instance in which our teachers or ourselves have not proved faithful? But we are persuaded other things of you.

"We believe, on the contrary, that your object was rather to prove the faithfulness of pupils and teachers. The necessity of hope is laid in the constitution of mind. The stern warrior is not free from her influences; the worn out soldier as he lays him down upon the verdant earth, finds in her a pleasant companion; be guiding the tardy hours as they pass and pouring joy into his troubled heart. She dissipates the gloom which hides his Mecca from his view and leads him on to deeds of valor, of glory which will gain for him, a crown of unfading laurels, to adorn his care worn brow.

"Now it becomes us to mention the honor of this college and its founders. We feel the weight of responsibility and, when we go forth from under your protection, we feel truly grateful that you have so loved our sex as to bestow upon us the privilege of being educated. When we contemplate the kind and tender mercies with which our lives have been crowned, and more especially this inestimable favor which you conferred we can but exclaim, 'So! The lines have fallen to us in pleasant places.'

"In return you have the earnest desires of our hearts for your success in this noble enterprise. May it continue to prosper as it has done, and may many hundred students flock together to partake of the advantages you have prepared. We have endeavored to be faithful to our college but since we no longer mingle with its dear associations since its wall shall no longer echo to our voices, we know, ah!, yes, we feel that we could have been more devoted to its interest, that we could have loved it more even as we do now when we must tear ourselves away from its sacred threshold. Praying Heaven will bestow its choice blessings on you, and our college, we part with a sad farewell.

"Beloved schoolmates: Allow a few words from us. 'Hope on your youthful brow has settled, And visions sweet your thoughts employ'. And may we ask what these bright dreams are which allure you on? Are they that when you have finished your course here, you can say in all good conscience that I have done all I could; that when you depart from these dear old walls you will leave a spotless character—a good name, embalmed in the memories of loving teachers; in a word, that you may be all that proud parents and devoted teachers desire!

"If so happy are your anticipations. Delightful will be the realization. Strive to attain your noble hope. When the heart sinks, think of the battle of life which is being contested all around you, of Madame De Stael, Charlotte Brontë, Mrs. Horton, Hannah More, Mrs. Heineins and a host of others; who have made their lives glorious; and then if spirit fails, your faith is small. Surely with these examples pointing us to a higher, noble life it were unwomanly to falter and faint by the wayside.

"Buffet your way through difficulties, wring from the world an acknowledgement of your worth. 'And never from thy tempted heart, Let its integrity depart, When disappointments fill thy cup, Undaunted nobly drink it up, Truth will prevail and justice show, Her tardy honors sure but slow, Bear on, bear nobly on.' Begging your kind hearts to bear with us, we must bid a last adieu. "How can we leave you; how can we tear our yearning hearts from the scenes of happiness we love so well? But though our bodies be far removed yet our spirits linger around you; they shall haunt your resorts upon the college green, and there would fain mingle as in by gone hours, in your merry laugh, in your youthful sport. 'Tis so hard to bid adieu to you forever! Our warmest and purest affection have twined themselves around you and yet, we must be severed.

"No more we gain your number. No, no more voices we shall hear. You will again assemble to listen to the instruction of cherished teachers. That best privilege is no longer ours. We go hence; we leave you forever, but as our last request we ask to be remembered. That a kind thought may sometimes stray in your musings to us, school-mates of former days. 'Tis sweet to remember and be remembered by those we love.' Adieu! Adieu!

"To you whose names and memories it will be our delight to cherish. Kind Teachers we have assembled in this hall for the last time. But we would not leave you before we had unburthened (sic) our grateful hearts. All gratitude is due to you who have been so faithful in your instructions, so true the interests of your students. It has devolved upon you especially to train the rude germs of thought; to draw out the latent energies of the untutored mind; and moreover to administer reproof of the earring. The influence that you exert on this sphere is such as will endure until the last knell is sounded, yea, it is stamped upon the very brow of time, and will be felt when the last wave lands its myriads upon the shore of Eternity.

"Would that we could tell, would that the world knew how faithfully you have discharged every duty. In sickness, in health, the same cheerful countenances have ever greeted us, the same clear voices have illustrated the truths of sciences, the same patient spirits have borne us up. Who would chide us for offering our pure and lasting affections to your noble benefactors. Will you loved teachers spurn our unworthy libations? Freely we give it, for it bursts forth spontaneously from our grateful hearts. Now dear Teachers, all with the kindest wishes of our hearts for your success and happiness we must say farewell—a sure farewell to you and all the delightful associations of our youth!

"To our venerable President we must offer a special parting thought. While it has been your duty in common with others to impress upon our minds the truths and realities of science and nature it has further been your delight to point us 'from Nature up to Nature's God'. The silver sheen of age has already covered the clear, calm brow. Your head is whitened with the frosts of accumulated winters that will never melt. All these admonish us, that you are rapidly journeying to that 'undiscovered country, from whose bourn no traveler returns.' Soon, ah! soon you must be torn from all endearing associations and gathered home with the Faithful. May your works ever follow you!

"My dear Classmates; Our school days are passed! The time so swiftly flown has had its joys and sorrows, but the occasional disturbances which have invaded our little band, have passed away; we forgot them. Memory now claims only scenes that are brightest. In after years we shall revert to these as the joyous days of yore— days of association with the friends of our youth. But alas! the bitter is mingled with the sweet. The time for parting comes, and 'tis with deep and heartfelt emotion that I think of it. But first let me say, though I am no sage adviser, Direct your trust to the unerring Guide above us. Will you allow one who feels an interest in your well fare (sic) to give a few words in parting counsel?

"In after years when your minds are filled and hearts wretched, and torn by things of this world; then let it not be in vain that the voice of Nature—the murmurings of that something righteous and holy implanted within us—shall invade the inner citadels of your hearts and speak in soft wooing tones, 'Come unto me, all ye that are weary and heavy laden and I will give you rest'—You have a friend that will ever be true and faithful. May Faith, Hope, and Love lighten your days on earth!

"We, soon, too soon must part; leave our beloved haunts; the seats which we once occupied shall know us no more forever. New comers shall fill our places in the hour of prayer, other voices shall mingle in songs of praise. We go to our long deserted homes. We know we all shall never meet again. Our barks tossed by wind and tide perchance may be thrown together, but oh! how much will have been the changes wrought by time. Our hearts, now fresh and joyous may then have drank the bilious cup of human woe. Disappointments may have blighted the germs of hope. Who knows the future? God only knows, 'But while there is life there is hope'.

"When shadows gather thickly around; when the mists of disappointments hide from your anxious view the long looked and wished for headland toward which you press; droop not, faint not; battle on again bravely with these glorious words of cheer—Nil desperandum? Who can despair? Who in this bright world glorious with sweet sounds and forms will sink beneath the shadows as a tempest bursts over head, when we know the bright sunshine succeeds the storm, and the future is all before us radiant with the light of Hope. But what ever be your fate, loved class mates, prosperity or adversity, my sincere prayer for you is that you may be sustained by that hope which is an anchor of the soul, sure, and steadfast.

"Now run, my bursting heart—say farewell to your companions of my college days? Do I gaze on the faces that I shall never more behold? Sad, sad reality, 'Though no more on earth we meet, Yet again where all the joy and ill and Change of life are passed, We hope to meet in Heaven. Yet again we hope to meet you When the day of life has fled, Then in Heaven with joy to greet you, Where no face with tears is shed' I bid you all affectionate farewell.

"We may roam far over land and sea, after our separation but we will never lose the light of the halcyon days of school life. We shall ever cherish as sacred our 'Alma Mater' and like the wandering Jews ever toward this place shall we pray as the Jerusalem of our hearts, the temple of our affections. And now dear friends, instructors and class mates we extend to you all a heart felt— Good Bye."

Senior Class of 1865   "The Mystic Seven"
Anna Kirksey
Ophelia Graves
Ella Stell
Emma Pistole
Nannie Smith
Sallie Cannon
Berta Smith

Item 8
LETTER FROM BERTA SMITH TO JOHN WOOTTERS

December 1866

Address   Capt John H. Wootters
            Present

Capt Wootters

Fannie came to see me the same today that you left, also? Ad.
Thiley?, Amanda White hill. Mrs. Michelle and Jo M the next day
the worthy Capt.

Wilson honored us with his presencc. Fannie will go home this
afternoon, (Sunday) and wishes me to go with her. We both hope to
see you at Dr. Meriwethers Tuesday. Do not fail to come. I would wait
until your return but do not think you care much about going with
me. Fannie and I went to church today and I am sorry to tell you
that I behaved miserably, could hardly preserve my gravity at all.

Adieu! Adieu! Your true friend, Berta

(The following was written on the back of the letter by John
Wootters in his hand)

Marshall Dec 17th 1866

Darling girl, does she know how dear she is to me? Little does
she think how much I love her but in time she will appreciate my
devotion. Will you not dearest one. Me thinks I hear her answer
"Yes, I will love you"

Item 9

Palestine (Sunday) Dec 30th/66

My Dear Darling

I know you will say when you get this that I ? it small so I would not have to write much to fill it but it won't be "pretty" and "sweet" "and good" for you to say so for I thought it was larger until I had ? it still if it is small My love is not. Berta I am ? away from you and I begin to fear that it will be ? cry when I have to go away instead of you. (I know you say "as if men could cry") but I don't intend to go away often for it is a part of my life to be

Page 2.

with as near you. I think I must love you a thousand times better than I did one week ago for your image is constantly before me and not one moment passes but that I think of you my own precious one. I never was half so happy in life as I have been since I love you, for I know I am loved by the best woman upon earth and all my ambition now is to prove myself worthy of the dear girl that I love not less than life. I came from Crockett here yesterday it was bitter cold and I am not well from it today.

Page 3.

I leave in the morning for "Mound Prairie" Linnear Colony" "Pine Bluff" and "Fairfield" I want to reach the latter place Thursday if possible and will try to get to your home Friday or Saturday night but if I fail do not be uneasy for I may be detained at Pine Bluff longer than I expect.

Capt. Wall told Nettie that it was going to be "Monkey Show" I am getting frightened ? it makes me nervous to think of it. You ought not to have put it off so long. We will both be timid having to think of it so long. It seems that the last three days have been a month. Take care of yourself, darling.

Affectionately yours,

John H. Wootters
My love to Pa & Ma

Item 10

Envelope address   Capt John H. Wootters
                              Present

Home

January 9th 1867

Capt. Wootters

The girls arrived this morning bringing with them the cheerful,
smiling Mr. Aldrich. We, or rather I spent the afternoon very
pleasantly enjoyed the girls company very much. I am not such a
very sad creature after all, and I will scold you good for saying
so, when I see you. You are not much afraid of my scolding
though I believe so I will have to give vent to my feelings in some
other manner.

I received some letters from you a few days since. Was glad to
read the gentle and affectionate encouragement you gave some
hope we will be happy in each other's love. The girls tell me to tell
you some good for them.

I leave it entirely to your imaginative faculty. Think of something
that will please, cheer and comfort.

Ever ? –

Berta

Item 11

Obituary of Anna Jane Pouncey – Died June 9, 1874.

Departed this life on the 15th inst., Mrs. Anna Jane Smith, wife of Mr. John Smith of Houston County, in the 63rd year of her age.

She was born in Marlboro District South Carolina, was the daughter of Maj. James and his wife Mrs. Anna Pouncey who were one of the most influential and excellent families in that county. In early life she gave satisfactory evidence of conversion to God and united with the Baptist Church of which she remained a devoted member until her death.

In 1834 she was united by marriage to Maj. John Smith. The marriage ceremony was performed by Rev. Robert Nappier, a Baptist minister of great worth and usefulness. Several years after their marriage they removed to Texas and settled on the Trinity River, in Houston county, where they remained in the enjoyment of a high degree of domestic happiness until separated by death.

For several years previous to her death she was quite an invalid, which prevented her from mingling with and enjoying the society of her friends as she would have done. All, however, who knew her were impressed with her excellence of character and her deep and earnest piety. Though seldom able to attend the house of God, she was ever ready to give a reason for her hope in Christ. She delighted in religious conversation and seldom permitted an opportunity to pass without introducing the sacred theme, but it was in the circle of her own peaceful home that her noble traits were more fully known and appreciated and her influence felt. There she leaves an impression which time itself cannot efface.

The ordeal through which she was called to pass was trying and of long continuance. She bore it, however, with Christian fortitude, after saying "Thy Will Be Done." Her death was calm and peaceful bringing forcibly to mind that Divine declaration, "Precious in the sight of the Lord, Is the death of his saints." She has left a husband, daughter and two grandchildren together with many loving friends to mourn her loss.

"Sister, thou wast mild and lovely,
Gentle as the summer breeze,
Pleasant as the air of evening
When it floats among the trees."
Dearest sister, though has left us,
Here thy loss we deeply feel,
But 'tis God, who has bereft us,
He can all our sorrows heal.

W, D, B

Item 12
LETTER ADDRESSED TO
MRS. BERTA WOOTTERS, CROCKETT

Daly, Tx – August 19th 1882

My Dear Daughter

Smithie seems to think he must go home this morning. I dislike for him to go alone but he seems not to mind it. I have not had as much of his company as I wished (?) caring to have to be at (?) long to Mrs. S. She is at home at last but Oh Me! a mere wreck I am much disappointed in her improvements in health. I now see no chance for her. The dread disease consumption has evidently got full hold and I fear that her days are numbered and that the numbers will be very few.

Mrs. Raney & Willie are both here at present but Willie is going home now (?) and Mrs. R (?) go on Monday. I would be very glad if you could come before long when you are able.

I feel very sad about her condition to be left alone again at my old age is very gloomy but our Heavenly Father does all things right and I will be sub (?)

Your loving Father –John Smith

Item 13
OBITUARY LISTINGS FROM HOUSTON COUNTY, TEXAS, 1890 FROM ANCESTRY.COM

MAJOR JOHN SMITH

In the death of Major John Smith, Houston County loses one of its oldest and valuable citizens. The deceased was a native of North Carolina, and moved to Texas previous to the war. He located in Houston County on the Trinity River, or near there, and engaged in the planting business. He owned one of the finest plantations in East Texas, and was regarded as one of the county's most successful planters.

For several years he has done nothing other than exercise supervision over some farming interests of his son-in-law, Capt. Jno. H. Wootters.

Major Smith was a gentleman after the old school type—highly educated, intelligent, courteous, and patriotic. He leaves but one child, the wife of Capt. J. H. Wootters, with whom he has passed the latter years of his life.

REV. J. P. PRITCHARD

Rev. J.P. Pritchard, who died at the residence of his son, William Pritchard, Feb. 11, 1890, was born of English parents in Charleston, SC, Sept. 1806. During his infancy his parents returned to London, England, where he remained until his tenth year, when he returned , an orphan, to America.

In his Twenty-second year he was married to Miss Eliza Henderson, of Charlotte, NC, with whom he lived hapily (sic) until her death, Sept. 29, 1880. Soon after his marriage he made a profession of religion and joined the Presbyterian church. Two years later he united with the Baptist church, of which he was a member until his death. More than fifty years he was a faithful minister of the gospel.

He moved to Texas in the year 1854. One year later he came
to Houston County. He served the Crockett church as pastor a
number of years, besides a number of other churches in this and
Leon County. Notwithstanding he was more than 83 years of age,
he continued to preach occasionally until his last sickness.

Six children of 13 survive their father of who are, Mrs. John
Miller, Mrs. Henry Leaverton, Mr. William Pritchard, Miss Tidy
Pritchard, of Crockett; Mrs. Lummy Thomas, now a resident of
Florida; and Dr. Tom Pritchard, pastor of First Baptist Church,
Wilmington, NC.

JUDGE A.E. GOSSETT – DEAD – 1890
It becomes our painful duty this week to record the death of Judge
A.E. Gossett, an old and highly respected citizen of Crockett, which
occurred Monday morning last at his residence near this city.

He was an old pioneer, having settled in Texas 56 years ago, and
was a veteran in the war between Texas and Mexico, and at one
time owned the land on which Crockett now stands. He was, at
the time of his death, 78 years old.

Mr. Gossett was a member of the Masonic Order and was buried
on Tuesday morning by that fraternity. All the business houses of
the town closed and his remains were followed to the grave by a
vast concourse of friends and relatives. The Courier tenders to the
widow and other bereaved relatives its sympathies in their loss.

OBITUARIES – Judge A.E. Gossett
Departed this life, Judge Andrew E. Gossett, at his residence near
the town of Crockett at 5 o'clock a.m., on the 24th of March, 1890.

Judge Gossett was confined to his bed about ten days with an
attack of la grippe; relapsed, then bronchitis set up, and though all
was done for him that medical skill could do, aided by the efforts
of a kind and devoted wife and affectionate children, yet the grim
monster, Death, had marked him for his victim and he had to go.

Judge Gossett was born on the 19th day of July 1812, in the County
of Hardeman in the State of Tennessee. He came to Texas in 1832,
and located in Houston County, and was a patriot and lover of
his country. He aided in ridding the county of the savages who
infested it and in beating back the Mexican hordes, and living to
see the development and prosperity of that county.

As an honest man, he held many offices of trust. He was the
first sheriff of Houston County; subsequently a justice of the
peace, county commissioner for a series of years and then county
judge. Judge Gossett leaves a kind and devoted wife and four
affectionate, grown children—two of them the fruits of a former
wife, who has been waiting "over the river" for him for a number
of years, and two by his disconsolate widow—and many friends
who mourn their irreparable loss.

Item 14

Friday, January 22, 1892. *The Courier* –
Published Every Friday at Crockett

In Memoriam of Capt. John H. Wootters

It becomes my sad duty to record with you an event of more than
ordinary significance in the death of our esteemed and beloved
fellow citizen, Capt. John H. Wootters, who departed this life at his
home in the town of Crockett on Thursday, the 21st day of January,
1892, surrounded by a broken hearted and distressed family and a
sympathizing community.

He was just attaining the meridian splendor of life when his
virtues were known and his usefulness to society broadened till
his death creates affliction not only for his interesting family
but also for the town and community in which he lived. He was
born August 12, 1839, in Queen Anne's County, Md. In 1860 he
immigrated to and settled in the town of Crockett, State of Texas.
In 1861, in the month of July, he volunteered his services and
joined Capt. E. Curry's company, the first company raised in this
county, and went with that gallant band of boys to the hottest of
the fight, landing in Virginia and becoming a part of that grand
old Hood's Brigade whose deeds of valor and heroic devotion
furnish rich material for the patriotic historian and prolific
themes for the poets happy conceptions. He passed through the
firery (sic) ordeal of the defense of Richmond and shared the
glory of the grand achievements of Lee's and Jackson's armies;
was wounded and disabled in skirmish line at Bermuda Hundred,
but resumed and continued service until the confederate flag was
finally furled.

At the close of the war he returned to his home and engaged in
active business and in 1867 intermarried with Berta, the daughter
of Col. (sic Major) John Smith who had come from North Carolina
and settled in Houston county in the year 1857; afterwards in 1858
(sic 1868), he became a partner in the house of Duble & Wootters,
of Galveston, also conducting a mercantile business and extensive

farming at and near Daly in Houston County, giving his principal attention to such business and trusting to his partner, Mr. Duble, to manage and conduct the Galveston house. The Galveston business after about five years got in bad shape. Capt. Wootters assumed control for the purpose of liquidation and did all that an honorable man could do in justice to its customers and friends, but this misfortune carried away all his earnings and left him to start life anew. He did not become disheartened and spend his time in repining but with renewed energy and determination, plunged again into the battle of life as one conscious of his own powers and nerved by a sense of duty that knew no such word as "fail."

He joined the Baptist church at Daly in Houston County and afterwards transferred his membership to the Baptist church at Crockett, where he remained an active, useful and honored member to his death. He joined the Masonic order at an early period and was there esteemed for his good fellowship. He joined the Knights of Honor at or soon after its organization in Crockett about fifteen years since. He has attended with great regularity the reunion of his old Hood Brigade, and this was one of his chief pleasures of life; always dwelling in anticipation of the happy meeting of old comrades. He leaves a widow and five children, the eldest, Dr. John Smith Wootters, who graduated at New Orleans about a year ago and is now attending a third course at Jefferson Medical College in Philadelphia; one other bright boy, Leon Blum Wootters, five years old, and three bright promising and lovely daughters, Ethel, Lucia and Fannie, ages respectively, 14, 12 and 8.

Capt. Wootters (sic) was especially distinguished for his public spirit and his quiet, unostentatious charity and kindness to the poor, the helpless, the sick and distressed; the widow and orphan always having his solicitude and care and active sympathies.

His burial was postponed to await the return of his son till Sunday the 24th inst. The corpse was to the last lifelike and retained up on its face the pleasant good natural expression that, in life, won his way to the hearts of all who knew him. The services were conducted by the Rev. Mr. Armstrong, of Palestine, the minister, Rev. Mr. Gaddy, being confined by the prevalent disease. Mr.

Armstrong's remarks, brief, pointed and from a loving heart, took lodgment and was responded to by every heart in the vast concourse assembled to do honor to one of Crockett's noblest dead.

At the conclusion of the services an invitation was given to his friends to view the dead, and the vast throng joined in sympathy, mingling tears and sorrow with the distressed and mourning family. The scene was truly pathetic and the heart not moved would be made of stone. So passed away one of Crockett's noblest men. He will be missed from his church and other orders in which he stood as a worthy and useful member. He will be missed from the business circle where he had become an important factor in all matters affecting town or community. He will be missed by the widow, the orphan, the poor, the friendless. Let us emulate his virtues and place a veil over his faults if he had any.

Requiescat in pace.

A Friend

Item 15 ††
TRANSCRIPT OF LETTER FROM MRS. SAMUEL LANDRUM (MARY RAINS LANDRUM) TO MISS ETHEL WOOTERS(SIC) {WOOTTERS} POSTMARKED CHILTON, TEXAS MAY 21, 1905

May twenty-second, ninteen(sic) {nineteen} hundred and five

Miss Ethel Wooters, Crockett, Texas

Dear Miss Wooters,

I congratulate you on being one of the prize winners of the Chronicle's contest. I had hoped you would win the first prize. Are you a granddaughter of Mrs. Anna (Pouncey) Smith? I met with that lady long ago at Major Lenoir's in Alabama. She was on her way to Texas. Mrs. S. had one daughter and two sons—Lucius and Philander and Berta. I have often wondered where Mrs. and family had settled in Texas since I came in 1868. My eldest sister Rowena (Rains) Birdsong married Mrs. Lenoir's brother James Pouncey Cargill, both died many years since. Five children survived them, all had families. The two boys died since my visit there in '92 and '93. Mary married Mr. Downey and has a large family. Ellen married Singleton and they lived near Putnam in Maringo (sic) {Marengo} County. Willy Putnam lives near Clay Hill Maringo County. The sons' families lived near there also.

Ella Cocheran was visiting Major Lenoir's at the same time when Mrs. Smith was there. I visited her when I was on a visit in the early '90s. She had a large family, and recently lost a little girl and after a few years another daughter died from an accident of which you may have heard. After some years, they moved to Lexington, Kentucky where Ella died and I hear the family since then moved back to Alabama but I do not know anything of them for four or five years and through friends.

If Berta the little girl if your mother is living, give her my kind remembrance and ? the time you may spend if you will write to me at your leisure. I have often wished I could meet with the family again.

I am sincerely Mrs. Samuel Landrum (Mary Rains Landrum) Chilton, Tx.

†† *This letter written about sixty years after the relocation of the family of John Smith and Anna Jane Pouncey Smith from North Carolina to Texas is the best documentation of the route that they followed on this journey. The letter refers to another child, a son named Philander who died shortly after the family arrived in Texas. No information about him has been located and he is not included in this story.*

Item 16
OBITUARY OF MRS. BERTA SMITH WOOTTERS
FEBRUARY 1915.

The Crockett Courier Volume XXVI – No. 3 Crockett, Texas,
February 11, 1915
(Issued weekly from the Courier Building)

The End of a Noble Life
The announcement of no single death could have caused more
genuine sadness than the announcement, early Saturday (sic.
Friday) morning of the death of Mrs. Berta Wootters, whom all
knew and loved so well. All knew her, because she had been
going in and out among our people for a lifetime; and all loved
her, because she had done so many acts of kindness and charity
during all this time. Mrs. Wootters was a good woman in every
sense of the word and one of the most charitable. Charity with
her was not alone an act of the bestowing of material things, but
of the mind and heart as well—never an unkind word was said
by Mrs. Wootters. Devoted to her family, her devotion did not stop
there. Her heart also went out to the young men and women of
the town, whom she delighted to advise and counsel with, but
never a word of reproach would she utter. There is cause for the
universal sadness that is now overspreading our town.

Mrs. Wootters died a little after 6 o'clock Saturday (sic Friday)
morning. She had been out the day before, but had complained of
not feeling well at times—of a shortness of breath. She retired as
usual, but between 5 and 6 o'clock in the morning she called her
daughter, Mrs. Painter and complained of a difficulty in breathing.
Her son, Dr. Wootters, was summoned by telephone, and at about
6:10 her spirit had peacefully passed out.

Relatives and friends at distant points were notified, and the
funeral was not held until Monday afternoon, awaiting the arrival
of a son from Santa Fe, New Mexico. Those here from a distance
were: Mr. and Mrs. Willis Higginbotham, Stephenville; Dr. and
Mrs. P.R. Denman, Houston; Mr. and Mrs. L.B. Wootters, Santa Fe,
New Mexico; Walker King, San Marcos.

Funeral services conducted by the Baptist pastor, Rev. M.L. Sheppard, were held at the family residence Monday afternoon at 2:30 o'clock. The home and the front yard were thronged with sorrowing friends who had come to pay the last tribute and respect and esteem to a departed loved one. The funeral procession was one of the longest in the history of this city. At the cemetery the newly-made grave was banked and hidden with flowers—evidence of the appreciation, esteem and love in which this good woman was held.

Mrs. Berta Wootters was the daughter of Major John Smith and his wife Anna Jane. She was born in Bladen County, North Carolina, on the 4th day of September, 1847, and was therefore 67 years old.

Her parents moved to Texas in 1857 and made their home in the western portion of Houston county on a large Trinity river plantation owned by Major Smith. She was educated by private tutors and at the Fairfield Female Academy at Fairfield, Freestone County. It was while attending this college, on April 26, 1863, that she became a member of the Baptist church, which church she remained a constant member of until her death. She had two brothers—Philander, who died at the age of 15, and Lucius who lived to the age of 19. Lucius was a member of Sibley's Brigade during the civil war and was mortally wounded at the battle of Valverde, N.M.

She was married to Captain J.H. Wootters at her father's Trinity River plantation by the Reverend Joseph P. Pritchard on the 17th day of January, 1867. She moved with her husband to Crockett in 1877, where Captain Wootters was engaged in the mercantile business until his death on Thursday, January 21, 1892.

Mrs. Wootters, immediately upon her arrival in Crockett placed her letter of church fellowship in the First Baptist Church of this city. She was one of the organizers of the Dorcas Aid Society of the Baptist church—one of its first officers, as well as one of its most active and enthusiastic members.

Mrs. Wootters had seven children—Lena, who died at the age of 11 years; Dr. J.S. Wootters of this city; Ann Berta, who died at the age of 6 years; Sarah Ethel, who married Willis Higginbotham of Stephenville; Lucia, who married J.H. Painter of this city; Frances who married Dr. P.R. Denman of Houston; L.B. Wootters of Santa Fe, New Mexico. There are seven grandchildren.

Item 17
TRANSCRIPT OF "ANTE-BELLUM WOMEN CHERISH TEXAS COLLEGE MEMORY," THE *HOUSTON CHRONICLE*, SUNDAY, SEPT. 28, 1930

Ante-bellum Women Cherish Texas College Memory
Famous Institution Near Fairfield, Which Was Attended by Daughters of Planters From Many Southern States and Around Which the Halo of Romance Lingered for Many Years, Has Been Destroyed But the Picture of Its Former Glory Is Ineffaceable in the Minds of Many Women in Freestone County.

An aristocratic old building with white pillars and verandas kept a lovely vigil under the tall oaks near Fairfield, in Freestone County, for many years until it was razed a few years ago, leaving only the bricks and stone to mark the location of the old cellar basement. Several women in Freestone and neighboring counties, women in the evening of life, found that their eyes dimmed when they learned that the old Fairfield College was no more. For here, in the quaint little rooms, the college girls of ante-bellum days, daughters of the planters of the Southland, held their secret midnight feasts, whispered their hopes and fears to one another, here in the drawing rooms held their parties wearing their quaint billowing skirts and demure lace mitts and on the long verandas as a bevy of young girls gathered one morning to say goodbye to a company of young boys who had donned the gray.

The Fairfield Female College was erected in 1858. The need for it became apparent with the quick growth and development of Freestone County, one of the largest slave-holding sections of Texas before the war, and the more progressive citizens and wealthy planters realized the great need of educational facilities for their daughters. Definite action for the college came in 1857. It was established by the authority of the legislature. A board was selected and invested with the power to grant diplomas to all pupils deemed worthy, and to "perform all acts necessary to put in operation and perpetuate a first class female institution of learning."

The fame of the college spread and from all over the state and from other Southern states girls came to attend it. They were girls of a romantic and unique period. They came from the great plantations of the Southland, and they came from the homes of pioneering strength and foresight.

A slim little woman, Mrs. Henry Childs of Fairfield, to whom death came, a few days ago, lay in her bed by a window with soft white curtains and told of her girlhood at the old college. She unfolded a life of romance and excitement and interest which dulls the so-called exciting existence of the modern college girl.

Mrs. Childs spent her earliest childhood on the great plantation of her father, Doctor Winters of Columbus, Miss. Then came the journey to Texas. The little girl and her mother and sisters and brothers rode in a carriage. It was part of the long caravan composed of their cattle, horses, wagons and their slaves. When the long hours grew too wearisome the mother gave commands for the wagons to be stopped and the children climbed out to wade in the little streams that ran across the road or to gather the first autumn leaves, the nuts and the winter grapes that hung in purple bunches from the vines that swung across the path of the travelers.

"I thought Texas was the most wonderful place in all the world," Mrs. Childs said. "It was all so different from the life we had known on the big plantation near Columbus. At first I went to a little log cabin school, where the big girls went barefooted and carried their snuff boxes in their apron pockets. The woods were filled with interesting things. There were the wild turkey, bear and wolf, but, best of all, the shy deer, which at last became so tame that one day they came right up to our fence and looked over at a little tame dear that we had. My chief pet and delight was my beautiful saddle horse, Ramon.'

"When the college was founded my father placed Elmira, my sister, an unusually lovely girl and ever since then I have been attached to a place. I was (?) yet and gaieties were (?) the campus in the evenings, our secret lunches when the lights were supposed to be out. Sometimes (?) other times it was sent to us from homes, but wherever it came from it was the basis of a happy and enthusiastic evening as we gathered by the sheltered light of a candle."

"We heard the proclamation of war with mingled wonder and misgivings. Most of us were very young. Life was beautiful and lovely. We listened to the announcements in chapel. We saw the stern and solemn faces of our elders and then forgot it in our play."

"But one day is stamped upon my memory forever. The first company of our boys was leaving. They rode up to the college steps in the morning, gallant, carefree, must have been spring, because I remember that the girls were wearing light, fluffy dresses. How lovely it all was. I remember that William Moody was captain of the group. A young girl named Molly Rather presented him with a Confederate banner, and our eyes dimmed as she said:

> 'Take this banner and beneath
> The war clouds encircling wreath
> Guard it till our homes are free;
> Guarded, God will prosper thee.'

"Emma Anderson who later became Mrs. Chandler of Buffalo, made a little patriotic speech to them, and they galloped away. We who were left standing there on the veranda wondered what (?) this (?) Embroidered names on knapsacks (?) the soldiers, and soon began to listen and look for names, for the war had taken on a sense of personal danger to those we loved."

A few years ago when P.D. Browne of Fairfield, taking his master's degree from the University of Texas, decided to use for his thesis the History of Freestone County he asked Mrs. Chandler to tell him something about her days at the college before the war. Mrs. Chandler wrote just before her death. "The first I remember hearing of the college was when a neighbor stopped at my brother's house one morning and told him that a college for girls was being built in Freestone County. My brother turned to me and said: 'You are going to attend that college.'

In those days we had nothing but little log houses with one teacher who boarded with some patron who had room to spare. My brother with whom I was staying at that time, lived about nine miles south of Fairfield on the Fairfield and Centerville road. The old stage coach carried the mail between the two places three times a week and I would go to the college on Monday and come back Saturday. Dr. H.L. Graves was the president, a gentleman of the old school, a descendant of the Lees of Virginia."

The rooms at the college were large and comfortable. We had a library, a spacious chapel, dining rooms and other comfortable accommodations. I remember particularly that each room had two large windows, that reached to within a foot of the floor, making it easy for girls bent on mischief, and there were some then even as now, to slip in and out again. The water came from a well in the back yard. A large bell stood on the corner of the gallery. It was rung about 6 o'clock in the morning at 9 o'clock at night."

"We had several hours of recreation after school closed, when we would walk or occupy ourselves as we liked. But we were not allowed to cross certain boundaries. We went to our rooms and were supposed to study a half hour. After the nine o'clock bell rang at night each girl was supposed to stay in her room. One of the teachers, usually Doctor Graves, would knock at each door inquiring if all were in. If any visitors were there they would slip out at a convenient window and be demurely studying or at some other necessary talk when he knocked at their door. After he had gone downstairs they would very likely slip back and finish the innocent piece of mischief they were engaged in at the time of the interruption."

"If we failed to march in with the others at the sound of the bell we did without a meal until the next. Sometimes we would smuggle biscuits or teacakes or whatever was easy to hide, and secretly take it up to the unfortunate one who had been locked out. We wore roomy sleeves, sometimes built for smuggling. Nobody was allowed to leave the table until all had finished. Then Doctor Graves would tap a bell, each girl would rise and move her chair back against the wall, face about and march with her mate across the table, up the stairs to her room or out on the grounds."

"We had no sports such as tennis or golf, but we played ball, ran races and played hop-scotch. We had a good sized campus. The whole place was lined with the old-fashioned hedge rose. Misses Mollie and Betty Graves, Doctor Graves' daughters, had a lovely rose garden. Sometimes they allowed us to walk in it and pluck a rose or two. I have a cutting of the hedge rose in my back yard. It is an immense bush and is blooming today."

"A negro woman named Tempy waited on the rooms. I remember how we hired Tempy to smuggle us something to eat, and after the teachers had gone to bed we would have a midnight feast. Sometimes we were surprised in our illicit little capers, but we usually 'got by.' On one occasion, however were caught red-handed. There was only one teacher we could cajole, and it happened that she was the one who went the rounds. We had the feast spread in our room and were having the time of our lives when somebody knocked. We had to go to the door, and when we opened it Miss Betty stepped into the room. We all rushed to her, threw our arms around her and begged her not to give us away. So we made her stay and help eat our purloined supper and promise not to report us."

"I shall never forget our dances, and wonder what the college girl of today would have to say about them. No boys were thought of, of course, so some of the tallest girls would act as young men. They would dress as near the part as our wardrobe would allow. They would make up a very ferocious mustache and assume very distinguished names. I do not remember that were ever caught in this kind of fun, which would have been immediately banned."

"Henry Lee son of Doctor Graves, was the only boy that went to the school and we teased him unmercifully."

"When the war came, my brother joined the army and I became a regular boarding student. I remained there until 1865. I was thinking the other day of my years there, of how Sunday we went to church with Doctor Graves and his corps of teachers. There was never any disturbance."

"At dinner, when our name was called, during the week we were supposed to relate some historical fact we had learned that day. On Sunday, we gave a verse from the Bible."

"There is another distinction for the college I must not miss. We had a nobleman for a music teacher, a descendant from the house of Sobieska, Poland. He was in the Southern army, was wounded at the battle of Shiloh, was discharged and came to Fairfield, where he taught music. He was quite a dandy. His little black mustache curled up and his black hair was worn in ringlets. His name was Count Rudolph von Godski. And so I took lessons from a Polish nobleman and played in a concert!"

"Although the college was open as a school for a number of years preceding (sic) the war its glory died with the surrender of General Lee. Poverty walked in the South where luxury had reigned before. Sadness, bewilderment and desolation hung over the great plantations. The days of reconstruction were upon the people, that peculiar and ghastly period of Southern history."

Mrs. Childs went home from the college to be with her people, who sat many nights with weapons about them, fearing marauding bands.

The years went by, the land bloomed again, at last Mrs. Child's daughter, Inez, was a student at the college, which was now open to both boys and girls. "But the spirit," said Mrs. Childs, "was dead. Never again was it to know the beauty, the charm and the romance of other days when young girls wandered arm in arm through the rose gardens and under the tall oak trees. They told me one day that the stately old building had passed into private ownership and was being razed. That was one of the saddest days of my life. There came to be an almost unbearable longing to stand in my old room once again, to walk down the lengths of the old verandas."

"If I could have done it, I am sure there would have been an echo of girlish laughter from the old halls, a flutter of billowing skirts along the campus walks."

APPENDIX II

1. FAIRFIELD FEMALE COLLEGE

Fairfield Female College was located in Fairfield, Freestone County, Texas. On February 13, 1858, a group of town leaders incorporated as the Freestone County School Association "to put in operation and perpetuate a first class female institution of learning." The Baptist State Convention endorsed the college but it was not an official Baptist institution. It may have opened in the bottom floor of the Masonic lodge in Fairfield. In November 1854 the Leon Pioneer reported, "The Masonic hall, quite imposing, is nearly complete. The lower room of the hall is occupied by Dr. Moore, who has under his charge a flourishing school composed of young ladies." W. B. Moore and principal (in 1856) H. V. Philpott were members of the Fairfield Masonic Lodge.[102]

Construction of a two-story building, located a mile southwest of the county courthouse, was completed in early 1859, and classes began in February. About seventy girls were in attendance for the first session. The school was chartered on February 8, 1860, along with a male academy that failed. Henry L. Graves was selected president of the new college. Graves had previously served as president of Baylor University at the town of Independence, Texas and of the Baptist State Convention. He taught ancient languages and moral and intellectual philosophy. Other offered courses included mathematics, English literature, music, and ornamental art. In addition to the college curriculum, a graded preparatory department was offered. The length of each session was twenty weeks, and tuition was fifteen to twenty dollars for prep school and twenty-five dollars for college classes. The students, faculty, and Graves and his family lived in the school building and were attended by nine slaves, who did maintenance, housework, cooking and serving.

In February 1861, the same week that the Secession Convention in Austin passed the Ordinance of Secession, the college property was put on sale at public auction. Graves bought all the property, including ten acres of land on which the buildings were situated, for $5,000. Assisted by three women teachers, he operated the

---

[102] *Shields, D.R. Fairfield Female College, Handbook of Texas Online.*

school until it closed. Attendance was good in 1861, and during the war a number of refugees descended on the area, bringing enrollment to its highest levels at about 200, but also causing a housing shortage. The war continued and attendance dropped. In December 1869 Graves and the other owners of the college and property sold their interest to Alice M. Adams for $1,500 and the assumption of $5,000 indebtedness against the school. In the following years the Fairfield Masons annually appointed a school committee to provide education for the children of deceased master Masons living in the jurisdiction of the lodge. The college was closed in 1889. In 1936 the state of Texas erected a marker at the site. The Houston Chronicle, Sunday, Sept. 28, 1930, 'Ante-Bellum Women Cherish Texas College Memory'.[103]

[103] *Appendix I, Item 17.*

2. JEFFERSON DAVIS, PRESIDENT, CONFEDERATE STATES OF AMERICA

Jefferson Davis (1808-1889) was born in Todd County, Kentucky, on June 3, 1808, the youngest of ten children in the family. His father served in the Continental Army during the American Revolution. The family moved to Louisiana and then Mississippi where he attended school before entering the U.S. Military Academy in 1824. After graduating in 1828, he served seven years in the army under Colonel Zachary Taylor in Wisconsin at the time of the Black Hawk War. For the next ten years he was a planter in Mississippi, became active in Democratic Party politics and was elected to the United States House of Representatives in 1845. With the onset of the Mexican War he resigned his seat in Congress, raised and trained a volunteer regiment, the Mississippi Rifles, and served as their Colonel. He insisted on providing the best possible equipment for his troops and armed them with the newly developed Model 1841 percussion rifle. His regiment contributed to the United States victory at the Battle of Monterrey and played a decisive role in the Battle of Buena Vista. In 1847 he was elected to the U.S. Senate and subsequently served as the Secretary of War under President Franklin Pierce. On his return to the Senate he was Chair of the Committee on Military Affairs.

These experiences and the knowledge he had gained made him cautious about secession as he was certain that such would lead to war and that the Southern states lacked the military resources to prevail in a prolonged conflict. Once secession became likely he resigned from the U.S. Senate, was named Provisional President of the Confederate States of America at a Constitutional Convention and inaugurated on February 18, 1861 at Montgomery, Alabama. During that convention he had urged caution in secession and after his election had appointed a Peace Commission to meet with the government in Washington, D.C. The commission was authorized to offer to pay for any federal property on southern soil and to assume responsibility for their share of the national debt but not to discuss terms of reunion.

The newly inaugurated U.S. President Lincoln and his Secretary of State William Seward refused to meet with the Confederate commissioners as doing so could indicate recognition of the legitimacy of their government. The Federal troops in Charleston, South Carolina, commanded by Major Robert Anderson, had relocated to Fort Sumter and refused the order to surrender from Confederate Brigadier General P.G.T. Beauregard. President Lincoln sent a fleet of armed ships to resupply the fort and the first to arrive on April 11 was the Harriet Lane.[104] The commission never had the opportunity to act as the bombardment of Fort Sumter on April 12, 1861 had ended any opportunity for a peaceful resolution.[105] Once it became apparent to Davis and his cabinet that the newly inaugurated President Lincoln intended to reinforce that fort, they approved the bombardment by General P.G.T. Beauregard and the war began.

Following the collapse of the Confederacy in the spring of 1865, Davis evacuated the capital in Richmond and was captured in southern Georgia. Although indicted for treason, Davis never faced trial and was released on bond in 1867. He spent most of the remainder of his life in Mississippi where he completed writing "The Rise and Fall of the Confederate Government" in 1881. This helped restore his reputation and for the remainder of his life he was viewed as a hero throughout the South. On June 14, 1875, he was offered the presidency of the newly established Agricultural and Mechanical College of Texas (now Texas A&M University) but declined the appointment. He died in New Orleans on December 6, 1889 at the age of 81 years.[106]

---

[104] *The U.S. Coast Guard cutter, Harriet Lane, was to play a role in the Battle of Galveston in 1863. The ship, named for the niece of U.S. President James Buchanan had served as a very popular "First Lady" during the administration of the only bachelor U.S. President (1857–61). Miss Lane later married Henry Eliot Johnston of Baltimore, but none of their children survived them. Upon her death in 1903, she left her sizable estate to begin what is now St. Alban's School at the Washington National Cathedral and the Department of Pediatrics at the Johns Hopkins Hospital in Baltimore.*

[105] *Crofts, Daniel W. Reluctant Confederates: Upper South Unionists in the Secession Crisis.*

[106] *Campbell, Randolph B. and Bishop, Curtis. Davis, Jefferson. The Handbook of Texas Online.*

3. DESSERETTE – THE SMITH PLANTATION IN BLADEN COUNTY, NORTH CAROLINA

Information about the Smith family and their plantation life in North Carolina was learned from a visit to Bladen County in 2013. The home survived the Civil War and after one hundred-fifty years has been carefully preserved by the present owners, Commander George S. Council, Jr. USN (Ret.) and his wife, Patricia Averitte Council. They graciously permitted this author to visit Desserette and learn of its history. Details of the architecture and history are on the National Register of Historic Places Nomination Form. This was approved by the U.S. Department of the Interior, National Park Service in1987 and is available on-line.[107]

Major John Smith and Anna Jane Pouncey married on February 20, 1834 at her family's plantation in the Society Hill, South Carolina area and established their home in Bladen County, N.C. where his family had lived since the colonial era. It is unknown where the couple lived immediately following their wedding but it is estimated that the existing Desserette home was built in about 1840. The home is about two miles from the Cape Fear River, in the vicinity of the town of White Oak, about half way between Elizabethtown and Fayetteville. In 1840 the river and two roads which ran parallel to it were the primary transportation routes in the county. There were numerous landing sites on the river between the port of Wilmington and Fayetteville approximately 110 miles upstream.[108]

One of these landings, known as Prospect Hall, served as a post office between 1832 and 1866. A letter to Mrs. John Smith from her niece, Rebecca Crosland dated October 7, 1841 was sent to Prospect Hall, about one mile above the site used by the Desserette plantation for shipping.[109] Other landing sites were used for shipping or for storage of pine logs used for fuel by the steam driven paddle-wheel boats.

[107] *Bladen County, North Carolina, National Register of Historic Places.*
[108] *Cromartie, S. The Cape Fear River: Road to Bladen County Landings.*
[109] *Appendix I. Item 3. Letter from Rebecca Crosland, October 7, 1841.*

A federal post office was established at Desserette in 1853 and John Smith's brother, Thomas, was appointed the first postmaster. John Smith assumed that role in 1855, serving until 1857 when he and his family moved to Texas.

Desserette included 3,400 acres and produced considerable amounts of livestock and corn. These commodities were primarily food for John Smith's family and his forty-seven slaves. The income of the plantation was from commodities referred to as naval stores. These were products stored for later use by naval ships and included pine tar, pitch and turpentine. These were critical for the maintenance of wooden-hulled ships and in great demand by the British navy and merchant fleet. They had been highly valued since early colonial times. Lumber production was also active as Desserette produced 200,000 board feet of lumber annually during the 1850's. This industry depended on the abundant supply of longleaf pine trees that covered much of this plantation and the tidewater areas of the southeast.[110]

These commodities are not widely recognized now but were critical to the economy of the South from early colonial days to the mid-nineteenth century. Pine tar was made by slowly burning pine branches and logs in kilns and was used to paint the riggings that held masts and rails in place on the ships. Its other uses were as a lubricant, such as axle grease, preservatives for fence posts and as medication for livestock wounds. Pitch was made by boiling pine tar and the concentrated product, when heated, was applied to the bottom and sides of wooden ships to make them watertight. Turpentine was produced by distilling gum collected from cuts made in living trees. Its use in the colonial period was limited to medicinal purposes, as a water repellant for cloth or leather and in the manufacture of soap. The use for turpentine increased greatly between 1800 and 1860 when it was used for lamp lighting in homes and public areas. When combined with alcohol, the mixture was known as camphene or palmetto oil and was in great demand until 1860 when it was replaced by a cheaper illuminant, kerosene.[111]

[110] *Walbert, D. Naval Stores and the Longleaf Pine.*
[111] *Johnson, L. Naval Stores, North Carolina History Project.*

Although 3,400 acres is a large tract, the logging practices of that time would eventually deplete the forest resources. This, and the increasing profitability of cotton production, were factors in the changing emphasis of John Smith's efforts at Desserette after 1850. The need for additional land suitable for cotton production was an impetus for him to look westward for the expansion of his business. It must have been difficult for the family to leave their friends in Bladen County, the Old Shiloh Baptist Church at nearby Baker Lake and their home which was surely as comfortable as it was beautiful.

The main house is a two-story structure with a third floor attic and it rests on a high brick foundation. It is in the Greek Revival style with some late Federal Period interior details. It has a hipped roof with two interior plastered brick chimneys that each served two fireplaces on both floors. The exterior of the house was of overlapping cypress plank siding that has survived to the present. The interior is in the Greek Revival style with fluted pilasters and decorative molding, wainscoting and railings. Hallways divide both floors which are joined by a single-flight stairway.

Directly west of the house is a one-story two room frame building covered in original lapped cypress siding and corner boards which was the original kitchen for the home. Two large fireplaces were used for cooking. There is also a frame smoke house of cypress weatherboard. Hardwood logs would have been stored there and used for the preservation of meat. It is likely that the design of the home and other buildings were models for what was built on the new property in Texas.

The buildings have been carefully protected and restored by Patricia and George Council, Jr. and the grounds reflect their skills as master gardeners. Desserette is a worthy reflection of a by-gone era and represents a part of our nation's heritage and history that is beautifully preserved.

4. THE AMERICAN REVOLUTION IN NORTH CAROLINA, THE BATTLE OF ELIZABETHTOWN AND THE FAMILY OF MAJOR JOHN SMITH.

Major John Smith's family had a tradition of military service as most of the men from the Carolinas. The Roll of Colonel Thomas Clark's First North Carolina Battalion indicates that Thomas Smith, the grandfather of John Smith, enlisted on July 25, 1776 in the 1st North Carolina Regiment and was still on active duty with that unit as of September 8, 1778.[112] During that time they had been present at the defense of Charleston, South Carolina in 1776. In February 1777 they were transferred from the Southern Department to George Washington's main army and Thomas Clark became Colonel of the 1st Regiment. As part of the North Carolina Brigade they fought in the Battles of Brandywine and Germantown where their commander, Brigadier General Francis Nash was mortally wounded in October 1777. General Nash is remembered as several states named towns in his honor, including Tennessee. In June 1778 the 1st Regiment was in the Battle of Monmouth and subsequently their brigade was sent south, arriving in Charleston in March 1780. The regiment was captured in the Siege of Charleston on May 12, 1780 and Colonel Thomas Clark and 287 men, including Thomas Smith were captured. They were paroled later that year and when the regiment was reformed the next summer, Smith reenlisted on May 15, 1781. As a member of Dixon's Company he saw action at the Battle of Eutaw Springs on September 8, 1781 when their company was serving under Brigadier General Jethro Sumner and the command of Major General Nathanael Greene. The military roll shows that Thomas Smith completed his service on May 21, 1782.

Major John Smith's father, James Smith, had been engaged, according to tradition, as a fourteen-year-old youth in the Battle of Elizabethtown in Bladen County where James and his wife Elizabeth Clark later established their home and where their son John had lived from his birth. This patriot victory, while not widely known outside of that area, was an important success and eliminated the Tory threat in the territory between the Cape

[112] *Appendix I. Item 1. North Carolina Regiment Records.*

Fear and Pee Dee Rivers. James had been a youth of exceptional physical and mental maturity and in August 1781 had journeyed from Jones to Duplin County to deliver supplies on behalf of his father, Thomas, who was away for duties with his regiment. While in Duplin County, James' patriotic zeal and ability attracted the attention of Colonels Thomas Brown and Thomas Robeson Jr. and he was permitted to join the difficult march to Elizabethtown.[113]

The Tories having driven many of the Whigs from their homes, had ravaged Bladen County, insulting and plundering the most respectable families, burning private dwellings and destroying a great amount of valuable property. Sixty Whig patriot militiamen were hiding in Duplin County and in late August 1781 they marched toward Elizabethtown under the cover of night. Colonel Robeson realized that his small band would need more than bravery to overcome the 400 Tories and British regulars in the town. Sallie Salter, daughter of an influential family in the area proved to be an effective spy for the patriots as she entered the Tory camp selling eggs to the troops. She gathered information that helped Colonel Robeson devise an effective strategy. That night his small band crossed the Cape Fear River one mile below the Tories and early on the morning of August 27 attacked from different positions with rapid reloading of their weapons. The deception caused chaos among the Loyalists who were convinced that they were under attack by a vastly larger force. After their commanders were killed, the Tories scattered and their troops were decimated. This rout had devastating effects on the British sympathizers in the area which remained peaceful until Cornwallis' surrender at Yorktown in October 1781.[114] This event confirms that the American Revolution in much of the south pitted neighbor against neighbor and was in reality a civil war.

[113] Tew, Jerome D. Battle of Elizabethtown. The Sampson Independent. 2012.
[114] Ibid.

5. HISTORY OF THE WELSH NECK BAPTIST CHURCH

A small group of Baptists from the counties of Pembrokeshire and Carmarthenshire in Wales were motivated by deep religious convictions, for which they faced persecution, "to resolve to seek their future in America." In the spring of 1701 they had constituted a church with Thomas Griffith as their minister, met at Milford Haven Waterway in Wales, embarked on the ship "James and Mary" and landed in Philadelphia on September 8, 1701.[115] The initial group of sixteen persons received courteous treatment from the earlier settlers in the William Penn colony and they were advised to settle in the area of Pennepec where other Welsh-speaking immigrants had settled since the mid-1680s. Over the next year and a half their number had increased to thirty-seven and in 1703 they purchased from William Penn what was known as the Welsh Tract of over 30,000 acres in Newcastle County. This area was initially in the province of Pennsylvania but a later boundary change placed most of their land in Delaware. In Pennepec their numbers grew and they became part of the congregation of the Pennepack Baptist Church founded in 1688. On their removal to the Welsh Tract they affiliated with the Pencader Hundred Baptist Church in New Castle County, Delaware.[116] Over the next thirty years their group continued to grow in numbers and in prosperity and they established the Welsh Tract Baptist Church. Several families had become slaveholders, which put them at odds with others of their faith and congregation. By the mid-1730's a number of the Welsh Baptist community were influenced by publicity concerning the availability of suitable land for farming in the Carolinas. In May 1731, Benjamin Franklin published in the Pennsylvania Gazette the accounts of Hugh Meredith that made favorable mention of the prospects of the area.

---

[115] *The Church at the Welsh Tract, in the County of Newcastle upon Delaware. http://www.gpp-5grace.com/graceproclamator/pp0199welshtractchurch.htm.*
[116] *Gilmore, G. W. The New Schaff-Herzog Encyclopedia of Religious Knowledge, 1:467–469.*

Welsh settlers had moved to the Cape Fear River area in 1725 but encountered hostile Indians who killed the family of a Thomas James. The continuing influx of people from Pennsylvania and other colonies had eliminated the threat of the Indians and many colonists of Welsh ancestry had moved into the area of Bladen County. In the early 1730's the royal governor of the province of South Carolina granted ten thousand acres in the upper Pee Dee River area. More than thirty families immigrated from the Welsh Tract to South Carolina beginning in 1735. These colonists, led by James James, Esq., and the slaves that some brought with them located in an area known as Welsh Neck near a town later named Society Hill. James James, Esq. had served as an Elder Deacon in the Pencader Hundred Baptist Church and as a Justice of the Peace in Pennsylvania and was both prosperous and respected by the Welsh community.[117] He and his three sons, Abel, Daniel and Philip and their spouses were important members of the Welsh Neck community, as this South Carolina frontier area was known. James James, Esq. was the great-grandfather of Sarah James Kolb, the grandmother of Anna Jane Pouncey Smith, the spouse of Major Smith. It had not taken long for the Welsh Baptists to form a church in their new homeland. In 1738 eight families founded the Welsh Neck Baptist Church. Their first pastor was the son of James James, Esq., the Reverend Philip James who was ordained on April 4, 1743. Philip James, born in 1701 in Pennepec, Pennsylvania served Welsh Neck Baptist Church until his death in 1753. The Welsh Neck Baptist Church had a far greater influence on the spiritual life of the South Carolina frontier than its small size and remote location might suggest. By the end of the eighteenth century it had served as the mother church of over thirty-five congregations in this area of westward expansion. In its early years it preserved much of its Welsh heritage but by 1777 it had 197 members the majority of whom were not of direct Welsh descent.[118]

[117] Jordan, J. W. "Colonial and Revolutionary Families of Pennsylvania." p.781.
[118] Johnson, L. "The Welsh in the Carolinas in the Eighteenth Century." North American Journal of Welsh Studies, Vol. 4, 1 (Winter 2004)

One of the major contributions of this religious community was its association with musical practices that became such a distinctive part of evangelical Christianity. Hymn singing became a part of Baptist worship throughout the South and some of this could be traced to the Welsh Neck influence.[119]

[119] *Ibid. p. 19.*

Figure 11

(SEE IMAGE IN GALLERY)
Pennepack Baptist Church, Philadelphia, Pennsylvania
(text from the marble marker in front of the church)

Pennepack Baptist Church

In the latter half of the seventeenth century Baptists from
England and Wales settled in the Country of Philadelphia.
Their gathering as baptized believers led to the formation of the
Pennepack Baptist Church.

In 1686, Elias Keach, son of the famed English Pastor,
Benjamin Keach arrived in America. Though unconverted,
he presented himself as a minister of the gospel. His name
secured for him the opportunity to preach and the
aforementioned group of believers, in need of a pastor were
among those who gave ear to his message.

Pennepack is a mother to Baptist Churches in Pennsylvania, New
Jersey, Delaware and beyond. Her influence extended throughout
the colonies and her early pastors traveled far and wide
preaching the gospel and organizing churches.
The great evangelist, George Whitefield, preached
on these grounds to about two thousand people May 10, 1740.

Elias Keach returned to England in 1692.
John Watts, second Pastor of the church is buried here.
Other early pastors include:
Evan Morgan, Samuel Jones, Joseph Wood,
Abel Morgan, Jenkin Jones and Peter Vanhorn.

The present rock building was constructed in 1805
during the ministry of Dr. Samuel Jones and his remains are
buried behind the meeting house in which he preached
for over fifty years. Other pastors and many of the faithful
saints of God rest in these hallowed grounds.

W.T. Brantly wrote the following words after visiting here in 1829:

"We always look with feelings of veneration upon the habitation
which may be regarded as the cradle of the greatness or goodness
and on which antiquity has marked its deep impressions.
In passing over such scenes, we seem to hold communion with
the reposing spirits that once enlivened that solitude, and to
identify them with the names and incidents which gladden and
diversify the present moment. We look back on the generous
anxiety with which their bosoms throbbed, when they laid those
foundations on which others have built. We call to mind their
mingled feelings of hope and fear, when they stretched the cords,
and planted the stakes of their tents; and fixed
a habitation for their God.
Will the generations which are to come after us build up,
or demolish these feeble beginnings."

Baptist historian Morgan Edwards
records the details of this event.
"He performed well enough till he had advanced pretty
far in the sermon. Then stopping short, looked like a man
astonished. The audience concluded he had been seized with a
sudden disorder; but on asking him what the matter was received
from him the confession of the impostate with tears
in his eyes and much trembling."

The deceiver became the first convert of his own preaching
for from this time he dated his conversion!
Keach repaired to Elder Thomas Dungan, who as Cold Springs
in 1684, founded the first Baptist Church in the colony of
Pennsylvania. Dungan administered the ordinance of baptism to
Keach and the young preacher returned to Pennepack.

The Pennepack Baptist Church was constituted in 1688.
It is recorded that "by the advice of Elias Keach and
with the consent of the following named persons viz:
John Eatton, George Eatton, John Baker, Samuel Vaus,
Joseph Ashton and Jane his wife, William Fisher,
John Watts and Elias Keach, a day was set apart
to seek God by fasting and prayer in order to form
ourselves into a church. Where upon Elias Keach was
accepted and received as our pastor and we sat down
in communion at the Lord's table."

The same year, 1688, Elder Dungan died, and in 1702,
the Church at Cold Springs was absorbed into the Pennepack
Church. Though not the first established, to
"Ye Olde Pennepack" belongs the distinction of being the oldest
Baptist Church in Pennsylvania. It is also one of the oldest
Baptist Churches in America.

In 1707, Pennepack, with four other Baptist churches,
Middletown, Piscataway and Cohansey in New Jersey,
and Welsh Tract in Delaware, became constituent members of the
Philadelphia Association, the first Baptist Association in America.
Therefore, my beloved brethren, be ye steadfast, unmovable,
always abounding in the work of the Lord,
for as much as ye know that your labour is not in vain
in the Lord. 1 Corinthians 15:52

Marker placed by the Baptist History Presentation Society
May 8, 2007

FIGURE 12

(SEE IMAGE IN GALLERY)
Welsh Tract Baptist Church, New Castle County, Delaware.

The Welsh Baptists, who arrived in Pennsylvania in 1701 and worshipped at the Pennepack Baptist Church, purchased a 30,000 acre tract from William Penn and relocated there in 1703. They built a church known as the Meeting House at Iron-hill in New Castle, Delaware. The original log building was replaced by the present structure (above) built in 1746. The James' lived across the Welsh Tract Road from this church where they owned a tavern which was said to have later sheltered Generals Washington, Greene and Lafayette when they had been atop Iron Hill spying on the British in the nearby Chesapeake Bay. At one time the Welsh Tract Road passed behind this church building and continued up and over Iron Hill. Traces of this abandoned road can still be seen southeast of the church. The oldest tombstone in the walled cemetery is inscribed in Welsh and dated 1707.

6. SAMUEL MAY WILLIAMS OF GALVESTON, TEXAS

Samuel Williams moved to Texas is 1822 as one of the original settlers in Stephen F. Austin's land grant. Williams was born in 1795 in Rhode Island, and his father was a sea captain, instilling in him a love of the sea and its ships. He became an apprentice to his uncle, a Baltimore commission merchant, a position that led to his living in Buenos Aires and learning the Spanish language and business practices. On his return to the United States, he settled in New Orleans before moving to Texas. With his language and business skills he became Austin's lieutenant and managed colonial and business matters during Austin's frequent absences. His service as postmaster of San Felipe and revenue collector for the State of Coahuila earned him 49,000 acres which he chose to locate on prime farm land with river access. By 1833 he and his partner, Thomas F. McKinney, formed a mercantile company and soon were the dominant cotton brokerage in the Brazos River area.[120]

During the Texas War of Independence from Mexico he used his credit to purchase arms in the United States. With his own resources he purchased a warship to protect his shipping interests and is considered the "Father of the Texas Navy." He relocated his business to Galveston where he was an investor in the Galveston City Company that developed the Tremont Hotel as well as the commission house and wharf. The brokerage partnership was assumed by Henry, Samuel's brother and the firm became H.H. Williams and Company. Samuel Wiliams was an early leader of Masonry in Texas and served as Grand Master of Masons in Texas in 1840. During the latter years of his life he concentrated his efforts on banking and political support for his friend, Sam Houston. Williams died September 13, 1858 leaving his wife, four children and a home in Galveston that is still preserved by the Galveston Historical Commission.[121]

[120] Briseno, E.X. Samuel May Williams-Texas Pioneer, Businessman and Freemason (http://www.grandlodgeoftexas.org)
[121] Henson, Margaret S., Williams, Samuel May, Handbook of Texas Online.

7. THE U.S. PRESIDENTIAL NOMINATION AND ELECTION OF 1860

The United States Civil War was certainly the most devastating event in the nation's history and had far-reaching effects on virtually every aspect of its subsequent experience. The loss of over 700,000 lives during the four years of the war and an unknown loss of productivity from disability and shortened life spans of injured men had profound effects on the demographics, politics, the economy and the role of the United States as a military presence and world-wide influence of the nation. While the war began as a result of the secession of the southern states, the factors that led to that tragic event were complex and had culminated in the U.S. Presidential election of 1860.

The political environment of the United States had, since its founding, evolved along the lines of controversy concerning the focus of power and influence in a central authority (Executive branch) or in the diffusion of authority to the states (Legislative branch). This had initially involved the competition between Federalists (the party of Hamilton, Adams and Washington) and the Anti-Federalists (Jefferson, Madison and Monroe). After the election of Jefferson over John Adams in 1800 his party, the Democratic-Republicans, dominated the political arena. With the demise of the Federalist Party after the War of 1812, they were the only national political party.

In the election of 1824, sectionalism became a dominant political factor and the Democratic-Republican congressional caucus presented four nominees for the presidency. None received a majority of the electoral votes (Andrew Jackson-99, John Quincy Adams-84, William Crawford-41 and Henry Clay-37) and the outcome was decided in favor of Adams by the vote of the House of Representatives. Jackson's faction would become the Democratic Party and the factions of Adams and Clay would become the National Republicans, later known as the Whigs and eventually the Republican Party. By 1856 the geographic distinction was complete and, although James Buchanan of the Democratic Party was elected, the Republican candidate, John C.

Fremont needed only to have won a pair of states to have been elected. The Republican support was exclusively from states opposed to slavery and their prospects for victory in the non-slave states of Pennsylvania, New Jersey, Indiana or Illinois made their eventual success likely. For the Democratic Party to prevail, they would need to carry most of those four northern states.

The issue of slavery as a political factor had been present since colonial times and although slavery had existed throughout the colonies, it was eventually banned in some of them. The opposition to it was both religious and economic as it gained support in areas where the agricultural economy required a larger labor force to produce marketable commodity products. In colonial times this product was tobacco requiring intensive labor and which was also limited by the availability of suitable land.

One of the first restrictions on the spread of slavery was the Northwest Ordinance, approved by the Congress of the Confederation of the U.S. in 1787. This prohibited slavery in the territory northwest of the Ohio River and was passed again by the U.S. Congress in 1789. The ordinance was supported by southern states as it would keep these new territories from competing in the production of tobacco. This ordinance also established the Ohio River as the boundary between slave and non-slave states.

From the earliest years of the union, it was recognized by many leaders from both the north and south that phasing slavery out of the economy was needed. Compensation of the owners and provisions for the freedmen would be required. Perhaps Benjamin Franklin was the best chance for such to be considered in the new constitution but with his death in 1790 the impetus for gradual emancipation was lost.

By 1790 the economic significance of slave labor to the southern states was such that their ratification of the Constitution depended on a compromise that accepted its existence. The next thirty years were profoundly influenced by the expanding industrial revolution in Great Britain and the invention of the cotton gin by Eli Whitney in 1793. These events led to greatly increased demand for cotton and the ability to deliver this product was thought to require the expansion of slave labor. Cotton production greatly enhanced the wealth of the southern states and any restriction on slavery was rejected by many of the white inhabitants.

The last opportunity to peacefully change this viewpoint was lost with the passage of the Missouri Compromise in 1820 that prohibited slavery in the new lands of the Louisiana Territory north of the 36-30 parallel except for the new slave state of Missouri. The Tallmadge Amendment would have forbidden the further introduction of slaves into Missouri and children of slave parents born in the state would be free at the age of 25 years. The defeat of this amendment in the U.S. Senate indicated that any attempt to peacefully resolve the slavery issue would be unlikely to succeed.

During the next decades the sectional conflict over slavery focused on its extension into the newly acquired territories of Texas and the lands gained after the Mexican War. Such actions as the Wilmot Proviso and the Compromise of 1850 failed to resolve the issues and the Kansas-Nebraska Act of 1854 clearly drew the lines between legislative supporters for the continuation or the restriction of slavery. This debate gave life to the newly formed Republican Party and split the Democratic and Whig Parties. The election of 1856 as noted above clearly defined the subsequent debate and the nominating process of the parties for the 1860 election and predicted the nation's future.

The outcome of the election of 1860 was sealed by the fracturing of the Democratic Party at its convention in Charleston, S.C. in April 1860 when delegates from all of the "cotton states" led by William Yancey of Alabama walked out over a platform dispute and the remaining delegates were unable to select a candidate. The Democrats reconvened in Baltimore in June and again the southern delegates left when the party failed to support the requirement of the expansion of slavery into territories even though it was rejected by the local voters. The remaining Northern Democrats nominated Stephen A. Douglas, Senator from Illinois, who favored self-determination for the territories. Yancey and the Southern Democrats met in Richmond and nominated John Breckinridge of Kentucky who was a former Senator and the current U.S. Vice-President for the presidency. The Republican Party met in May and in a contentious process nominated Abraham Lincoln who was considered a moderate on the slavery issue. The party platform made it clear that slavery would not be allowed to spread further and adopted other positions including tariffs protecting northeastern industry, the granting of free farmland in the west to settlers and the funding of a transcontinental railroad which assured that there would be no support for their party in the south. A smaller group which rejected both party platforms created the Constitutional Union Party which narrowly selected John Bell of Tennessee over Sam Houston, Governor of Texas as it's candidate. This party advocated compromise to save the union and preserve the Constitution.

The results of the election on November 6, 1860 were no surprise and clearly predicted the conflict that could not be peacefully resolved. Abraham Lincoln received 180 of the 303 electoral votes but had only received 39.8% of the popular vote and had no support in the southern states. Breckinridge received 72 electoral votes but only 18.1% of the popular vote. He carried all of the slave states except Virginia, Tennessee and Kentucky who voted for Bell (39/12.6%). Missouri was the only state carried by Douglas who received 29.5% of the popular vote.

On December 20, 1860 the state of South Carolina voted to secede and was followed by the cotton states in the next three months. The Peace Commission failed to achieve any compromise legislation for the lame duck congress. After Lincoln's inauguration on March 4, 1861 and the beginning of the Thirty-seventh Congress, controlled by the veto-proof majority of Republicans, the inevitable war began.

From a distant perspective it can be concluded that this catastrophic event was a result of the unwillingness of the national leaders, the states and individual Americans to seek compromise and to resolve issues. This failure would have disastrous effects. Sadly, a nation that had been created by compromise was dissolved by the failure to work toward that goal which is essential for a democratic union to exist successfully.

8. COLONEL ABEL KOLB AND THE AMERICAN REVOLUTION IN SOUTH CAROLINA

The gathering of information for the story of Berta Smith and John Wootters often brought my attention to the generations of family that preceded Berta and their experiences in South Carolina and in Pennsylvania in the early days of the eighteenth century. Much of this information is derived from a book written by the Right Rev. Alexander Gregg, "History of the Old Cheraws." The volume, published in 1867 and reprinted in 1925, is available in DVD format from dmkheritage.com. Alexander Gregg, the first Episcopal bishop of the Diocese of Texas was elected in 1859 and he moved his family to Texas from Cheraw, S.C. where he had been rector of St. David's Parish since 1846. Gregg was born on his father's plantation near Society Hill, Darlington County, in 1819. During his youth and adult life he would have known many of the people with the names of Kolb, James and Pouncey who were relatives of Anna Jane Pouncey Smith, Berta's mother.

One individual often mentioned in Gregg's history is Colonel Abel Kolb, the grandfather of Anna Jane Pouncey whose service in the American Revolution is not only worthy of description, but was a defining experience in the lives of subsequent generations of his family and of their slaves. Values and personal ethical beliefs are transmitted to subsequent generations, not through our genes, but through the examples of our lives and the truths that are taught to our children and grandchildren. Hence, there is merit in relating the story of this American patriot. The story also relates an aspect of the First War with Great Britain that is not widely appreciated.

Abel Kolb, the son of Peter Kolb and Ann James, was born in 1750 in Society Hill, S.C. Abel's grandfather, Johannes Kolb and several of Johannes' brothers who were Mennonites had emigrated in 1707 from the German town of Wolfsheim (now in Rhine-Palatinate) to Germantown, and later the Skippack Township of the Colony of Pennsylvania. Johannes' wife Sarah was likely a member of the Welsh Baptist community in Pennepec. They had eight children before the family emigrated to the Welsh Neck area of the Pee Dee

River in South Carolina. This arduous journey between 1732 and
1735 would have traversed the Great Wagon or Fall Line Roads.
Their infant child, Peter, grew up at Kolb's Neck on the river where
his father built a mill and operated the Cashway ferry.

Peter married Ann James, the daughter of Rev. Philip James
who served as the first pastor of the Welsh Neck Baptist Church,
of which the Kolb family were members. Peter and Ann had six
children, the fifth being Abel Kolb, born in 1750. Abel married
a cousin, Sarah James, and they owned a six hundred acre
plantation near the town of Society Hill. The residence was a
two-story brick building on the east bank of the river. They had
two daughters who survived to adulthood, Ann, born in 1773
(who married Major James Pouncey) and Sarah (who married
Philip Pledger).

Abel Kolb enlisted in the South Carolina militia and was
commissioned captain on September 25, 1775. By 1780 he was
lieutenant colonel and was taken prisoner on May 12, 1780 at the
surrender of Charleston. He was then appointed colonel of the
Cheraw District Regiment and served under Francis Marion who
became brigadier general in January 1781. Kolb was a member
of the Welsh Neck Baptist Church and was elected a member of
the colonial House of Representatives for the Cheraw District. He
was a member of the St. David's Society that promoted educational
opportunities in the district.

After the patriot victory at the battle of Cowpens on January
17, 1781, Kolb led his regiment, under General Marion, in battles
at Georgetown and Wiboo Swamp. On April 27, 1781 his troops
routed a large force of Loyalists but on returning to his home
on April 28, he was captured by fifty North Carolina Tories and
was fatally shot in front of his wife and two daughters. The home
was plundered and burned and an historian wrote, "That was
a sad day for the people of Cheraw District when Abel Kolb fell
by the hand of the foe. He was recognized as the leader of the
patriot influence, in command of his regiment, in the prime of life,
vigilant, active, daring, he commanded the respect and confidence
of his countrymen far and near."

A number of the slaves owned by Ann and Abel Kolb, who might have escaped to freedom at the time of his murder, chose to remain with the family, making it possible for Ann Kolb and her daughters to rebuild their lives. The respect and loyalty that these slaves and Ann Kolb's family shared was evident in the family of her granddaughter, Anna Jane Pouncey Smith, mother of Berta Smith.

9. THE WALLINGS OF HOUSTON COUNTY, TEXAS

James R. Walling and his wife, Martha Mobley Walling settled on a farm in the Daly's Community of Houston County in 1838 after their move from Tennessee. While in Tennessee they had two children, Amanda (b. 1836) and Robert (b.1837) and after their move had five other children, including Hosea (b.1839). Their farm was adjacent to one owned by Richard Pennington and his wife, Polly Walling Pennington, the sister of James Walling. Other brothers and sisters joined them in Houston County and had notable experiences in Texas. A brother, Joseph Walling, filed the first request for permission to free a family of his slaves. This request was presented to the 3rd Texas Congress by Houston County Representative, Joseph A. Parker, but was denied.

Another brother, A. Elisha Walling, joined the Mier Expedition, a short-lived incursion in December 1842 across the Rio Grande River in retaliation for a Mexican invasion of the Republic of Texas.[122] In September 1842 a force of 1200 Mexican soldiers captured San Antonio. Their occupation of the city lasted but ten days and there was much disagreement as to the appropriate response by the fledgling Republic. President Sam Houston urged that Texas not retaliate but the "War Hawks" in the Texas Congress over-ruled his admonitions and created a poorly organized force of 750 men under General Alexander Somervell. Of this force, about 200 Texans entered the Mexican town of Mier where they met a large Mexican detachment. On December 25, 1842 they had success against the Mexicans until the lack of food, water and ammunition led to their surrender. One hundred-seventy six Texans were captured including A. Elisha Walling. This led to the "Black Bean Episode" in which the prisoners were forced to draw from a jar containing 159 white beans and 17 black beans. Those with black beans were immediately executed and the others placed in prisons where many died. The prisoners, including Walling, were eventually released in September 1844. These events were among a number of issues that led to the Mexican War of 1846-47.

---

[122] *Gunn, Jack W. Mexican Invasions of 1842. The Handbook of Texas Online.*

In 1860, Robert Walling, son of James and Martha Walling, was employed as an overseer for Redden (sic. Redding) S. Pridgen on his farm in the Daly's Community area. Redding Pridgen was born in Alabama in 1822, the son of Wiley Washington Pridgen and Mary Baker Pridgen. He served as captain in McCowan's Company, First Mounted Texas Riflemen in the Mexican War. With the onset of the Civil War, R. S. Pridgen recruited a company at Elkhart (then in Houston County) on June 22, 1861. Robert, his brother, Hosea, and their younger friend, Lucius Smith, joined that unit, later known as Company H, 5th Regiment, Texas Mounted Volunteers after their official organization on September 1, 1861 in San Antonio. This unit was cited in an official report of the Battle of Val Verde as deserving "great credit for their coolness and gallantry." It was in this battle on February 21, 1862 that Lucius Smith was fatally wounded. Hosea died on March 14, 1862 from wounds received in the battle and Robert died of pneumonia on March 11[123] at the field hospital in Socorro, New Mexico.[124]

---

[123] *Redding Scott Pridgen, Hosea Walling and Robert Walling, www.findagrave.com*
[124] *Taylor, J. Bloody Valverde. p. 107.*

10. SIBLEY'S BRIGADE AND
THE WAR IN THE WEST
(SEE IMAGE IN GALLERY)

In 1861, as the states that would constitute the Confederacy seceded from the union, their governments ordered the federal military presence within their boundaries to relinquish properties and equipment to the states' jurisdiction. After the Texas Secession Convention and the overwhelming popular vote in February, Brigadier General David E. Twiggs, commander of the U.S. Army troops in Texas turned over the munitions and arms and peacefully evacuated his troops. Twiggs, a native of Georgia, born in 1790, had a distinguished career through the War of 1812 and Mexican War. He had served as commander of the forces in Texas since 1857, except for part of 1860 during a sick-leave absence when replaced by Colonel Robert E. Lee. Twiggs resigned his U.S. Army commission and was the senior Confederate major general until his death in 1862.[125]

There was significant sympathy for secession in southern New Mexico and, at a conference of residents on March 3, 1861 in the Mesilla Valley, they voted to declare the lands below the 34th parallel as the Confederate Territory of Arizona. While U.S. Army officers such as Twiggs and Lee opposed secession, their consciences required that they cast their lots with the people and states of their births and they joined the Confederacy. Such an ethical dilemma was not a problem for Henry Hopkins Sibley, a U.S. Army officer stationed in New Mexico. He was descended from an early New England family, was born in Louisiana and grew up in Missouri. He graduated from West Point in 1838 and during his extensive military career had demonstrated a high degree of initiative and inventiveness. He created the Sibley Tent and Stove used by the U.S. Army for many years. He had served with distinction in the Mexican War and had continued his career in the western territories. His activities, however, had been impaired by recurrent abuse of alcohol that earned him the nickname "the Walking Whiskey Keg." He had recently been promoted to Brevet Major of Dragoons when, in April 1861, he

---

[125] *Thomas W. Cutrer and David Paul Smith, Twiggs, David Emanuel, The Handbook of Texas Online.*

resigned his commission and began a journey from New Mexico through El Paso and San Antonio to Richmond, Virginia.[126] A charming and charismatic speaker, Sibley persuaded President Jefferson Davis to assign him to lead a brigade of cavalry to seize the territory of New Mexico for the Confederacy. He anticipated that the U.S. Regular Army would be thinly deployed for Indian containment and that the New Mexican volunteers would not be able to stop him from capturing Fort Craig and subsequently Fort Union. This could give him control of New Mexico and the opportunity and supplies to take the territory of Colorado with its gold resources and possibly the other western territories that had been gained during the war with Mexico. He was commissioned a brigadier general and authorized to raise a brigade of 3200 men.

In July 1861 Sibley returned to San Antonio and the organization of his mounted brigade proceeded rapidly. In the spring of 1861 there was great enthusiasm for the new Confederacy and units began to form throughout Texas for military service. In the northern part of Houston County, Redding S. Pridgen began recruitment for a company of mounted troops. Pridgen had come to Texas as a youth with his large family and served in the Mexican War in Captain McCowan's Company, First Mounted Texas Riflemen where he had known Captain Tom Green, another company commander in the regiment. Pridgen and his wife, Elizabeth owned a plantation in Houston County, south of Elkhart and his overseer was Robert Walling. On June 22, 1861 his company, known as the Horse Cavalry Company, was organized at Daly's Community near Elkhart Creek. The following are listed on the muster role: Captain R.S. Pridgen, 2nd Lt. R. Chadwick (Elijah Chadwick, overseer of the Smith Landing Plantation), 3rd Sgt. Robert Walling, and privates, Hosea Walling and Lucius (Philander) Smith.[127] The muster role of December 1861 officially lists Elijah Chadwick as the bugler of the company and a private. As information concerning General Sibley's brigade spread, the company went to San Antonio and became Company H of the Fifth Regiment, Texas Mounted Volunteers, commanded by Colonel Tom Green.

[126] *Taylor, J. Bloody Valverde: A Civil War Battle on the Rio Grande.*
[127] *Mainer, T. Houston County in the Civil War. p.95-6.*

After several months of intensive training, the brigade was ready and eager for action. On October 21, 1861, following a grand parade through San Antonio, the brigade began its trek to El Paso and the invasion of New Mexico. The seven hundred mile journey to Fort Bliss on the Rio Grande River traversed desolate and arid terrain. Over 500 of the Confederate soldiers were lost to illness on this venture but by mid-December the force had reached El Paso. 400 men of the Second Regiment, Texas Mounted Rifles, commanded by Major Charles Pyron joined the brigade. These troops had initially been under the leadership of Lieutenant Colonel John Robert Baylor and had been dispatched to the southern New Mexico area in July 1861 to encourage Confederate sympathies.

The first unit to cross the border into New Mexico was the Fifth Regiment under Colonel Tom Green, including Company H with Lucius Smith and Hosea Walling. The entire brigade, now numbering 2600 men, soon followed north along the Rio Grande towards Fort Craig and the Union Army, commanded by Colonel Edward R.S. Canby. Within two weeks the troops neared Fort Craig and the movements of the Confederate force prompted Colonel Canby to send troops from the fort to meet the invaders at Valverde.

Valverde, or the "green valley", referred to three fords across a placid stretch of the Rio Grande River and a village about three miles upstream on higher ground not affected by malaria which plagued the lower bottom land in the warmer months. The village, with its ninety residents was about ten miles north of Fort Craig, which was the only military impediment to General Sibley and his Army of New Mexico.

On February 21, 1862 occurred the critical battle of the western campaign. The specific troop movements during that battle are superbly described in the book "Bloody Valverde: A Civil War Battle on the Rio Grande, February 21, 1862" by John Taylor beginning with his description of the dawn of the day: "although the morning was cold, some alert Texans may have noticed a faint reddish-tinged morning star just above Sagittarius in the southeastern sky. Mars, the god of war, was also up early that cloudy February day."[128]

[128] Taylor, J. Bloody Valverde. p. 41.

The intensity of the fight was very high and the encounter had not been going well for the Confederates by late in the afternoon. General Sibley had withdrawn from his command due to disability (likely alcohol related) and Colonel Tom Green assumed leadership of the entire force. The Texans were assailed by an artillery battery positioned on high ground. Colonel Green called for Company H and C of the Fifth Regiment, led by Major Samuel Lockridge, to join with the First Battalion of the Seventh Regiment led by Lieutenant Colonel John S. Sullivan to capture this battery of six guns under the command of Union Captain Alexander McRae. McRae was a native of North Carolina and graduate of West Point who had remained loyal to the Union.

At 4:00 PM Colonel Green divided his troop of 750 men into three waves for a frontal attack on the battery, and at his final urging said, "Boys, I want Colonel Canby's guns! When I yell, raise the rebel yell and follow me." The balance of the day was to change with his words, "Up, boys, and at 'em!" The waves of Texans armed with shotguns, pistols and Bowie knives covered the distance of seven to eight hundred yards to the Union battery which was protected by units of New Mexican Volunteers. These untested troops had never experienced anything as terrifying as a half-mile semi-circle of screaming Texans dashing headlong toward them. McRae's battery was able to fire several rounds from their guns, but, despite heavy losses, the Confederates continued their assault. As they neared the artillery placement, the terrified volunteer troops panicked, and the line of the Tenth U.S. Infantry Battalion collapsed with the loss of the battery.

Although clearly their victory, Sibley's Brigade suffered a ten percent casualty rate with 71 dead, including Lieutenant Colonel Sutton and Major Lockridge.[129] Private Lucius Smith was mortally wounded. Captain Pridgen later reported that Smith had charged the Union position without the slightest hesitation, successfully dispatching several of the enemy with his shotgun and two pistols before receiving a wound to his body. After the rout of the Union forces, his comrades, including Elijah Chadwick, brought Lucius to their camp. Through the night he had been ministered to by

[129] *Ibid. p. 75–84.*

Powhatan Jordan, the Captain of Company A and a distinguished physician from San Antonio, but Smith died the next morning. Hosea Walling was also critically wounded and died several days later. Robert Walling had been injured and within two weeks died of pneumonia.

Although the Battle at Valverde was clearly a defeat for the Union troops, the Texans had not been able to pursue the enemy to complete their victory or to capture Fort Craig due to the darkness of the winter evening on the 21st and a truce that the Union commander had requested. General Sibley concluded that an assault on the fort the next day would not be successful due to the strength of the fortifications and the loss of horses and pack animals which severely compromised their resources.

The Sibley Brigade continued northward occupying Albuquerque and Santa Fe but failed to improve their deficiency of winter equipment and ammunition. Five weeks after the battle at Valverde, units of the Second Texas Cavalry of Major Charles Pyron and the Fourth and Fifth Regiments under Lieutenant Colonel William Scurry met forces from Fort Union at Glorietta Pass and successfully drove them back through through the mountain gap. General Sibley had failed to securely guard their supply train, and a Union detachment was able to march around the Texans and burn most of their wagons, destroying the Army's equipment. Dr. Powhatan Jordan was promoted to major after his brave and effective leadership at Glorietta Pass. The Confederate losses in the campaign were severe, amounting to almost one thousand of the men that had left San Antonio the previous year. Dr. Jordan remained behind when the troop headed towards El Paso as there were many sick and wounded Texans unable to evacuate. It was later learned that he and other Texans were taken prisoner and transferred north to Camp Douglas in Chicago. Within the next year they were freed after an exchange of prisoners.

The brigade limped back to San Antonio by June and later served the Confederacy at the battle of Galveston and in Louisiana at the battle of Mansfield. General Richard Taylor assumed command of the brigade in early 1863 due to Sibley's problems with alcohol. The McRae cannons captured during the fateful battle would be known as the "Valverde Battery." These guns and their unit, which included Elijah Chadwick, would serve as a rallying point for the brigade until the end of the war.[130]

[130] *Ibid. p. 109.*

11. THE 1st TEXAS REG'T, HOOD'S BRIGADE – 1862: THE PENINSULA CAMPAIGN, SECOND MANASSAS AND THE MARYLAND CAMPAIGN

The companies that would constitute the 1st Texas Regiment reached Richmond, Virginia by August 1861 and, with the 4th and 5th Texas Regiments, became the Texas Brigade, commanded by General Louis Wigfall. The Southland had been elated by the victory at Manassas on July 21, but this battle awakened both the Union and Confederate populations to the reality that the casualties from the war would be greater than previously imagined. The Lincoln administration's immediate goals were to maintain control of border states (Maryland, Kentucky, Tennessee and Missouri) and to establish an effective defense of Washington, D.C. Their military strategy was a three-fold plan to blockade the southern ports, secure the Mississippi River and capture the Confederate capital at Richmond. After the war began in March 1861, the most intense action in the next year was found in Kentucky and Tennessee as the Federals sought to secure the Ohio and Mississippi Rivers, culminating in the crucial battle of Shiloh on April 6-7, 1862. This victory led to the Union advance into the state of Mississippi and the Federal victory at Vicksburg in July 1863, resulting in their control of the Mississippi River and the effective isolation of the western states of the Confederacy.

After the Confederate victory at Manassas, only a few miles from Washington, the war in the east became a defensive standoff and both sides reorganized their armies. The Union Army of the Potomac, commanded by General George B. McClellan, was charged to secure the capital at Washington and to capture Richmond. The Confederates were commanded by General Joseph E. Johnston and the Texas Brigade was enlarged by the addition of the 18th Georgia Infantry and assigned to the defensive line at the Potomac River. Wigfall was elected to the Confederate Senate in November and command was given to Colonel John Bell Hood who had been commander of the 4th Texas Infantry Regiment.

The brigade was moved from the Potomac to defensive lines south of the Rappahannock River in March 1862 in anticipation of McClellan's invasion of Virginia. This invasion, known as the Peninsula Campaign, began in mid-March with the landing of over 120,000 men at Ft. Monroe on the peninsula between the York and James Rivers with Richmond as their goal. By May that offensive had advanced only as far as Williamsburg and McClellan was surprised by Johnston's withdrawal of his troops to more secure defensive positions nearer the capital city. McClellan tried to intercept this withdrawal by an amphibious landing of 11,000 men further up the York River at Eltham's Landing, near the key rail and roadway intersections at West Point and Barhamville, Virginia. During the fight on May 7 the Texas Brigade had its first combat engagement. They were able to drive the Union troops back to the protection of their gunboats after Johnston had directed them "to feel the enemy gently and fall back." Later, with a sense of humor, Johnston asked Hood, "what would your Texans have done, sir, if I had ordered them to charge and drive back the enemy?" Hood's answer was, "I suppose, General, they would have driven them into the river and tried to swim out and capture the gunboats."[131]

A critical battle of the Peninsula Campaign, known as Seven Pines, took place between May 27 and June 1 with many casualties but did not involve Hood's Brigade to a great extent. The Federal advance on Richmond was halted, but General Johnston was wounded and unable to continue his command. Jefferson Davis replaced him with Robert E. Lee who became commander of the Army of Northern Virginia and reorganized the army, adding Hampton's Legion of South Carolina infantry to the Texas Brigade. Lee adopted a more aggressive stance and the Peninsula Campaign culminated in the Seven Days Battles (June 25-July 1, 1862) ending the immediate threat to Richmond as the Union troops were withdrawn to the Wasnington, D.C. area.

[131] *Sears, Stephen W. To the Gates of Richmond: The Peninsula Campaign. p. 86.*

During the Seven Days Battle, Hood's Brigade had its first major combat opportunity at Gaines' Mill (Farm). The brigade served in General Whiting's Division and was called upon to attack a strong Union defense. The brigade charged, breaking the Union line which withdrew across the Chickahominy River in defeat. This was Lee's first victory in the war and established the Texans as an elite fighting force in his mind and throughout the army.[132] Losses by the Texas Brigade were severe as every field officer was killed or wounded. The commander of the 1st Texas Regiment, Colonel A.T. Rainey, was wounded and the commander of Company I, Lieutenant J.L. Sheridan, was killed.[133]

The last battle of the campaign at Malvern Hill on July 1 went badly for the Confederates but McClellan and his army, with their morale crushed, were withdrawn by Lincoln to reinforce General Pope in northern Virginia. The Confederates incurred severe losses at Malvern Hill and the other battles of the Peninsula Campaign which demonstrated that direct infantry attacks against fortified fixed positions with modern weapons would result in immense human loss and suffering. The Enfield 1853 Rifle-Musket used by the Confederates and the Springfield Model 1861 of the Union forces could be fired at a rate of three rounds per minute with accuracy up to five hundred yards in experienced hands. The military tactics that had been taught for the previous century were not compatible with such deadly weapons. It was apparent that fatalities and injury would far exceed any previously experienced in warfare.[134]

[132] Ibid., p. 236–40.
[133] Chilton, F.S. Dedication of Monument to Hood's Brigade, Austin, TX, 1910.
[134] Bilby, J. Civil War Firearms: Their Historical Background and Tactical Use.

For the month following Malvern Hill the Texas Brigade recuperated in Richmond where thousands of ill and wounded soldiers were treated at large hospitals such as Chimborazo. The brigade received some replacements including a new company formed in Trinity County—Company M—which arrived on August 8 when they received orders to march north. They were assigned to Longstreet's command and they marched toward the Bull Run Mountains. The Texas Brigade and others were directed to clear Thoroughfare Gap of Union troops and after doing so they led Longstreet's troops to the eastern side of the mountain to support Stonewall Jackson's wing. The next afternoon Hood's Brigade led the charge at the Chinn Ridge, overwhelming two regiments of New York Zoaves. By the end of the day the Union troops were in full retreat but not in the state of panic that had characterized the first battle at Manassas in 1861. The Union army had ten thousand troops killed or wounded, but the Confederates, low on ammunition and weary from battle, had not succeeded in their original objective of completely destroying those forces.

Lee, who was jubilant with the success of his army, immediately sent them through the Shenandoah Valley and crossed the Potomac River into Maryland to meet McClellan and the Army of the Potomac near the town of Sharpsburg and Antietam Creek. Lee had several objectives in this invasion, namely to resupply his army from the northern farms that had not been affected by the war as had those of Virginia, and to further demoralize the northern population prior to the Congressional elections of 1862. Victories at that time could make the people and the government unwilling to continue the fight. He had also hoped to incite upheaval in the slave-holding state of Maryland and to enhance European support and recognition of the Confederate States of America.

Lee concentrated his forces, out-numbered two to one, in strong defensive positions at Sharpsburg. On September 17 occurred the bloodiest single day in American military history. By skillfully deploying his forces, Lee fought the Federals to a standstill and the following day was able to withdraw south of the Potomac River. The Confederates had 10,316 casualties (31%) and the Union 12,401 (25%). McClellan did not take the offensive on July 18, permitting Lee to withdraw safely. Four days later, Lincoln issued the Emancipation Proclamation, and the chance to gain support from France or England for the Confederacy was lost.

The 1st Texas Regiment lost 186 of the 226 men engaged at Sharpsburg Company I lost it's commander, Captain R. W. Cotton and six other men were killed and thirteen others wounded on that day. The 1st Texas regimental flag was left on the battlefield during the conflict and not returned to Texas for fifty years. Hood's division suffered greatly and after the battle when asked where his division was, Hood told Lee that "they are lying on the field...my division has been almost wiped out."[135]

John Wootters was promoted to Senior First Lieutenant and given command of the company.[136] The division spent the next several months in Winchester, Virginia where they restored some of their vastly depleted manpower. The 3rd Arkansas Infantry was added and Hampton's Legion and the 18th Georgia were transferred to other brigades.

[135] McPherson, James M. *Crossroads of Freedom: Antietam, The Battle that Changed the Course of the Civil War. p. 116-131.*
[136] *Appendix I. Item 6. Military Record of the 1st Texas Reg't.*

FIGURE 14

RESTORED FLAG OF THE 1ST TEXAS
INFANTRY REGIMENT
(SEE IMAGE IN GALLERY)

Flag Carried by the 1st Texas During the Peninsula Campaign,
at Second Manassas and Antietam

This flag was reported to have been made by the wife
and daughter of the regiment's first colonel, Louis T. Wigfall and
at least the star was said to have been made from material of
Mrs. Wigfall's wedding dress. In the summer of 1862 the four
battles named on the flag were added. At Antietam
on September 17, 1862 the 1st Texas Regiment lost 186 of its 226
men including nine standard bearers of this flag. It was captured
by a Federal soldier who was awarded the Congressional
Medal of Honor for the deed. The flag was returned to Texas in
1905 and is in the Texas State Library and Archives.

12. GENERAL ALBERT SIDNEY JOHNSTON AND THE BATTLE OF SHILOH

A consideration of the Civil War and the state of Texas must include an awareness of the critical battle at Shiloh and the Confederate commander, General Albert Sidney Johnston. The battle of Shiloh, at a town located in southwestern Tennessee between Pittsburg Landing on the Tennessee River and the Shiloh Church near the state of Mississippi border, took place April 6-7, 1862, and was a Union victory that had profound effects on the perception of the war by the public and by military leaders, both North and South. This two-day battle was the costliest in American history at that time with over 23,000 casualties. It established the certainty that the war would be longer and at greater loss than anyone had previously imagined. Although the initial reports from the field did not reflect well on the Union commander, Major General U.S. Grant, subsequent analysis indicated that his ability to regroup and attack on the second day had produced a major victory and justified President Abraham Lincoln's statement when Grant had been criticized: "I can't spare this man; he fights."

Following the battle at Shiloh, the Confederate army was unable to prevent the Federals from advancing into northern Mississippi and securing their hold on western Tennessee, giving them the access that would lead to the siege of Vicksburg and control of the Mississippi River the next summer. This would isolate the western states of Louisiana, Arkansas and Texas from the rest of the Confederacy. For President Jefferson Davis and many of the Confederate troops, a great loss to their cause was the death of General Albert Sidney Johnston, the commander of the Army of Mississippi and perhaps the outstanding military strategist in the field at that time. His surprise attack on April 6 nearly routed the Union forces but his fatal wound late in the day was a factor in the failure to pursue these gains and led to the success that the Federals had on the following day.[137]

---

[137] *Foote, Shelby. The Civil War: A Narrative, Volume 1, p.336–340.*

Albert Sidney Johnston, born in Kentucky in 1803, considered Texas his home as he had moved there in 1836 after the death of his wife and his resignation from the U.S. Army, eight years after graduating from West Point. He served in the army in the Texas War for Independence from Mexico and later was a Brigadier General and Secretary of War for the Republic of Texas. He resumed his U.S. Army service in the Mexican War as Colonel of the 1st Texas Rifle Volunteers.

While managing his plantation, China Grove, in Brazoria County, Texas he served as Colonel of the 2nd U.S. Cavalry in the West and was promoted to Brigadier General in 1857. At the outset of the War Between the States, Johnston was commander of the U.S. Army Department of the Pacific in California. When Texas voted to secede he resigned his commission and after a trek across the southwestern desert and Texas, reached Richmond, Virginia. His former schoolmate and friend, President Jefferson Davis, appointed him a full General and commander of the Western Department. His death at Shiloh represented the highest ranking officer on both sides to be killed in combat and it was a serious blow to the Confederate effort. Johnston may have been the only individual to be a general officer in the army of three different nations. His death was even more tragic when it became apparent that the simple remedy of a tourniquet on his right leg may have prevented his death from bleeding from a lacerated popliteal artery.[138]

---

[138] Flachmeier, J. F. Johnston, Albert Sidney. The Handbook of Texas Online.

13. BATTLE OF GALVESTON

In 1860 the city of Galveston was the largest in Texas and rapidly growing as it was not only the major seaport but also the center for banking, commerce and culture. The expanding cotton production in Texas fueled this prosperity as the city's wharves saw 194,000 bales in 1860 representing three-fourths of the state's production. It might be expected that the idea of secession from the union would not be welcome to such a city but after the election of Abraham Lincoln the spirit of separation became strong and in the statewide vote, Galvestonians voted for secession 765 to 33. Any chance of success for secession depended on the sale of the cotton production of Texas and the other states of the lower South to the markets in Europe to provide the funds to obtain the materiel needed to succeed in the war. The Confederacy had virtually no capacity for the production of firearms, artillery and ammunition for the military. Preventing this trade was the highest priority of the Federal Navy and on July 2, 1861 the blockade of Galveston began with the arrival of U.S.S. South Carolina, a screw-propelled steamer that was able to effectively close the port's activity.[139]

As part of the Union blockade of Texas, Commander William B. Renshaw led his squadron into Galveston harbor to demand surrender of the most important Texas port on October 4, 1862. Brigadier General Paul O. Hebert, commanding the Confederate District of Texas, had removed most of the heavy artillery from Galveston Island that he believed to be indefensible.[140] The Union ships held the harbor, but the 264 men of the Forty-second Massachusetts Infantry, led by Colonel Isaac Burrell, did not arrive until December 25 to occupy Kuhn's Wharf and patrol the town.

---

[139] Cotham, E. T. "Battle on the Bay: "The Civil War Struggle for Galveston."
[140] Barr, A., "Galveston, Battle of," Handbook of Texas Online, Published by the Texas State Historical Association.

When Major General John B. Magruder replaced Hebert in the fall of 1862, he began to organize for the recapture of Galveston. For a naval attack he placed artillery and dismounted cavalry from Sibley's Brigade, led by Colonel Thomas Green, aboard two river steamers, the Bayou City and the Neptune, commanded by Captain Leon Smith. Magruder sent infantry and cavalry, led by Brigadier General William R. Scurry, and supported by twenty light and heavy cannons, across the railroad bridge onto the island to capture the federal forces ashore. These Confederate leaders had been a part of the New Mexico invasion in which Lucius Smith lost his life and the cannons that were captured by his fatal charge at the battle of Valverde contributed to this effort. The Union commander, Renshaw had six ships that mounted twenty-nine pieces of heavy artillery to support his troops in the town.

At 3:00 a.m. on New Year's, January 1, 1863 the Confederate gunboats armed behind cotton bales appeared and General Magruder launched a land attack which was devastating for the unsuspecting Federals. The Confederates captured the Harriet Lane; the U.S.S. Westfield ran aground attempting to avoid capture and was blown up by her own crew. Both Commanders Wainwright and Renshaw were killed and the other Union ships sailed out to sea, abandoning the federal infantry in town.

Magruder had retaken Galveston with twenty-six killed and 117 wounded. Union losses included the captured infantry and the Harriet Lane, about 150 casualties on the naval ships as well as the destruction of the Westfield. The port remained under Confederate control for the rest of the war but the reinforced blockade prevented a resumption of trade on a meaningful scale.

14. BATTLE OF FREDERICKSBURG

The Texas Brigade had been assigned to the Winchester, Virginia area after the disastrous battle of Antietam where their ranks had been decimated by the ferocious combat in September 1862. Due to the effective withdrawal of General Lee and the failure of Union General McClellan to pursue the Confederates when there was an opportunity for a fatal blow to have been delivered to the Army of Northern Virginia, the Texans had a two month respite in which they partially replenished their supplies and manpower. By mid-November the troops were anxious to resume supporting the efforts of their comrades and were pleased to receive orders to begin marching toward the east. The Texas Brigade left their camp in Winchester, marched south through the Shenandoah Valley, turned east through the Manassas Gap in the Blue Ridge Mountains and marched south of Culpepper Court House to the vicinity of Cedar Mountain, Virginia. An official inspection at that location confirmed the poor level of supply for the men, especially the lack of adequate footwear so critical for infantry regiments. By the end of November they had reached the Rappahannock River near Fredericksburg as a part of General Longstreet's force. Company I, received clothing made by the ladies of Houston County and the First Texas received five hundred pairs of the much needed shoes.[141] They soon experienced very cold weather with heavy snow and the men in part kept warm by building breastworks on a ridge known as Marye's Heights to the west of town.

By December 13 the Union troops had crossed the river and occupied the city of Fredericksburg which they looted and virtually destroyed by their depredations. In the morning of that day the Union troops had brief success in an attempt to flank the Confederate defenders but when this was countered, General Burnside ordered an attack on Marye's Heights. This area was well protected by artillery coverage with strong defensive emplacements. Repeated Union attacks met with failure and

[141] *1st Texas Voluntary Infantry Regiment, Nineteenth Century Living History Association.*

enormous numbers of casualties. This was a stunning defeat of a vastly larger Union force, later determined to be the largest single battle in American military history with 114,000 Federal troops and 72,500 Confederates engaged in the conflict. The Union army had over twice the casualties of the army of General Lee. General Burnside withdrew his defeated forces across the river and their disastrous campaign ended. Burnside attempted to resume his offensive but the poorly planned venture known as the "Mud March" failed and Lincoln replaced him as commander of the Army of the Potomac with Major General Joseph Hooker.[142]

Hood's Division was sent to southeastern Virginia for what was known as the Suffolk Campaign to obtain supplies for the army. They succeeded in that mission but they were not present for the battle at Chancellorsville at the end of April which was considered General Lee's greatest victory.

[142] *See Appendix II. Item 21. Union Army Generals*

15. SUMMER OF 1863 – GETTYSBURG AND THE TURNING POINT OF THE WAR

At the beginning of the year, the hopes of the Confederacy were high following the rout of the Union forces at Fredericksburg in December 1862. After the failure of the Mud March, Lincoln replaced General Burnside with Joseph Hooker as commander of the Army of the Potomac. In the spring, Lee sent two divisions from Longstreet's Corps including Hood's division, to southeastern Virginia to counter a possible threat from troops landing at Norfolk on the Peninsula, to protect Richmond and to forage for badly needed supplies in North Carolina (Suffolk Campaign).[143] Lee had great difficulty providing adequate food for his troops and forage for their horses and by April he had only about 60,000 men on the defensive line at the Rappahannock River.

At the end of April, Hooker began the expected Union offensive, crossing the river with over 130,000 men. Despite the Federal numerical superiority, Lee split his army and was able to prevent the Union advance. Hooker withdrew to defensive positions and Lee boldly dispatched Stonewall Jackson's entire corps to flank the Union force, resulting in a decisive victory. This battle at Chancellorsville has been called Lee's "perfect battle" but the Confederate losses were great with over 20% of his troops killed or wounded, including his most capable field commander, Stonewall Jackson. Although the Union losses were greater in number, they could be replaced, unlike the Confederates. Hood's division, including the Texans, was unable to move from southern Virginia in time to participate in this battle.[144]

---

[143] Breiner, TL. Pork Belly Politics, Cincinnati Civil War Round Table.
[144] McPherson, J. Battle Cry of Freedom, p. 638–46.

After this success Lee was perhaps overconfident in the ability of his army and he led his troops north through the Shenandoah Valley to begin an invasion of the north. This invasion included about 72,000 Confederates who crossed the Potomac River in mid-June despite inclement weather and logistical delays to meet about 94,000 Federals, now under the command of General George Meade. Hooker was replaced by Meade only a few days before the impending battle at Gettysburg but his troops occupied strong defensive positions.

On July 1 the battle began with the Confederates' success in driving back the Union troops. On the afternoon of July 2, the 1st Texas engaged in some of the fiercest fighting of the war and demonstrated its mettle in the capture of the Devil's Den. Hood was seriously wounded early in the engagement, and over a three-hour interval the 1st Texas had twenty-four men killed and fifty-four wounded. The 4th and 5th Texas and the 3rd Arkansas regiments of the brigade had even greater losses. Company I reported five killed including the Jones brothers and William House who had been with Lieutenant John Wootters at the Houston County flag ceremony two years previously.[145]

Between July 1 and 3, 1863 more casualties occurred than in any battle in American military history with over 46,000 killed or wounded. The names of some of the locations in that battle, including Little Round Top, the Wheatfield, Devil's Den, Peach Orchard, Culp's Hill and Cemetery Ridge, represent revered monuments to the bravery and sacrifices of both sides in the war. On July 4, Lee began his withdrawal as an anticipated attack by the Union Army of the Potomac did not occur. Meade did not pursue Lee's army which was able to cross the Potomac River and move safely to its positions at the Rappahannock River.[146] This retreat signaled the end of the last attempt by the Confederates to take the war into Union territory.

---

[145] Mainer, T.N. *Houston County in the Civil War, p.23-4.*
[146] Foote, S. *The Civil War, A Narrative, Volume Two, p.467-581.*

Of equal importance in the ultimate outcome of the war was the fall of the City of Vicksburg, Mississippi to the Union forces led by General U.S. Grant on July 4. This victory gave the Federal forces control of the Mississippi River and effectively cut off major troop movements from the western states to the raging battles in Virginia, Tennessee and Georgia. For Texans this battle was of special importance as it was the last major engagement for the 2nd Texas Infantry Regiment. They had served well with the Army of Mississippi, led by General Albert Sidney Johnston at the battle of Shiloh on April 6-7, 1862. They were cited for bravery for their action in the Hornet's Nest at Shiloh and in October 1862 had success at the battle of Corinth, Mississippi. At Vicksburg the 2nd Texas, led by Colonel Ashbel Smith, defended a fortification known as the Second Texas Lunette and withstood two Union assaults. The siege of Vicksburg lasted forty-six days and the Confederates surrendered on July 4, 1863 due to the prospect of starvation. The decimated 2nd Texas Infantry Regiment was furloughed to Texas as paroled prisoners of war.[147]

With the defeats at Gettysburg and Vicksburg, it was apparent that the dwindling Confederate armies in the east could not long withstand the increasing numbers of Federal troops.

[147] *Chance, J E. Second Texas Infantry, Handbook of Texas Online.*

16. THE TULLAHOMA CAMPAIGN AND THE BATTLE OF CHICKAMAUGUA

The Tullahoma Campaign between June 24 and July 3, 1863 is less widely recognized than the concurrent battles at Gettysburg and Vicksburg. It was an important chapter in the ongoing conflict between the Confederate Army of Tennessee led by Major General Braxton Bragg and the Union Army of the Cumberland led by Major General William S. Rosecrans. This campaign took place in middle Tennessee between the cities of Nashville and Chattanooga in terrain marked by deep valleys and rugged ridges, passable only through gaps which would be vigorously defended by those in their possession. The campaign, a Union victory, was accomplished with less bloodshed than was characteristic of many Civil War battles but it would have profound effects on the outcome of the war.

The Union victory at Hoover's Gap in the campaign saw the introduction of a new weapon, the Spencer repeating rifle. This weapon contributed to the Union success and ultimately changed military tactics for decades in America and around the world. This weapon, used principally by cavalry units, could fire twenty rounds per minute instead of the three or four with the Enfield or Springfield musket rifles.[148] At that time, mounted cavalry would dismount and function as standard infantry units but in succeeding decades the use of these rifles by troops on their mounts would become the standard for the Indian wars that were to come. The development and deployment of the Spencer repeating rifle demonstrated the vastly superior manufacturing capacity of the Northeast and predicted the critical role of a nation's manufacturing capability to the success of their military for future generations. The Confederacy had only very limited manufacturing capacity and were dependent on the importation of firearms and supplies from Europe that was severely restricted by the effective Union Navy blockade of most southern ports. The Tullahoma Campaign, a Union Army success, drove the Confederates from Middle Tennessee but Rosecrans did not pursue Bragg and "give the finishing blow to the rebellion" as

[148] *Walter, John. The Rifle Story, Greenhill Books, 2006. p 69-71.*

he was urged to do by Secretary of War Edwin M. Stanton.[149]
The Texas Division had little rest after the very difficult battle
at Gettysburg in which Major General Hood had been wounded
but was able to remain with his command. Only two months
after that battle, the Texas Division was directed to march to
the mountainous area of northwest Georgia with Lieutenant
General James Longstreet to support Bragg's Army of Tennessee.
Longstreet would command the left wing of this army, including
his corps, with the Texas Division and Hood who had recovered
sufficiently from his wound. They faced sixty-thousand well
entrenched Federals at Chickamaugua Creek, about ten miles
south of Chattanooga in what was to be one of the bloodiest
battles of the war.

On the morning of September the nineteenth, Union troops
resisted repeated Confederate attacks on their positions on the
eastern slopes of Missionary Ridge. The First Texas Infantry,
commanded by Lieutenant Colonel Phillip A. Work with the rest
of the Texas Brigade, commanded by Major General Jerome B.
Robertson, had been deployed to the left side of the Confederate
line. By mid-afternoon they were ordered to move forward
and after vicious fighting they attacked across the Lafayette-
Chattanooga Road and drove the Federals from the top of a ridge
which they were able to hold. Over the next hours a desperate
struggle swirled around a farm known as the Viniard House.
By nightfall they had maintained their advance, but at a terrible
cost, with the First Texas losing twenty-two men. Casualties were
heavy for each of the four regiments of the Texas Brigade.

On the next day General Longstreet's command was able to take
advantage of a miscalculation by the Federal commander that
left a gap in the Union line. That half-mile gap allowed the Texas
Brigade and other Confederate troops to pour through, routing
the Federal defenders and sending their main force fleeing
toward Chattanooga. Only the bravery and determination of the
Federal Major General George H. Thomas saved the Army of the
Cumberland from total defeat. Rosecrans was subsequently able
to take advantage of the strong defenses of Chattanooga and for

[149] *Foote, S. The Civil War: A Narrative. Vol. Two. p. 668-675.*

the next three months held the city despite a Confederate siege. The Texas Brigade was directed to the siege of Knoxville and as 1863 ended they prepared their winter camp about forty miles northeast of that city.[150]

Chickamaugua had been a significant success for the Confederates but as Lieutenant John Wootters expressed, many more such victories would be the end of the war for the Texas Brigade and the 1st Texas Regiment as there were only one-hundred men in his regiment still fit for duty at its conclusion. Of the 65,000 Confederates in the battle, over one-quarter (18,454) were killed, wounded or missing. The Texas Brigade suffered 540 of its 1250 men killed or wounded. General Hood had been hit by a minie ball in the right thigh, shattering the bone and requiring amputation, limiting his ability to serve in the field with the troops for the remainder of the war.[151]

---

[150] *Cozzens, P. This Terrible Sound: The Battle of Chickamaugua.*
[151] *Foote, S. The Civil War: A Narrative, Volume Two. p 741.*

17. THE BATTLE OF SABINE PASS

In September 1863 as the maelstrom swirled about the Texas Brigade in north Georgia, the last meaningful attempt by a Federal force to invade Texas took place at the Battle of Sabine Pass.[152] An invasion had been anticipated since the recapture of the City of Galveston by the Confederates on New Year's Day. The fall of Vicksburg on July the fourth, however, made gunboats and troop transports available to the Union forces. By August, Major General Nathaniel P. Banks, the Federal commander in New Orleans had decided to invade Texas at Sabine Pass in the southeast corner of the state. His plan was to land a large force and use the existing rail line to move his troops westward to capture Houston and Galveston. On September the seventh, his armada arrived at Sabine Pass including nineteen troop transports with five thousand men and four gunboats armed with 9-inch bore-rifled cannons capable of firing 135-pound shells a distance of three miles.

Since the beginning of the war, Sabine Pass and southeast Texas, had been defended by over one thousand troops. By September 1863 all but forty-seven men had been reassigned to support Confederate efforts in Louisiana or to defend against Comanche Indian raids in the Fort Worth area. Captain Frederick Odlum, Lieutenant Dick Dowling and their troops, known as the Davis Guards, were assigned to the newly constructed Fort Griffin and armed with four 32-pound 6-inch guns and two 24-pound 5-inch guns. The troops consisted mainly of Irish immigrant longshoremen from Houston and Galveston whose work had been limited by the Federal Navy embargo and for whom enlistment in the Army at least offered the possibility of some excitement and a paycheck. Over several months of practice they had honed their artillery skills within the twelve hundred yard range of their weapons.

[152] *Barr, A. Sabine Pass, Battle of. The Handbook of Texas Online.*

On September the eighth the Union gunboats entered Sabine Pass and fired on the fort from a distance far beyond the range of the Confederate guns. Not receiving return fire, the Federals concluded that Fort Griffin had been abandoned. Captain Odlum had gone onboard the Confederate cotton-clad gunboat Uncle Ben and left Lieutenant Dowling at the fort with the option of spiking the guns and retreating if he should so choose. Instead, Dowling kept his troops out of sight in secure areas underground while he remained above until he saw the Union gunboats steaming forward. The Confederates emerged from hiding, aimed their weapons at the 1200 yard markers and when the Union boats were in range they opened fire with deadly accuracy. The steam drums of the two lead ships were pierced with resulting explosions that killed many of the Union crewmen and disabled the boats, blocking the Sabine Pass channel. The gunboat, Clifton, raised a flag of surrender and the remainder of the fleet withdrew in a hasty retreat toward New Orleans. The forty-seven Texans had suffered no injuries at all but were now faced with the prospect of dealing with over 350 prisoners. Soon the Uncle Ben arrived as did Company F of Griffin's Battalion which had set out from Beaumont to support the contingent at Sabine Pass on hearing the sounds of the bombardment earlier on that morning.[153]

Hence the most serious invasion threat of Texas was stopped, and although minor Federal occupations of other coastal sites occurred, no further major actions were experienced in Texas during the remainder of the war. Although this victory greatly encouraged the Texas population, the enthusiasm was not to have significant effects on the war effort as the blockade of the coast and the Mississippi River continued to effectively isolate the western states of the Confederacy.

[153] *Block, W.T. The Battle of Sabine Pass–Its Causes and Effects.*

FIGURE 7

(SEE IMAGE IN GALLERY)
Major Richard William (Dick) Dowling, C.S.A.
January 14, 1837 – September 23, 1867

Born in 1837 near Tuam, County Galway, Ireland, Richard
Dowling emigrated to New Orleans in 1846 during the Irish potato
famine. In 1857, Dick married Elizabeth Anne Odlum in Houston.
By 1860 he had owned 3 bars, installed Houston's first gas
lighting in his home and business, and was a charter member of
Houston Hook and Ladder Company No. 1.

During the Civil War, Dick was First Lieutenant, Company
F, Cook's Regiment, First Texas Heavy Artillery. He was in
command at Fort Griffin in 1863. On September 8 he held
fast with only 6 cannon and 47 men inside the fort
despite rumors of a federal invasion and orders to
retreat. Twenty-seven ships carrying Maj. Gen. William B.
Franklin and 5,000 Union troops sailed into Sabine Pass;
Dowling and "the Irish Davis Guards" shot so accurately
that Franklin's forces surrendered in 45 minutes. The
Confederate Congress called the Battle of Sabine Pass
"One of the most brilliant...achievements... of the war."

Discharged as a Major in 1865, Dick reopened his most
famous bar, "The Bank of Bacchus." In 1866 he formed the
first oil company in Houston. By 1867, he owned more
than 22 square blocks of downtown Houston and vast
lands across Texas. Dick Dowling died of yellow fever at
age 30 and is buried in Houston's St. Vincent's Cemetery. (1998)

18. WALKER'S TEXAS DIVISION, THE RED RIVER CAMPAIGN AND THE BATTLE OF MANSFIELD

Walker's Texas Division, known as Walker's Greyhounds, including the brigade of Brigadier General T.N. Waul, had been assigned to the command of Lieutenant General Richard Taylor in February 1864 to meet the advance of the Union Army's Red River Campaign. This Federal military initiative was designed to capture Shreveport, the temporary capital of Confederate Louisiana, as it was a major supply depot and a gateway to Texas. This campaign was authorized by President Abraham Lincoln and General in Chief Henry Halleck, but opposed by generals Grant, Sherman and Banks. Major General Nathaniel P. Banks, as commander of the Federal Army of the Gulf, led 30,000 Union troops up the Red River with plans to connect with Major General Frederick Steele who was in command of Federal troops in Little Rock and Fort Smith. These Arkansas-based Union troops were countered by Confederate forces led by General Edmund Kirby Smith, the commander of the Trans-Mississippi Department and Major General Sterling Price. This Camden Expedition resulted in a Federal disaster as between April 10 and 30, 1864 they suffered over 2,500 casualties and the loss of many supplies. The Federals retreated to their fortifications in Little Rock and elsewhere and the Confederates freely roamed rural Arkansas.[154]

---

[154] Baker, W.D. The Camden Expedition of 1864, Arkansas Historic Preservation Program.

On April the eighth the Federal troops led by Major General
Banks reached an area a few miles south of Mansfield where the
road from Natchitoches to the town of Mansfield crossed a road
leading to the Sabine River and Texas. It was at this location that
General Taylor had decided to take a stand against the invading
Federals with troops including Walker's Texas Division including
Brigadier General Tom Green's cavalry and the support of the
Valverde Artillery Battery. The Confederates determined their
battle plan by midday when the Texans had joined General
Taylor's troops which included Louisiana infantry commanded
by General Mouton who led the opening charge and was fatally
wounded. The Texas Division with Waul's Brigade in their front
joined the fight. They advanced with fixed bayonets to within fifty
yards of the Federals, fired their weapons and, with the Texas
yell, they charged. The terrified Union troops abandoned their
artillery and fled only to be encircled by Walker's Texas Division
with over one thousand being taken prisoner. The Federal troops
suffered severe losses including twenty cannons, their wagon
train and a thousand horses and mules along with nearly seven
hundred men killed or wounded. This battle at Mansfield was
followed in the next two days by the battle at Pleasant Hill in
which Confederate Brigadier General Scurry was fatally wounded
and several subsequent skirmishes in one of which Brigadier
General Tom Green was killed. Although the Confederates scored
a decisive victory and stopped any further attempt by the Federals
to invade Texas, their losses were very severe.[155]

---

[155] Leatherwood, A. Red River Campaign. The Handbook of Texas Online.

19. THE U.S. PRESIDENTIAL ELECTION OF 1864

The political turmoil in the North that accompanied the Presidential nomination in the summer of 1864 offered a glimmer of hope to the Southland. It was clear that there was great dissension in the Union and significant support for an immediate peace settlement with the Confederacy.[156] The other extreme view, however, was held by many members of President Lincoln's Republican Party who wanted more aggressive legislation concerning the slavery issue and opposed Lincoln's overtures to groups of Unionists in some Confederate states. These so-called "Radical Republicans" proposed the nomination of John C. Fremont, a former U.S. Senator from California. The Republicans loyal to Lincoln had enough concern about his party's ongoing support to join with some Democrats, who also favored continuing the war, to establish the National Union Party, which in early June did select Lincoln as their nominee for President.

The Democratic Party was deeply divided by the issue of war or peace and was influenced by a group of antiwar activists known as "Copperheads." Democrats opposing these pacifist views considered them to have similarities to the poisonous snake by that name but the Peace Democrats proudly accepted the description related to the "head of Liberty" which was on the copper penny that they proudly wore as badges. The deeply divided Democrats at their convention in late August, nominated General George B. McClellan of New Jersey, the former Commanding General of the Army. He favored continuing the war and rejected the platform that called for an immediate negotiated peace. If the Confederate army could win convincing victories, the support for the war would certainly continue to diminish in the North and perhaps the Southland could succeed in gaining independence. Continuing casualties by the Confederacy gave a pervasive sense of urgency to this view as the lack of replacements for their fighting force was an inescapable reality.

---

[156] *Library of Congress, Presidential Election of 1864: A Resource Guide (http://www.loc.gov// rr/program/bib/elections/election1864.html)*

The political mood in the North abruptly changed with the victory of Major General William T. Sherman over the Confederate forces led by Lieutenant General Hood on July 22, 1864 and with the conclusion of the siege of Atlanta on September 2, the reelection of President Lincoln was assured.[157]

[157] *Goodwin, D.K., Team of Rivals: The Political Genius of Abraham Lincoln. p.627-667.*

20. THE 1864 OVERLAND CAMPAIGN –
FROM THE WILDERNESS TO COLD HARBOR

The Union Army and its strategy for the war were restructured in the early months of 1864 following the appointment of Ulysses S. Grant as the Commanding General of the United States Army. The previous Federal leadership had often failed to capitalize on opportunities to significantly improve their prospects of ending the war. Grant had clearly shown a willingness and ability to fully engage the now dwindling Confederate forces and in March 1864 he was given overall command. He devised a strategy that called for moving his commanders in the western theater and Nathaniel Banks and his army were transferred from Louisiana to capture Mobile, Alabama. Benjamin Butler was moved from New Orleans to command the Army of the James and to threaten the city of Richmond from the east. Grant would direct the Overland Campaign against Robert E. Lee and the Confederate Army of Northern Virginia to eventually capture the capital at Richmond.

During May, Major General Butler, a political appointee, proved to be as ineffective in this mission as he had been in his earlier military ventures. He was stopped by a force about one-half the size of the Federal force in the Bermuda Hundred Campaign in Virginia by Confederate General P.G.T. Beauregard. Grant had assumed command of the Union Army of the Potomac and on May the fourth his Army, led by Sheridan's cavalry, crossed the Rapidan River to meet Robert E. Lee's army. The battlefield was only a few miles west of the site of the monumental struggle at Chancellorsville one year earlier when the Confederates' devastating attack had routed the Union line. The area in Spotsylvania and Orange Counties, known as the Wilderness, encompassed rugged terrain and dense scrub that would improve the chances of the vastly outnumbered Confederates by limiting the effectiveness of the Union artillery. On May the fifth, the Second and Third Corps commanded by Lieutenant Generals Richard S. Ewell and A.P. Hill engaged the significantly larger Federal forces to a stand still. On the next morning the greatly reinforced Union II Corps under Major General Winfield Scott Hancock successfully drove back the troops of A.P. Hill when Lieutenant General James Longstreet and his 12,000 man First Corps including the Texas Division arrived at midday after their journey from Tennessee.

General Lee, in his enthusiasm with the arrival of the expected reinforcements, attempted to personally lead the Texas Brigade in a charge against the Union line. The Texans, now numbering only 800 men, were aware of the importance of General Lee for their ultimate success and refused to advance until their revered leader withdrew to safety after their cry, "Lee to the rear!" Within two hours of their attack, Longstreet's First Corps had regained the ground lost on that morning and drove the Federals a mile further, splitting their forces and inflicting great losses on the enemy. Before daylight faded in this struggle, Major General John B. Gordon joined the battle with a Division of the Confederate Second Corps, further devastating the Union line and capturing nearly 1,000 prisoners. The horror of that days conflict with over 25,000 casualties was climaxed by a terrifying incident in which hundreds of wounded soldiers still on the battlefield perished in a brushfire that broke out between the two lines during the dark of night. The screams of the wounded soldiers of both armies that were burned alive in front of their fellow troops would remain in the minds of the survivors forever.[158]

Although Lee's forces inflicted 17,666 casualties on Grant's army while losing 7,800 Confederates, the Federals were able to replenish their losses. Although savoring a tactical victory, the Confederates were facing a war of attrition that they ultimately could not win. Although Grant was forced to withdraw from the battle at the Wilderness he was true to his statement that "there will be no turning back."[159] He would resume his attack and within a few days would engage the Confederates at another major battle only ten miles to the southeast at Spotsylvania Court House. Another major setback to General Lee was the critical wounding of General Longstreet only a few miles from the site of

[158] *Ibid. p. 183.*
[159] *Ibid. p. 188–191.*

"Stonewall" Jackson's fatal wound a year earlier. Longstreet, the most capable of the Confederate corps commanders and beloved by his troops who referred to him as "Old Peter," a name given him as a youth by his father because of his determination, would be a severe blow to the Southland.

Major General Richard H. Anderson replaced General Longstreet as the Commander of the First Corps, including the Texas Division under Major General Charles W. Field. After the appalling events of May the sixth at the Wilderness, General Grant withdrew his forces from the field but instead of retreating to the north they turned south with plans to seize the village of Spotsylvania Courthouse. This refusal to retreat following a withdrawal from a battle and to stay on the offensive was a significant boost to the morale of the Army of the Potomac. Both armies moved rapidly in the direction of Spotsylvania Courthouse but General Anderson and the First Corps, which had marched all night from the stench of the Wilderness battlefield, arrived at a farm clearing known as Laurel Hill just before Union Major General Governeur K. Warren and his V Corps. The Federals launched an immediate attack but had no success and incurred heavy casualties. By the next day the Confederates had constructed a four mile defensive fortification which had only one potential weakness at an area known as the "Mule Shoe." On the morning of the tenth of May, General Grant attacked these positions but the well-placed Confederate artillery and poor timing of the Union attacks resulted in heavy losses and no success against the Confederate line. Late in that afternoon Union Colonel Emory Upton attacked a weak point at the Mule Shoe with an innovative infantry formation that was subsequently studied for years by military historians and tacticians. Their initial success could not be maintained and the armies continued almost constant combat through the twelfth of May when the fighting at the "Bloody Angle" produced perhaps the most intense firepower of the entire war with over seventeen thousand casualties in a single day.

By the twenty-first of May the two exhausted armies moved by parallel paths with General Grant being unable to flank General Lee's Army of Northern Virginia to their next encounter at the Battle of North Anna. Lee won the race to a position just south of the North Anna River where his engineers constructed an ingenious scheme of defensive earthworks that would reduce the manpower advantages of the Union forces. This "inverted V" configuration could not be successfully assaulted and Grant soon ordered his army in a wide flanking movement toward an important crossroads twenty-five miles to the southeast and directly east of Richmond. It was at this location, only a short distance from the site of the Battle of Gaines' Mill where, in 1862, Hood's Texas Brigade first demonstrated their fighting abilities, that the final engagement of Grant's Overland Campaign would occur.[160]

The goals of Grant's movement of the Union Army were uncertain in the first days following the Battle of North Anna, but a series of sparring engagements including an intense encounter by Major General Wade Hampton's cavalry indicated that the Federal forces were moving in the direction of an important crossroads named for the Cold Harbor Tavern at that site. The tavern, owned by the Isaac Burnett family, was not a port but did provide sleeping accommodations (i.e., harbor) but no hot meals, hence its name. The intersection located ten miles east of the Confederate capital, if occupied by Grant, would give him an easily enforceable location from which he could either attack the Confederate army or the city of Richmond. Both armies had received reinforcements but those joining the Army of Northern Virginia were seasoned veterans who were assigned from other fronts. The new Union troops were untested recruits but, their total number approaching 108,000 men, vastly exceeded the 59,000 troops that could be counted on by General Lee. The Confederates had used the delays of the Union forces on June the first and second to build intricate defensive fortifications extending about seven miles and anchored on the north by the Totopotomy Creek and on the south by the Chickahominy River preventing any possible flanking movements by the Federals. The earthen barricades would maximize the effectiveness of the Confederate artillery and disguise the location

[160] *Ibid. p.265–275.*

and strength of the entrenchments. The Union troops that had assaulted such fortifications at Spotsylvania Courthouse had knowledge of what faced them as the attack began before dawn on June the third. The Union advance faced withering fire and what little success they achieved was met by Confederate artillery with devastating results. By midday the Union assault was over and Grant's troops had suffered three to four times the casualties of the Confederates.

Over the next nine days the two forces were engaged in trench warfare with artillery and sharpshooters claiming as many victims as had been lost in the June third assault. During the Battle of Cold Harbor the Union army lost 13,000 men and since the beginning of the Overland Campaign in early May, the toll had been more that 52,000 Federal casualties. The Army of Northern Virginia had 32,000 casualties in that time costing the Confederates, a much higher percentage loss of their forces.[161]

On June the twelfth Grant removed his troops from the engagement to cross the James River and threaten the vital rail center to the south of Richmond and thus began the Siege of Petersburg which would last until the twenty-fifth of March 1865. In response to Grant's withdrawal, the 1st Texas Regiment was moved south and on June the thirteenth crossed the Chickahominy River and on the sixteenth crossed the James River near Drewry's Bluff. On June the seventeenth Field's Texas Division occupied defensive lines at Bermuda Hundred awaiting orders to march to Petersburg.

[161] *Ibid. p. 281-299.*

21. BERMUDA HUNDRED

(SEE IMAGE IN GALLERY)

The term 'hundred' refers to an administrative unit intermediate in size between a county and a shire—in the terminology of 17th century Wales and England—and was occasionally used in the colonies. Bermuda Hundred was incorporated in 1613 as the first town in the colony of Virginia and was named for the islands to be known by that name. The Bermuda Islands was the site of the grounding of an English ship, the Sea Venture, attempting to resupply Jamestown in 1609. The Sea Venture sank as a result of a severe hurricane but the one hundred-fifty passengers and crew survived and were stranded on the islands for nine months before building ships to continue to Virginia. Many passengers did not survive the experience including the wife and son of John Rolfe. He would later marry Pocahontas and he became wealthy from his plantation where he became Virginia's first successful tobacco planter. He lived at Bermuda Hundred until his probable death during the Indian Massacre of 1622 in which the Powhatan Confederacy of natives killed one-third of the colonists living in Virginia at the time. Another survivor of the wreck of the Sea Venture was William Strachey, a writer whose account of the incident was widely publicized and published in London and is thought to be the inspiration for "The Tempest" by William Shakespeare.

Bermuda Hundred, located near the confluence of the Appomattox and James Rivers was the site of the ineffective Campaign by that name led by Union Major General Benjamin Butler in early May 1864. The town is equidistant from Richmond and Petersburg, the latter being the goal of General Grant's next offensive after his disastrous efforts at Cold Harbor. The defensive line at Bermuda Hundred was the site of the last combat event for Captain John Wootters.

22. UNION ARMY GENERALS

For the new or casual reader of the history of the War Between the States, the frequent changes in the highest levels of leadership in the Federal Army are often confusing. The seeming disparity in the effectiveness of the Union and Confederate Generals is puzzling especially since most of the generals on both sides had attended the U.S. Military Academy and knew each other from their days at West Point. The more senior leaders had gained similar experience in the Mexican War or in the almost continuous warfare with the American Indians that was present in the early decades of the nineteenth century. The federal army had leaders that were the equal of their Confederate counterparts but the paradox is that it took two years before they were recognized and put in positions of significance. Many other Union generals had no military experience and were political appointments.

An explanation of this paradox may lie in the organization of the Union and Confederate armies, the political atmosphere in the two nations and the experiences of their Presidents. Jefferson Davis had as much military experience as any Chief Executive could have acquired prior to their election as Supreme Commander of the Armed Forces. Abraham Lincoln was a master politician but had no military experience.

The aged Winfield Scott led the Union Army as the Commanding General since 1841 and during his tenure had campaigned unsuccessfully in 1852 for the U.S. Presidency on the Whig Party ticket. Lincoln replaced him on November 1, 1861 with Major General George McClellan who concurrently commanded the Army of the Potomac. McClellan's own political views were much too sympathetic to the South to ever make him an effective commander of the Federal army and his political aspirations were contrary to the goals of Lincoln.

The political environment confronting Lincoln made it unfeasible to replace McClellan who had required great prodding after the disaster of the First Battle of Manassas to begin any offensive action. His Peninsula Campaign in the spring of 1862 was a dismal failure. He was replaced by Major General Henry Halleck as Commanding General on July 11, 1862 but retained the command of the Army of the Potomac. McClellan's first success was at Antietam in September 1862 but his failure to pursue his advantage when the Army of Northern Virginia was forced across the Potomac River from Maryland into Virginia sealed the end of his military career.[162] Major General Ambrose Burnside replaced McClellan on November 10, 1862. Burnside would lead the Union army in the debacle at Fredericksburg, demonstrating his ineptitude.

On January 26, 1863 Burnside was replaced by Major General Joseph Hooker, known as "Fighting Joe" due to a newspaper misprint of a telegraph message.

Hooker was in command in April 1863 at the battle of Chancellorsville which was a disaster for the Federals and perhaps Robert E. Lee's greatest success. Lincoln replaced Hooker only days before the critical battle at Gettysburg, Pennsylvania by Major General George Meade who performed well in that victory July 1-3, 1863. Meade, however, failed to pursue the severely depleted Army of Northern Virginia in the days following that battle and by the beginning of 1864, Lincoln realized that new leadership would have to be found if he was to have any military chance of ending the war and succeeding in the upcoming election of 1864.

[162] Goodwin, Doris Kearns. "Team of Rivals" p. 425–485.

In March 1864 Lincoln replaced General Halleck as Commanding General of the U.S. Army with Ulysses S. Grant who had shown the traits that would be essential for ultimate Union victory. His success at Shiloh in 1862 and at Vicksburg in July 1863 and his leadership in opening the Tennessee River for the resupply of Chattanooga convinced Lincoln that he would be able to provide the needed leadership for the Federal forces. "After Confederate General Bragg's beaten army drifted down the far slope of Missionary Ridge, securing the Union presence in Chattanooga, it was as certain as anything could be that Grant was going to be given the top command."[163]

When Congress approved the rank of Lieutenant General for Grant, one not authorized since General George Washington, he received a tumultuous welcome in Washington D.C. and immediately proceeded to the headquarters of the Army of the Potomac where he demonstrated political acumen by retaining General George Meade as their commander. Despite this organization of the leadership, the Federal forces in Virginia would always be known as "Grant's Army." After reviewing the condition of the Federal troops in the East, Grant altered the previous Union military plans. They would now include an invasion of Georgia to capture the great city of Atlanta and further divide the already fractured Confederacy. General Grant would make his headquarters with the Army of the Potomac from where he would personally direct the entire Federal military. His strategy called for the destruction of the Confederate Army of Northern Virginia through what would be known as the Overland Campaign and the eventual capture of Richmond.[164] During his leadership he proved to be a master of grand strategy with a thorough understanding of logistics. He made mistakes, but he learned from them. His success lay in promoting highly competent commanders for his troops and in always seizing and holding the initiative, never calling retreat and having an indomitable determination to win.[165]

---

[163] *Catton, B. Never Call Retreat., p.295.*
[164] *Ibid. p. 301–304.*
[165] *Generals of the Union, John Hinde Curteich, Inc., 2002.*

23. COLONEL ASHBEL SMITH, M.D.

Ashbel Smith can properly be called the renaissance man of early Texas history and his contributions to the state and the nation were extraordinary. He was born on August 13, 1805 in Hartford, Connecticut and graduated from Yale University at the age of 19. After teaching for two years in Salisbury, North Carolina he returned to Yale where he completed his M.D. in 1828. He studied in Paris during the cholera epidemic of 1832 and published a pamphlet on the disease. On returning to the U.S. he practiced medicine in Salisbury where he became involved in politics and was editor of a newspaper. In the fall of 1836 he was persuaded to move to Texas by a friend, James Pinckney Henderson.

After his arrival in Texas in 1837 he became a friend and roommate of Sam Houston who appointed him surgeon general of the Army of the Republic of Texas. He established the first hospital in Houston, served as the first chairman of the Board of Medical Censors and treated patients during the yellow fever epidemic in Galveston in 1839. In 1848 he helped organize the Medical and Surgical Society of Galveston and was a leader in the formation of the Texas Medical Association in 1853, serving as president from 1881-82. He had a respected medical practice in association with Dr. John Henry Bowers, making it possible for Dr. Smith to pursue his interests in public affairs, military service, education and agriculture. Smith served the Republic of Texas in a number of diplomatic roles including charge d'affaires of Texas to England and France from 1842 to 1844 and as Secretary of State in 1845. He represented Harris County in the state legislature for three terms. He served on active duty with General Zachary Taylor in the Mexican War and with the onset of the Civil War he organized Company C of the Second Texas Infantry. At the battle of Shiloh he received a severe arm injury, was cited for bravery and named commander of the regiment. During the siege of Vicksburg he led the Second Texas with distinction. Toward the end of the war he was put in charge of the defenses of Galveston and afterwards he and William P. Ballinger were sent by Governor Pendleton Murrah as commissioners to negotiate peace terms for Texas with Union officials in New Orleans.

He had great interest in education and urged the Texas Congress to establish a system of public education in the Republic. He championed public education for blacks and women and was one of the commissioners to establish an "Agricultural and Mechanical College of Texas for Colored Youth," now known as Prairie View AM University. As president of the Board of Regents of the University of Texas he led the effort to make it a first-rate institution of higher learning and worked to establish the Medical Branch in Galveston.

He was widely recognized for his contributions to the study of the climate, soil, vegetation and wildlife as well as the raising of livestock and crops on the Gulf Coast. He died on January 21, 1886, at Evergreen, his plantation home on Galveston Bay.[166]

[166] Silverthorne, E. Smith, Ashbel. The Handbook of Texas Online.

24. COTTON, FOREIGN POLICY AND THE TEXAS RIO GRANDE VALLEY

From before the onset of the war, thoughtful southerners knew that they lacked both the manpower and industrial base to succeed in a prolonged conflict with the northern states. Their optimism at the time, however, was high and was based on the one "weapon" that they possessed in abundance and which seemed, to some, certain to shift the balance of power in their direction. That resource for the Southland was COTTON—which had become the basic commodity for the industrial revolution. In the previous decades this had completely transformed the society and economies of Britain and France and made them world powers. Britain's economy was fueled by the textile industry and three quarters of the cotton was imported from the American South. During 1861 the seeming inevitability of British intervention to insure this supply of cotton became entrenched in the Confederates' minds and their policies.

To encourage British recognition, the Confederacy limited shipment of the 1861 crop and planted only half the usual cotton acreage in 1862. By the end of 1862 unemployment in Britain had soared and the Union and Confederate governments were engaged in a complex jousting of international law and public relations to gain the upper hand for support from the European nations. This intriguing story is well described by James McPherson in his classic text on the war.[167] Several factors worked in the Union's favor including the surplus of cotton inventory in British warehouses from bumper crops of 1858-60, the dislike of slavery by the British population, a reluctance of their government to risk involvement in the war and the relative ease with which the Union blockade could be breached by the Confederates.

[167] *McPherson, J. Battle Cry of Freedom. pp.369–391.*

The blockade of southern ports was the initial strategy of the Union navy and a number of memorable naval battles occurred. Developments in naval architecture and engineering eventually led to Union's dominance of the seas. Among these design advances were the screw propeller, iron-clad armaments of the ships and rifled artillery which the Union industrial base could produce.

Despite the Union blockade, Confederate ships managed to deliver a considerable amount of cotton to the waiting British ships in Havana, Nassau or Bermuda which was exchanged for Enfield rifles, ammunition and other goods. That the price of a bale of cotton in gold had increased six-fold during the war greatly encouraged bold seamen to take the risks of running the blockades. The contraband flow of cotton to mills in the north in exchange for clothing, shoes, medicine, gunpowder and other products also flourished although it was illegal on both sides of the conflict.

Cotton that escaped through Texas ports was generally bound for Havana or Mexican ports where it could be exchanged. The blockade of Galveston encouraged the transport of cotton to the Mexican border over land by routes such as the Old San Antonio Road or El Camino Real to border sites such as Villa de Dolores (south of Laredo) or the Presidio del Rio Grande (near the present day Mexican town of Guerrero) where it could be carried by paddle-wheel boats or over land to Brownsville. Incentives for this trade were greatly reduced by the closing of the Mississippi River to goods and troops from the western states after the battle of Vicksburg in July 1863.

Other factors effecting Union foreign policy included the threat of foreign intervention in Mexico by Britain, Spain and France who sought repayment of large debts incurred by the Liberal government after the success of reformist Benito Juarez in a civil war in 1857. In 1861, when the payments on the debt were suspended, the European nations landed forces at Veracruz and the French captured Mexico City in 1862. The British and Spanish withdrew but in 1863 Napoleon III of France installed Maximilian, Archduke of Austria as the Emperor of Mexico. The possibility of intervention by the French on behalf of the Confederacy and continuing trade of cotton via the Rio Grande port of Matamoros encouraged the Union to make another attempt at invading Texas.[168]

General Nathaniel P. Banks had replaced General Benjamin Butler as commander of the Department of the Gulf in December 1862 and was based in New Orleans. Butler, a political appointee, had demonstrated his military ineptitude at the battle of Big Bethel before First Manassas and it would be confirmed during the campaigns at Bermuda Hundred and Fort Fisher with the Army of the James in 1864. Banks, also a political appointment, had been ordered to establish a Federal presence in Texas to prevent trade between the state and Mexico and to discourage French support of the Confederacy. There was little to recommend his military skills as he had experienced great losses in the Shenandoah Valley against Stonewall Jackson in 1862 and ten-fold the Confederate casualties at the siege of Port Hudson on the Mississippi River in the spring of 1863. His first attempt in Texas resulted in the Union debacle at Sabine Pass in September 1863. In November he personally led a troop of between 3500 and 6000 men in a landing at Brazos Santiago near the mouth of the Rio Grande. The area was defended by only 150 Confederates, and he occupied the town of Brownsville without conflict and was able to claim that at least a small part of Texas was under Union control. The Confederates, commanded by General Hamilton P. Bee were able to destroy significant supplies of gunpowder and cotton before the Union occupation. The Federal presence never extended beyond the lower Texas coastline. Trade with Mexico had relocated several hundred miles up-stream and goods were transported by land to the Mexican ports.[169] The Rio Grande Campaign ended with the battle of Palmito Ranch on May 12, 1865, one month after Appomattox and was the last battle of the war.[170]

[168] *U.S. Department of State, Office of the Historian, French Intervention in Mexico and the American Civil War, 1862–67.*
[169] *Foote, S. The Civil War, Volume Two, pp. 870–72.*
[170] *Marten, James A. "Rio Grande Campaign," Handbook of Texas Online.*

In retrospect, the expectation that King Cotton would rescue the undermanned and undersupplied Confederacy proved to be an illusion. The Confederate soldiers suffered greatly from inadequate shoes, clothing and food and often relied on captured armaments for their protection. The U.S. Navy's effectiveness on the rivers and on the high seas deserves much credit for the Federal success. Those forces were pivotal in the capture of New Orleans and the Mississippi River early in the war and the captureof Mobile, Alabama and Wilmington, North Carolina in the last year of the conflict. During the remainder of the nineteenth century the U.S. Navy reached preeminence among the military forces of the world.

BIBLIOGRAPHY

1st Texas Volunteer Infantry Regiment. Nineteenth Century Living History Association, Inc. (http://texas-brigade. org/1st_tex/1tex.htm)

Baker, William D. The Camden Expedition of 1864. Arkansas Historic Preservation Program. Little Rock, AR.

Barr, Alwyn. Black Texans: A History of African Americans in Texas, 1528-1995. Norman, OK: University of Oklahoma Press, 1996.

Barr, Alwyn. "Battle of Galveston," Handbook of Texas Online. (http:// www.tshaonline.org/handbook/online/ articles/qeg01). Uploaded June 15, 2010. Modified March 4, 2011. Published by the Texas State Historical Association.

Barr, Alwyn. "Green, Thomas." Handbook of Texas Online. (http:// www.tshaonline.org/handbook/online/ articles/fgr38). Uploaded June 15, 2010. Modified March 4, 2011. Published by the Texas State Historical Association.

Barr, Alwyn. "Sabine Pass, Battle of. Handbook of Texas Online. (http:// www.tshaonline.org/handbook/online/ articles/qes02) Uploaded June 15, 2010. Published by the Texas State Historical Association.

Bilby, Joseph. Civil War Firearms: Their Historical Background and Tactical Use. Conshohocken, PA: Combined Publishing, 1996.

Bishop, Eliza H. "Houston County." Handbook of Texas Online. (http:// www.tshaonline.org/handbook/online/ articles/hch19). Uploaded June 15, 2010. Published by the Texas State Historical Association.

Bladen County N.C. Genealogy and History. (www.ncgenweb.us/bladen/).

Block, William T. The Battle of Sabine Pass – Its Causes and Effects. (http:// www.wtblock.com/wtblockjr/ battleof.htm).

Boles, John B. Masters & Slaves in the House of the Lord: Race and Religion in the American South, 1740-1870. Lexington, KY: The University Press of Kentucky, 1990.

Boles, John B. The South Through Time: A History of An American Region, Third Edition, Volume I and II. Hoboken, NJ: Pearson, 2004.

Braynard, O. Frank. S.S. Savannah, the Elegant Steam Ship. Athens, GA: University of Georgia Press, 2008.

Breiner, Thomas L. Pork Belly Politics or How Longstreet Brought Home the Bacon: James Longstreet and the Suffolk Campaign. Cincinnati Civil War Round Table, September 16, 1999. (http://www.cincinnaticwrt.org/data/ ccwrt_history/talks_text/breiner_ longstreet_suffolk.html)

"A Brief History of Public Education." Texas State Historical Association, Texas Almanac.

Briseno, E.X. "Samuel May Williams: Texas Pioneer, Businessman, and Freemason."

Browne, Philip Dale. "Graves, Henry Lee." Handbook of Texas Online. (http://www.tshaonline.org/handbook/online/articles/fgr14) Uploaded June 15, 2010. Published by the Texas State Historical Association.

Burns, Ken. The Civil War: A Film by Ken Burns. A production of Florentine Films and WETA-TV, American Documentaries, Inc, 1990.

Campbell, R.B. An Empire for Slavery: The Peculiar Institution in Texas, 1821-1865. Baton Rouge, LA: Louisiana State University Press, 1989.

Campbell, Randolph B. and Curtis Bishop. "Davis, Jefferson." The Handbook of Texas Online. Texas State Historical Association.

Carroll, H. Bailey. Texas Santa Fe Expedition. Handbook of Texas Online. (https://www.tshaonline.org/handbook/online/articles/fda42) Uploaded on June 12, 2010. Modified on January 18, 2013. Published by the Texas State Historical Association.

Cassel, Daniel Kolb. A Genealogical History of the Kolb, Kulp or Culp Family, and Its Branches in America, With Biographical Sketches of Their Descendants from the Earliest Available Records. Norristown, PA: Morgan R. Wills, 1895.

Catton, Bruce. The Coming Fury: The Centennial History of the Civil War, Volume 1. Garden City, NY: Doubleday and Company, Inc., 1961.

Catton, Bruce. Terrible Swift Sword: The Centennial History of the Civil War, Volume 2. Garden City, NY: Doubleday and Company Inc., 1963.

Catton, Bruce. Never Call Retreat: The Centennial History of the Civil War, Volume 3. Garden City, NY: Doubleday & Company, Inc., 1965.

Chance, J.E. "Second Texas Infantry." Handbook of Texas Online. (http://www.tshaonline.org/handbook/online/articles/qks04) Uploaded June 15, 2010. Published by the Texas State Historical Association.

Chilton, F.B. Unveiling and Dedication of Monument to Hood's Brigade on the Capitol Grounds at Austin, Texas. Houston, TX, 1911. From the Library of Congress Internet Archive.

Cotham, Edward T. Jr. Battle on the Bay: The Civil War Struggle for Galveston. Austin, TX: University of Texas Press, 1998.

Cozzens, Peter. This Terrible Sound: The Battle of Chickamauga. Urbana, IL: University of Illinois Press, 1992.

Cromartie, Shamella. The Cape Fear River: Road to Bladen County. (http://bladenroadwork.pbworks.com.) A Roadwork project by Bladen County Public Library and Bladen County Historical Society. North Carolina Humanities Council.

Crofts, Daniel W. Reluctant Confederates: Upper South Unionists in the Secession Crisis. Chapel Hill, NC: University of North Carolina Press, 1989.

Cutrer, Thomas W. "McLeod, Hugh." Handbook of Texas Online. (https://www.tshaonline.org/handbook/online/articles/fmc90) Uploaded June 15, 2010. Modified on April 3, 2011. Published by the Texas State Historical Association.

Cutrer, Thomas W. "Smith, Edmund Kirby." Handbook of Texas Online. (http://www.tshaonline.org/handbook/online/articles/fsm09). Uploaded June 15, 2010. Published by the Texas State Historical Association.

Cutrer, T.W. and D.P. Smith. "Twiggs, David Emanuel." Handbook of Texas Online. Uploaded June 15, 2010. Modified on March 8, 2011. Published by the Texas State Historical Association.

Dattel, Gene. Cotton and Race in the Making of America: The Human Costs of Economic Power. Lanham, MD: Ivan R. Dee, Publisher, 2009.

DeFazio, Joe. "Morse's Telegraph – A Gift Refused." From Preserving Texas History at Ancestry.com. (http://freepages.history.rootsweb.ancestry.com/~unclejoe/tx/telegraph.html)

Flachmeier, J.E. "Johnston, Albert Sidney." Handbook of Texas Online. (http://www.tshaonline.org/handbook/online/articles/fjo32) Uploaded on June 15, 2010. Modified on March 13, 2013. Published by the Texas State Historical Association.

Foote, Shelby. The Civil War: A Narrative, Volumes 1, 2 and 3. New York: Random House, 1986.

Frazier, Donald S. "Val Verde Battery." Handbook of Texas Online. (http://www.tshaonline.org/handbook/online/articles/qkv01) Uploaded on June 15, 2010. Modified on March 8, 2011. Published by the Texas State Historical Association.

Ferguson, Ernest B. "The Battle of Bull Run: The End of Illusions." Smithsonian Magazine, July- August, 2011: 57-64.

Gilmore, G.W. The New Schaff-Herzog Encyclopedia of Religious Knowledge. Vol. 1: 469-470. (http://www.ccel.org/s/schaff/encyc/encyc13/htm/TOC.htm)

Goodwin, Doris Kearns. Team of Rivals: The Political Genius of Abraham Lincoln. New York, NY: Simon & Schuster, 2005.

Gorman, M.D. Hospitals in Richmond During the Civil War, Civil War Richmond. From the Richmond Sentinel, May 17, 1864. (http://www.mdgorman.com/Hospitals/hospitals.htm).

Gorman, M.D. Information about General Hospital #9 in Richmond, VA during the Civil War, Civil War Richmond. (http://www.mdgorman.com/Hospitals/general_hospital_9.htm).

Gorman, M.D. Information about Howard's Grove Hospital in Richmond, VA during the Civil War, Civil War Richmond. (http://www.mdgorman.com/Hospitals/howards_grove_hospital.htm).

Gorman, M.D. Notice to All, Civil War Richmond. From the Richmond Examiner, May 17, 1864. (http://www.mdgorman.com/Written_Accounts/Examiner/1864/richmond_examiner_5171864.htm)

Gorman, M.D. Palmer CSR, Florida Hospital, Civil War Richmond. From the National Archives. (http://www.mdgorman.com/Written_Accounts/NARA/Palmer_CSR1.htm).

Gregg, Rev. Alexander. History of the Old Cheraws. Originally published in 1867. Austin, TX: DMK Heritage, republished in 2009.

Gunn, Jack W. "Mexican Invasions of 1842." Handbook of Texas Online. (http://www.tshaonline.org/handbook/online/articles/qem02) Uploaded on June 15, 2010. Published by the Texas State Historical Association.

Hall, Martin Hardwick. "Jordan, Powhatan." Handbook of Texas Online. (https://www.tshaonline.org/handbook/online/articles/fjo72). Uploaded on June 15, 2010. Modified on March 2, 2011. Published by the Texas State Historical Association.

Harper, Cecil, Jr. "Freedmen's Bureau." Handbook of Texas Online. (http://www.tshaonline.org/handbook/online/articles/ncf01) Uploaded on June 12, 2010. Published by the Texas State Historical Association.

Hazlewood, Claudia. "Augusta, Texas." Handbook of Texas Online. (https://www.tshaonline.org/handbook/online/articles/hna50) Uploaded on June 9, 2010. Published by the Texas State Historical Association.

Henson, Margaret Swett. "Williams, Samuel May." Handbook of Texas Online. (http://www.tshaonline.org/handbook/online/articles/fwi35) Uploaded on June 15, 2010. Published by the Texas State Historical Association.

History of Houston County, Texas 1687-1979. Compiled and edited by the Houston County Historical Commission, Crockett, Texas. Tulsa, OK: Heritage Publishing Company, 1979.

Johnson, L. "The Welsh in the Carolinas in the Eighteenth Century." North American Journal of Welsh Studies, Vol. 4, no 1 (2004): 12-19. (http://www.flint.umich.edu/~wllis/Lloyd2.pdf)

Johnson, Lloyd. "Naval Stores." North Carolina History Project. (http://www.northcarolinahistory.org/encyclopedia/103/entry/)

Joiner, Gary Dillard. One Damn Blunder from Beginning to End: the Red River Campaign of 1864. Lanham, MD: Rowman & Littlefield Publishers, 2002.

Jordan, John Woolf. Colonial and Revolutionary Families of Pennsylvania: Genealogical and Personal Memoirs. Volume II. Originally published by Lewis Publishing Co. in 1911.

King, C. Richard. "Ballinger, William Pitt." Handbook of Texas Online. (http://www.tshaonline.org/handbook/online/articles/fba52) Uploaded on June 12, 2010. Modified on March 1, 2011. Published by the Texas State Historical Association.

Leatherwood, Art. Red River Campaign. Handbook of Texas Online. (http://www.tshaonline.org/handbook/online/articles/qdr01) Uploaded on June 15, 2010. Modified on March 8, 2011. Published by the Texas State Historical Association.

Long, Christopher. "Daly's, Texas." Handbook of Texas Online. (http://www.tshaonline.org/handbook/online/articles/hrdzm). Uploaded on June 12, 2010. Published by the Texas State Historical Association.

Long, Christopher. "Gossett, Elijah" Handbook of Texas Online. (http://www.tshaonline.org/handbook/online/articles/fgohw). Uploaded on June 15, 2010. Published by the Texas State Historical Association.

Lowe, Richard G. Walker's Texas Division. Baton Rouge, LA: Louisiana State University Press, 2004.

Maberry, Robert Jr. Texas Flags. College Station, TX: Texas A&M Press, 2001.

Mainer, Thomas N. Houston County in the Civil War. Crockett, TX: Publications Development Company, 1981.

The Family of Col. Kolb and Some of their Neighbors. Marlboro County, South Carolina Genealogy Trails. (http://genealogytrails.com/scar/marlboro/hx_col_kolb.htm)

McPherson, James M. The Abolitionist Legacy: From Reconstruction to the NAACP. Princeton, NJ: Princeton University Press, 1975.

McPherson, James M. Crossroads of Freedom: Antietam, The Battle that Changed the Course of the Civil War. New York, Oxford: Oxford University Press, 2002.

Miller, Aragorm Storm. "Wootters, James C." Handbook of Texas Online. (http://www.tshaonline.org/handbook/online/articles/fwo61). Uploaded on April 21, 2011. Modified on April 25, 2011. Published by the Texas State Historical Association.

Moseley, Fred. "Depression of 1873-1879." In Business Cycles and Depressions: An Encyclopedia, edited by D. Glasner and T. Cooley, 148-149. New York, NY: Routledge, 1997.

Nance, John Milton. "Mier Expedition." Handbook of Texas Online. (http://www.tshaonline.org/handbook/online/articles/qym02), Uploaded on June 15, 2010. Published by the Texas State Historical Association.

National Register of Historic Places, North Carolina, Bladen County, Historic Districts. (www.nationalregisterofhistoricplaces.com/nc/bladen)

"Old San Antonio Road." Handbook of Texas Online. (http://www.tshaonline.org/handbook/online/articles/exo04). Uploaded on June 15, 2010. Published by the Texas State Historical Association.

Polley. J.B. Hood's Texas Brigade: Its Marches, Its Battles, Its Achievements. New York, Washington DC: The Neale Publishing Co., 1910.

Presidential Election of 1864: A Resource Guide From the Library of Congress http://www.loc.gov/rr/program/bib/elections/election1864.html

Proctor, Victoria. The Welsh Neck Baptist Church. Part One: Brief History. Marlboro County, SC Churches. (http://sciway3.net/proctor/marlboro/church/Welsh_Neck_Baptist.html)

Proctor, Victoria. The Welsh Neck Baptist Church. Part Two: An Abstract of the Records of the Welsh Neck Baptist Church, Society Hill, S.C. Marlboro County, SC Churches. (http://sciway3.net/proctor/marlboro/church/Welsh_Neck_Baptist2.html)

Roasting Ears Battle, August 23, 1864. Civilwartalk.com. (http://www.civilwartalk.com)

Robertson, James. The Untold Civil War: Exploring the Human Side of the War. Edited by Neil Kagan. Washington, DC: National Geographic Society, 2011.

Sears, S.W. To the Gates of Richmond: The Peninsula Campaign. New York, NY: Ticknor & Fields, 1992.

Sheehan-Dean, Aaron. Struggle for a Vast Future: The American Civil War. New York, NY: Random House, 2006.

Shields, Douglas R. "Fairfield Female College." Handbook of Texas Online. (http://www.tshaonline.org/handbook/online/articles/kbf01). Uploaded on June 12, 2010. Published by the Texas State Historical Association.

Silber, Irwin. Songs of the Civil War. Dover Publications Inc., 1995.

Silverthorne, Elizabeth. "Smith, Ashbel." Handbook of Texas Online. (http://www.tshaonline.org/handbook/online/articles/fsm04). Uploaded on June 15, 2010. Published by the Texas State Historical Association.

Stockard, Sallie W. The History of Guilford County, North Carolina. Knoxville, TN: Gaut-Ogden Company, 1902.

Taylor, John. Bloody Valverde: A Civil War Battle on the Rio Grande, February 21, 1862. Albuquerque, NM: University of New Mexico Press, 1995.

Tew, Jerome D. "The Battle of Elizabethtown." The Sampson Independent, 2012. (www.clintonnc.com).

The New York Times, February 1, 1864. "The Draft for Half a Million of Men." New York Times Complete Civil War, 1861-1865, edited by Harold Holzer and Craig L. Symonds. New York, NY: Black Dog & Levinthal Publishers, Inc, 2010.

The New York Times Complete Civil War, 1861-1865. Edited by Harold Holzer & Craig L. Symonds. New York, NY: Black Dog & Levinthal Publishers, Inc, 2010.

Walbert, David. "Naval Stores and the longleaf pine." Learn NC, a program of the UNC School of Education. (http://www.learnnc.org/lp/editions/nchist-colonial/4069)

Walter, John. The Rifle Story. Barnsley, UK: Greenhill Books, 2006.

Wilson, Anna Victoria. "Education for African Americans." Handbook of Texas Online. (http://www.tshaonline.org/handbook/online/articles/kde02). Uploaded on June 12, 2010. Published by the Texas State Historical Association.

Wolz, Larry "Kidd-Key College." Handbook of Texas Online. Texas State Historical Association. (http://www.tshaonline.org/handbook/online/articles/kbk02). Uploaded on June 15, 2010. Modified on October 24, 2011. Published by the Texas State Historical Association.

Wooster, Ralph A. "Murrah, Pendleton." Handbook of Texas Online. (http://www.tshaonline.org/handbook/online/articles/fmu15). Uploaded on June 15, 2010. Modified on March 3, 2011. Published by the Texas State Historical Association.

Young, N.B. "Houston and Great Northern Railroad." Handbook of Texas Online. (http://www.tshaonline.org/handbook/online/articles/eqh08). Uploaded on June 15, 2010. Published by the Texas State Historical Association.